Parish, Church and People

Parish, Church and People

Local studies in lay religion 1350–1750

Edited by S. J. Wright

Hutchinson

London   Melbourne   Auckland   Johannesburg

Hutchinson Education

An imprint of Century Hutchinson Ltd

62–65 Chandos Place, London WC2N 4NW

Century Hutchinson Australia Pty Ltd
PO Box 496, 16–22 Church Street, Hawthorn,
Victoria 3122, Australia

Century Hutchinson New Zealand Ltd
PO Box 40–086, Glenfield, Auckland 10,
New Zealand

Century Hutchinson South Africa (Pty) Ltd
PO Box 337, Berglvei 2012, South Africa

First published 1988

© S. J. Wright 1988

Set in Times 10/12pt
by Hope Services (Abingdon) Limited

Printed and bound in Great Britain

ISBN 0 09 173144 5

Contents

vi   *Contents*

Contributors

Nicholas Alldridge is a history teacher working in France. He is completing a thesis on sixteenth- and seventeenth-century Chester.

Jonathan Barry is a lecturer in the Department of History and Archaeology at the University of Exeter. He is currently writing a book on Bristol in the seventeenth and eighteenth centuries and is extending his research interests to cover social and cultural life in Devon and Cornwall in the same period.

Clive Burgess is engaged in research in late medieval English religious history.

D. M. Palliser is the G. F. Grant Professor of History at Hull University. He is the author of a book on Tudor York and has interests in all aspects of pre-industrial social and economic history.

Gervase Rosser lectures in the Department of Medieval History at Birmingham University. He is the author of a forthcoming book on the medieval town and is currently working on a book on the English medieval guilds.

Donald Spaethe works in the Department of Linguistics and Phonetics at Leeds University as an Arts Computing Development officer, and is preparing a book on parish life in seventeenth-century Wiltshire.

John M. Triffitt is an Assistant Producer with the History and Archaeology Unit at the BBC. His thesis is on parliamentary boroughs in south-west England, and he has a particular interest in the study of England's smaller towns.

Susan J. Wright has just finished a three-year appointment as an ESRC Research Fellow in the Department of English Local History at the University of Leicester and is currently studying the role of women in pre-industrial towns.

Abbreviations

BAO   Bristol Archives Office
BI   Borthwick Institute, York
BL   British Library
CCRO   Chester City Record Office
CDRO   Chester Diocesan Record Office
DCRO   Dorset County Record Office
HMC   Historical Manuscripts Commission
HRO   Hampshire County Record Office
HWRO   Hereford and Worcestershire County Record Office
LRO   Leicester Record Office
LJRO   Lichfield Joint Record Office
OCRO   Oxford County Record Office
PRO   Public Record Office
SCA   Salisbury Corporation Archives
SDR   Salisbury Diocesan Records
SPCK   Society for the Promotion of Christian Knowledge
Som. RO   Somerset Record Office
SRO   Shropshire County Record Office
STRO   Straffordshire County Record Office
VCH   Victoria County History
WDRO   West Devon Record Office
WRO   Wiltshire County Record Office
Worc. RO Worcestershire County Record Office

Bossy, *Christianity*: John Bossy, *Christianity in the West 1400–1700* (1985).
Dickens, *Reformation*: A. G. Dickens, *The English Reformation* (1964).
Hill, *Society*: C. Hill, *Society and Puritanism in Pre-Revolutionary England* (1964).

Sykes, *Church and State*: N. Sykes, *Church and State in England in the Eighteenth Century* (1934).

Scarisbrick, *Reformation*: J. J. Scarisbrick, *The Reformation and the English People* (1984).

Thomas, *Magic*: K. Thomas, *Religion and the Decline of Magic* (1971).

Note: Unless specified all publications are from within the United Kingdom.

Preface

In pre-industrial England religion pervaded many aspects of daily life. The local parish church acted as an important communal focus. Not only was attendance compulsory and time-consuming, but leisure pursuits were linked with the ecclesiastical year and secular activities, such as plays and markets, were often held within the church or in the surrounding churchyard. Religious precepts were taught in schools. Homilies and sermons offered advice on how to find the ideal partner and how the 'godly' family should be run. Of great importance also was the way in which the Church was able to provide 'psychological props' for dealing with and accounting for the misfortunes and uncertainties of daily life, whether through some of the more mystical elements of the pre-Reformation liturgy or through the emphasis on 'Divine Judgement'. There were many other ways too in which the spiritual and secular overlapped. Parish officials were involved in the administration of education and charity, although the state and local authorities gradually took over these roles; they were meant to keep an eye on the morals of their fellow parishioners, and they dealt with a range of other social issues through the medium of the church courts. As a result the Church frequently became a vehicle for local political disputes. Meanwhile, at the level of the individual, there were many reasons other than the purely pious for attending a particular church.

It was while trying to ascertain how and why certain church rate books were compiled that I became aware of how much remains to be discovered about the organization of parish life. Indeed, it is surprising that, although ecclesiastical historians have devoted considerable attention to the impact of the Reformation, to the emergence of the nonconformist sects, and to the relationship between the Church hierarchy and the state, relatively little has been published about lay attitudes to the Church and its teachings, or about the ways in which religious divisions reflected communal tensions and solidarities. Many questions, therefore, need to be answered. What was going on in the ordinary church-goer's mind when he or she attended divine service on Sundays? What were the social and political implications of church membership? How did periods of 'disequilibrium', such as the Reformation and the Civil War, affect the beliefs, not just of contemporaries, but also of future generations? Did people have a definite idea of the parish as a communal unit, or was it a very artificial concept? To some extent attitudes to the local church and its organs must have varied according to the nature of the settlement in question. In a small village, where all activities took place within the framework of the parish, the local church may have inspired greater loyalty and people have had a greater sense of communal solidarity than in the large town with a number of administrative units and a range of religious institutions. It is possible, too, that the local community was more closely knit at certain dates than others, and that the parish became a clearer ideological concept as local officials assumed more and more bureaucratic and social responsibilities from the late sixteenth century onwards.

As I read more extensively and talked to colleagues, it became apparent that these issues were beginning to interest other historians too. A group of us began to meet on a regular basis to discuss our research, and the idea of compiling a collection of essays based on local research slowly emerged. Although the question of lay piety was approached from very different angles we found that there were a number of common themes which needed to be aired and that many of the questions which were being asked of the medieval period or the years after the Reformation were just as relevant today. The climax to our informal workshops was a conference held in May 1986 at Leicester University. Not only was the occasion fun, as all good conferences should be, but we benefited tremendously from the lively debate which characterized the day. Thanks are therefore due to all those who attended for their support and comments, and in particular to Charles Phythian-Adams, Peter Clark, Evelyn Lord and Jane Swanscot who helped to organize the event. We should also like to acknowledge the help of Claire L'Enfant and Sarah Conibear of Century Hutchinson and the generous financial backing of the Nuffield Foundation, without which our meetings would not have been possible. But it is to the people who have been behind the scenes throughout the book's organic growth that we wish to dedicate the final product: to John Stedman, our 'stage manager' in May; to the partners who were deserted on many evenings; and above all, to Paul Gibson – 'butler', 'bursar' – the one who dealt with so many administrative loose ends.

Thank you!

S. J. Wright
1987

1 Introduction: the parish in perspective

D. M. Palliser

In 1701–2 an elderly yeoman of Shopshire, Richard Gough, wrote an account of his parish of Myddle.[1]* It is a fascinating document, and no other book, it has been said, 'gives such a complete and detailed picture of everyday life in a seventeenth-century parish'.[2] Gough's plan, however, is as revealing of the common assumptions of his time as any of his lively anecdotes of human behaviour. He started by drawing seating-plans of the parish church, and then described the families in the order of their pews. For the parish was the unit that mattered most to Gough and his four or five hundred fellow-parishioners, not the seven townships or hamlets in which they lived. Only in the church did large numbers meet regularly, and in that church seating was carefully ordered to reflect status, with the gentry at the front, yeomen and husbandmen in the middle, the servants of the gentry in the north aisle, and the cottagers at the back. Myddle church, like nearly all the 9000 or so parish churches in the land, was at one and the same time a reflection of the social and political order, as well as the religious order, of the community.

It is common enough for historians to argue that they are casting light on an important but neglected topic, but in this case it is no less than the truth. For despite the considerable output of recent writing on the Church in later medieval and early modern times, and especially on the English Reformation, the dimension here tackled by Dr Wright and her collaborators has been relatively neglected. The ecclesiastical hierarchy, the role of the state, the national causes and consequences of the Reformation, have all been analysed extensively, yet – apart from the Reformation period itself – little has been written on ordinary parishioners and their

*Superior figures refer to the Notes and references sections following each chapter.

attitudes to the Church and its teachings. Less still – even for the Reformation – has been written on the parish as a focus of loyalty as well as of administration, or on the unique blend of secular and ecclesiastical that underpinned it.

It is a regrettable lacuna for several reasons. In an age when economic, social and political historians are concerned increasingly with local communities and their interaction with the realm, ecclesiastical historians should share a similar concern, especially since – as these studies emphasize – there is no clear dividing line between 'social' and 'ecclesiastical' history. Reformation historians have recently been investigating how far the Reformation was imposed from above or instigated from below; either way, a detailed knowledge of change at the local level is necessary. If change from below was the motor, then we need to understand which groups and communities most instigated change and why; if from above, into which communities it would most readily penetrate and in which it found most resistance. And beyond the pathological picture of conflict, we need to ask, both for the pre-Reformation and post-Reformation periods, how the ordinary man, woman or child related to his or her parish or other local centres of loyalty. The history of 'the man in the pew', as Tindal Hart called him in a pioneer study, is of value in its own right. Pre-industrial English society was never monolithic, but consisted of an aggregate of many local societies.

It has been an awareness of the importance, as well as the convenience, of the parish as the basic secular and ecclesiastical unit that has led almost all county historians, from William Lambarde in the 1570s to the Victoria County History editors of our own day, to describe their shires parish by parish. A similar awareness led very early to a tradition of separate parish histories and descriptions, starting with White Kennett's antiquarian history of Ambrosden (1695), and including such diverse works as Gough's Myddle and Gilbert White's natural history of Selborne. Not all parishes, admittedly, were of such a convenient size as to make a meaningful administrative unit or a focus of loyalty. Nevertheless, taking England as a whole, the parish was the basic unit of local government (both civil and ecclesiastical), of worship, and of local loyalty, from late Saxon times until the eighteenth century, and in many rural and non-industrial areas to the present day. That does not mean that one should study it in isolation – country people have always had wider horizons, partly owing to a considerable degree of population mobility since the later Middle Ages at least – and we have been rightly warned to beware of 'the myth of the relatively isolated, self-contained and static rural community'.[3]

'Parish' derives from the Greek *paroikia* (Latin *parochia*), a word adapted by the early Church to mean 'a district under the spiritual charge of a bishop', and later (when the term 'diocese' was substituted for this) a district with its own priest. In England, since the Middle Ages, it has meant 'a township or cluster of townships having its own church, and ministered to by its own priest, parson, or parish clergyman, to whom its tithes and ecclesiastical dues are (or originally were) paid'.[4] Two complications to this neat definition, however, emerged between the sixteenth and eighteenth centuries. As more secular responsibilities were imposed upon the parish by the state, there arose the civil parish which in some cases came to cover an area which differed from that of the ecclesiastical parish. Some ecclesiastical parishes which were amalgamated in the sixteenth century, for example, remained separate units for purposes of rating or poor relief, while large ecclesiastical parishes were sometimes subdivided in the eighteenth century for civil purposes only. Furthermore, after 1689 there was no legal obligation to attend the parish church, and nonconformists were able to create communities based on a network of chapels and meeting-houses bearing little or no relationship to parochial geography. Nevertheless, the vast majority of church-goers before 1750 were members of the Established Church, and it may be legitimate here to use 'the parish' to mean a focus of community loyalty, worship and local government, while recognizing that it was by no means the only such focus.

Traditionally, Church history has concentrated on theology, doctrine and the upper levels of administration and leadership. Recently more attention has been paid to popular religion and to the laity, to such an extent that 'religion has become by definition popular'.[5] Yet the parish has not thereby become central, and few general works on the Church between 1350 and 1750 even have an entry for 'parish' in the index. There has been much research, it is true, on religion at the local level, but often concentrating on dissent, voluntarism or household piety rather than on the parochial and conformist communities which were the religious and secular context in which the great majority lived out their days. The parish church was, before 1689, the *only* public building intended for the assembly of the entire local community. Richard Hooker defended the solemn dedication of churches as a necessary ceremony 'to make them places of public resort' and to take away all private rights of ownership in them.[6]

The common theme of the following essays is the local community, usually, though not always, the parish. No attempt is made to provide a definition of 'community' on anthropological lines, for several different and overlapping kinds of community are under discussion. Suffice to say that what the contributors share is a community-based approach designed, as far as possible, to analyse the attitudes of ordinary people. The stress is on the parish and its alternatives as focuses of loyalty, ritual and belief; it would require another book to do justice to the parish as an organ of secular government, although it is considered here by Nick Alldridge and several other contributors.[7] Nevertheless, since the secular and ecclesiastical spheres overlapped so much, if indeed the two can be clearly separated at all before 1689, there is frequent consideration here of the parish in its dual role.

The parish before 1350

The following essays range over four centuries, their authors believing, rightly, that the impact of the Reformation can be overstated, and that there are significant continuities and parallels between the parish community of the late Middle Ages and its Protestant successor. There is a good deal to be gained by ignoring what Dr Edwards has called 'the artificial and tiresome historical frontier defences to be found around the year 1500'.[8] Yet if the sixteenth century has been overstressed as a break, it would be quite wrong to suggest that one could substitute for it the fourteenth or fifteenth century. The first studies begin then so as to depict the medieval Church in its final phase. The whole history of the English Church – of the undivided medieval Church and of its Church of England successor – is one of institutional continuity as well as of much flexibility and change within that continuity. It may therefore help to sketch briefly the early history of the parish before discussing the implications of the findings which follow.

Leaving out of account the Christianization of Roman Britain and the extent of its undoing by the pagan English invaders, England was converted to Christianity in the seventh century. The first stage of organization was the establishment of dioceses under bishops; only gradually were the priests under their obedience put in charge of defined geographical communities, first over large areas centred on mission churches (the minster system) and later in the tenth and eleventh centuries, over small subdivisions (the parish system). Dr Blair summarizes this development as follows:

Minsters played a crucial pastoral role in the . . . seventh and eighth centuries. . . . They were staffed by communities of priests who served big *parochiae* covering perhaps 5 to 15 modern parishes, and from whom the inhabitants of rural England first received the Church's ministry. Between the eighth and twelfth centuries thousands of little churches, founded by private lords and served by single priests, sprang up in the *parochiae*, assumed the pastoral functions of the minsters, and became the raw material of the fully-fledged parochial system.[9]

From the twelfth century onwards, the parish system was normal throughout England, though some of the old minster churches clung persistently to their rights of tithe, burial duty and so on.

Many parish boundaries remained unchanged from their first documentary record in the later Middle Ages to the time of the mapping of the bounds by the Ordnance Survey in the nineteenth century. However, parishes as social units may go back much further than the above sketch of ecclesiastical organization suggests. The estate boundaries specified in Anglo-Saxon charters often coincide with later parish boundaries, and in some cases one can go back further still; there are good reasons to think that many medieval parishes coincided more or less exactly with Roman, or even pre-Roman, estates.[10] In other words, by the time of the conversion to Christianity, much of the population already lived in communities sensibly based on the convenience of agriculture and landownership. When the missionaries arrived, they grouped such estates into larger minster parishes, and as the clergy became more numerous they reverted to the older, smaller units. If that is even partly correct, then much of the tenacious local loyalty of the parish community described in this book goes back a very long way.

Be that as it may, by the twelfth century the parish system was well organized in England, as throughout the Christian West, and everyone was deemed to be a parishioner of some church and to have both economic and spiritual obligations towards it. The Lateran Council of 1215 made annual confession to the parish priest and annual communion at Easter obligatory on all Christians, while the Council of Westminster (1200) ruled that the tithes of all newly cultivated lands must be paid to the parish churches within the bounds of which they lay, implying that all land lay within a parish. The Taxation of Pope Nicholas IV (1291) listed at least 8085 parishes and 457 parochial chapels in England and Wales; and since the number of benefices recorded in 1535 was 8838, it is clear that very few new parishes were created between those dates.[11] This is hardly surprising, because the parish clergy normally acquired the sole rights over tithes, marriage dues and burial dues, and were unwilling to see their income reduced.

The parish system was not utterly inflexible; in areas like Staffordshire, Lancashire and the West Riding of Yorkshire where a small population increased considerably between the Conquest and the Reformation, new parishes were created out of old dependent chapelries, while some of the churches serving villages deserted in the fourteenth and fifteenth centuries were demolished. In many other cases, however, vested interests blocked all attempts at change. Unseemly struggles might occur as a rector enforced his monopoly of burial in the parish churchyard, even over parishioners who lived at a distance, while new and thriving towns could find themselves without a parish church because the mother church in a nearby village forbade their independence. The townsmen's church at Market Harborough in Leicestershire was forced to remain a dependent chapelry to Great Bowden, and that of Kingston-upon-Hull to Hessle.

The consequence of freezing the parochial system in the high Middle Ages meant that some parishes became either too big or too small for the population. The natural response of growing communities was to modify or circumvent the system to bring it more nearly into line with demographic and social reality. Thus many growing villages and towns treated their chapels as parish churches so far as ecclesiastical law allowed, and made them the focus of loyalty for their communities. The men and women of Hull and Harborough did not cease to treat their chapels as their town churches simply because they could not keep their tithe offerings within the town, and they were even able to establish burial rights. In other cases, a guild could become a focus for a town's community loyalty where the parish church was inappropriate. At Stratford-upon-Avon the Bishop of Worcester laid out a new town over the fields of Old Stratford, in which parish it remained. Yet although Shakespeare's parish church of Holy Trinity is only half a mile from the town centre, the new burgesses wanted their own focus of loyalty, which they created through the Guild of the Holy Cross and its chapel. In any case it was natural for townsmen to establish alternative or complementary loyalties to parish churches through the form of guilds, as Dr Rosser shows, and it does not imply that the parish system was seriously out of joint.

Throughout most of medieval England the parish church remained the main, often the only, focus for the spiritual loyalties of its local community. The laity took a close interest in the building and its maintenance. Indeed, from the thirteenth century, they were responsible for maintaining the nave and for providing utensils and ornaments for services, and for these purposes they were represented by churchwardens chosen from among themselves.[12] The church and churchyard were the location for a wide variety of activities other than worship, despite clerical disapproval of the more profane ones. William de Pagula, in the early fourteenth century, instructed parish priests not to allow markets and fairs in churchyards, or games and stone-throwings, or those 'dissolute dances' and 'inhonest songs' customarily performed on the vigils of certain feasts.[13]

Continuity and change: 1350–1750

Between about 1350 and 1530 English parish churches continued to enjoy development as centres for communal loyalty and solidarity. The evidence, as Dr Burgess reminds us, includes the high proportion of medieval churches rebuilt, restored or enlarged in the Perpendicular style, the splendour of which has been persuasively emphasized by J. H. Harvey and others. Admittedly, surviving records rarely show how the work was financed and they are more likely to survive where wealthy donors proudly recorded their contributions, as with the Earl of Oxford and the clothier family of Springs at Lavenham in Suffolk (c. 1486–1525). At Bodmin, however, accounts survive to show that the rebuilding of 1469–72 was paid for by 460 people, nearly every adult in the parish, and that others too poor to give money or goods provided labour. For the nave of Solihull in Warwickshire in 1533–4, the leading townsmen clubbed together to supply timber, and seventeen people provided carriage for the materials.[14] Many of these churches housed parish guilds which played an important role in community life until their dissolution in 1547–8. A combing of some thousand York wills for the period 1501–54 revealed at least seven such guilds in different churches, and as they were only casually mentioned in bequests, the presumption is that all, or nearly all, parishes had one.[15] The existence of so many guilds is often a better explanation for the addition or enlargement of aisles than the growth of population, especially as the population was generally falling after 1350 while many churches continued to be enlarged. Often the process can be documented, as at Romsey in Hampshire, where Thomas Shotter in 1464–7 left 6s. 8d. for the 'fabric of the new aisle', and 20s. to the Brotherhood of St George which used it.[16]

The regular meeting of the parishioners in church helped to sustain not only a corporate identity but a collective memory. Agnes Maners of York left nine tenements to her parish church somewhere around 1500, being in return named in the parish bede-roll. She was prayed for by name until 1558, and witnesses still remembered the fact in 1585. Parochial loyalty could remain strong even when families moved away. Sir Martin Bowes, a London alderman and royal goldsmith, successfully interceded with York corporation in 1547 to preserve St Cuthbert's church there, since his grandfather and great-grandfather had been 'founders and patrons of the same churche and gave bothe books, bells and all other ornaments to the same'.[17] None of this is to suggest that other focuses of loyalty were unimportant: there could also be loyalties towards cathedrals and monastic houses (especially in the towns, the friaries), to chapels and hospitals, and to lay guilds and fraternities and other than parish guilds. The importance of such voluntary associations in the late Middle Ages is clear from the evidence presented by Dr Rosser as well as by Professor Scarisbrick and other recent writers.[18] None the less, they are best viewed as loyalties supplementing or overlapping with the parish rather than competing with it. When the rector of Holy Trinity, Goodramgate, York, gave a window to his church in about 1470, he depicted both the Corpus Christi and St Christopher and St George, patrons of the two great city guilds to which he belonged; he evidently saw no clash of loyalties.[19]

The choices open to laymen and laywomen were, of course, drastically reordered by the changes loosely but conveniently summarized as the Reformation, and yet again by the upheavals of the mid seventeenth century which A. G. Dickens has seen as 'almost . . . a second English Reformation'.[20] Christopher Hill has defined the main theme of these periods for the social historian of religion as 'the breakdown of the parish' with the spread of religious voluntarism, but it is a questionable and perhaps misleading definition of the late Middle Ages as well as of the Reformation. Patrick Collinson has suggested in reply that 'it may be proper to interpret the voluntary and quasi-separatist religious behaviour of the English puritans as the pursuit of religious and social instincts which had always existed both within and beyond the parish'.[21] Indeed, the removal of many religious alternatives to the parish at the Reformation – notably religious guilds and religious houses, and especially the popular friaries in the towns – may have increased the importance of the parish church. The Act of Uniformity (1559) added positive secular compulsion by requiring every inhabitant of the realm normally to frequent his or her own parish church. Even the cathedrals and collegiate churches were on the defensive, their endowments reduced and their very existence questioned; a draft parliamentary bill of 1589, apparently not introduced, proposed to suppress them altogether.[22]

The state's suspicion of rivals to the normal parochial framework was not new – it lay behind the 1389 inquiries into guilds – but it was now pursued more effectively. Between 1547 and 1642 the government showed itself uniformly hostile to extra-parochial religious loyalties of all kinds, and if the parish was a real community at this period (as is demonstrated below in the case of Chester) it partly reflects the lack of alternatives. It was no purely insular development; other Protestant regimes moved in a similar direction, as did the Roman Catholic states of the Counter-Reformation. As religious divisions hardened, both sides of the divide became deeply suspicious of alternatives to the framework of dioceses and parishes. One sign of the policy in England was the state's decision in 1538 to order registration of baptisms, marriages and burials by the parish clergy, an order renewed and extended in 1598. It depended on an assumption that all three events in the life-cycle would take place in the parish church or at least with the knowledge of the parish clerk.

At the same time, paradoxically, the amount of money spent on building and maintenance of parish churches was drastically curtailed. W. K. Jordan's figures for bequests in nine counties illustrate this very clearly in monetary terms, and the decline would be even steeper if inflation were taken into account.[23] Some of this was a natural result of suppressing chantries and simplifying the decoration of churches, but there was also much neglect of existing churches and an almost complete cessation of new church building between 1540 and 1660. A fervent Protestant like Philip Stubbes, in *A Motive to Good Workes* (1593), conceded that pre-Reformation Englishmen went 'far beyond' his contemporaries in church building, and that the condition of their 'stately edifices' was now 'lamentable'.[24] This does not mean, however, that parish churches had become less important, but that they were used in different ways. The services required a plainer interior; and furthermore, churches were still used for a wide variety of other, secular, purposes like schools and courts, even if some of the medieval uses of the church (like dinners and dances) were now being banned.[25]

The renewed emphasis on the centrality of the parish for worship coincided with, and was reinforced by, a new role for the parish in secular local government, as Nick Alldridge shows. It had long had a role as the smallest area of secular as well as ecclesiastical government, being for instance the normal unit of taxation whether imposed by parliaments or popes. Tudor and Stuart governments, however, imposed many new responsibilities on the parishes, to such an extent that new officials had to be instituted alongside the traditional churchwardens. A statute of 1555 imposed on parishes the maintenance of highways, and required each parish to appoint two surveyors, while from 1572 overseers of the poor were also to be appointed in every parish. During the following century the statutory duties of parish officials continued to accumulate, and it is hard to believe that the regular meetings of parishioners to choose or to assist their officers did not reinforce the sense of parish community. This is not, however, to deny that it may have also divided the parish, since in many areas big decisions were taken more and more by select vestries than by parishioners as a whole. Indeed, Wrightson sees the seventeenth century as witnessing a 'realignment of the vitally important middling group in rural communities, the yeomanry and minor gentry, the cocks of the parish' in which wardens and overseers distanced themselves from their neighbours and became 'willing auxiliaries' of the magistrates.[26]

Whether one should go so far or not, the parish certainly remained a key element in the maintenance of obedience and order, even during the period 1646–60 when the Church of England was disestablished and when Presbyterian and other ministers took over from rectors and vicars. Despite Hill's view of the 'breakdown of the parish' and the rise of voluntarism, sources like the diary of the Cheshire minister Adam Martindale show the law being enforced locally by the clergy and parish officers in the 1650s, much as in earlier decades. The same pattern continued after the re-establishment of the Church of England in the 1660s: the parish, at least in the countryside, remained a fairly effective organization. Richard Gough, himself a churchwarden at Myddle, gives little hint of any serious difficulty in keeping the parish harmonious and quiet in the late seventeenth century.

From 1662, of course, there were competing loyalties in the form of nonconformist churches, although that existence was for long a precarious one (they were not fully legalized until 1689, and as late as 1714 the Schism Act, had it received royal assent, threatened their existence in a last fling of state suspicions of alternatives to the parish). The studies by Dr Barry and Dr Triffitt remind us of how quickly they took root, especially in the towns, as alternatives to the established Church, creating 'enormous tensions once not all citizens participated fully in the parish'.[27] Yet it may not be perverse, from a twentieth-century perspective, to see them as complementing the Anglican Church as well as competing with it, helping to provide more local community focuses as much as to divide communities. It is certainly the case with the Methodists, at the very end of our period, that many of their chapels sprang up to serve communities lacking churches, especially in areas of large parishes and many townships like South Wales, Lancashire and the West Riding of Yorkshire. It needs also to be remembered that from Anne's reign onwards the Established Church did start new church-building on a significant scale, although not on the same scale as the nineteenth century. In the provincial towns alone some fifty churches were built or rebuilt between 1700 and 1750.[28]

Law and loyalty: a local perspective

This brief chronological survey has touched on some of the basic questions with which Wright and her fellow contributors are concerned. How far was the parish ever a real community and how far simply an administrative convenience? Or, to put it another way, how far was it a vehicle for order and discipline imposed from 'above', and how far a focus of loyalty freely given from 'below'? Did it become stronger or weaker as an ecclesiastical community over the four centuries (for it certainly grew in importance as a unit of secular government)? Did attendance at the parish church, and understanding of its rites and ceremonies, weaken, or was there simply more concern over, and documentation of, weaknesses that had always been present? Did participation by the poor, by women and by children change over time? How were religious beliefs reflected in office-holding and in political organization? To many of these questions there can as yet be only partial answers, and much of this volume represents an agenda for future research.

It is all too easy to take as a starting point the role of government, as have so many historians of the Reformation. Yet many parishes must have begun as voluntary associations of local communities to build and maintain a church, and continued to include a strong element of unforced loyalty; Alldridge persuasively stresses the 'assumption of a basic consensus' behind parochial government in Chester.[29] In 1798 in one Staffordshire village the churchyard wall was still being maintained by the parishioners 'in allotments proportionate to the land they occupy in the parish', perhaps in continuing recognition of the whole community's responsibility for upkeep of the church. An Oxfordshire churchyard wall was at the same period the liability of ten persons, apparently those whose land abutted the churchyard.[30]

The authorities in Church and state naturally held a different perspective. To them the parish was a subordinate unit of government and discipline. Bishops and archdeacons, both before and after the Reformation, summoned churchwardens to remedy defaults. Parliaments, after the Reformation, added an increasing burden of secular responsibilities. Congregationalism was never a practical issue, except to a limited extent during the Interregnum; clergy were appointed by bishops and patrons, and parish officers were expected to assist them. Yet even so, parishioners could find means to become involved in the running of their churches, as in the cases of Baldock (1462) and Oxford All Saints (1538) discussed below.[31] Two of the three churches of medieval Hedon in Yorkshire were built by the burgesses, and their 'unique proprietary relationship' was 'demonstrated by the election of the churchwardens at burgess meetings'; when the churches became redundant after 1476 their sites were regarded as corporation property. At Havering in Essex, a particularly independent-minded community, the churchwardens were, by the late fifteenth century, appointing their own priests without regard for the patron.[32] After the Reformation, some communities, especially in towns made sure of similar control by the simple expedient of buying the advowsons of their parishes, while those who could not do so often managed instead to fund lectureships under their control.[33]

As these examples suggest, lay initiative could be important before as well as after the Reformation. The traditional view is that late medieval initiatives were largely repressed and were driven into the channels of Lollardy and sedition,[34] but Rosser and Burgess remind us of the considerable scope for lay initiatives represented by fraternities and chantries, to which one could add pageants, plays and local shrines.

These opportunities for local initiative were swept away by the dissolution of religious gilds and chantries and, temporarily, a vacuum was created in local religious life. Deprived of the traditional vehicles by which they could influence the religious life of their locality, the laity naturally sought new opportunities.

Some were in direct continuity, as at Pilton in Devon, where people flocked to sermons on the site of a pre-Reformation shrine, and 'some offered as they did when they went on pilgrimage'.[35] As Rosser neatly puts it, at one level 'the assembly of zealous protestants takes its place in the same tradition as the medieval guild meeting'.[36] Another and quite different element of continuity was lay co-operation with the church courts. Hill has stressed their decline and their unpopularity after the Reformation, in particular over their pursuit of tithe payments; but Houlbrooke has demonstrated that they continued to function effectively, and with much lay support, certainly until the late sixteenth century. Their role in reconciling conflicts between neighbours and kin often made them valued by ordinary parishioners.[37] Another example of continuity of church practice, with the active support of the laity, was the annual perambulations of the bounds of the parish, exempted from the bans on religious procession in 1547 and 1559. These were a valuable means of reinforcing the community's sense of identity, and apparently continued to be carried out in many areas during the seventeenth and eighteenth centuries.

Yet it would be perverse, in stressing the continuities of community life before and after the Reformation, to minimize the significance of that revolution. For it was a revolution, and was perceived to be so by the laity in the parishes, whether they welcomed it or not. The wardens of St Andrew's, Norwich, affixed an inscription in the nave celebrating the fact that their church was

> . . . lately translated from extreme Idolatry
> A thousand five hundred and seven and fortie
> And in the first year of our noble King Edward
> The Gospel in Parliament was mightily set forward
> Thanks be to God. Anno Dom. 1547 Decemb.[38]

More conservative communities reacted differently, by co-operating to conceal Catholic furnishings, or to keep them in the church long after they had become illegal.[39] And when the Reformation had really triumphed in a zealous parish, it might be signalled by changes in government of an almost Genevan kind: at Dover at the end of the sixteenth century the municipal officers were elected at the communion table in the parish church.[40]

Similarly, the continuing effects of the Reformation in the seventeenth century should not be understated. From 1547 to 1642 the Church was perceived as an organization for all (a point stressed here by Alldridge), although Protestants had differing perceptions of the nature of that Church and the exercise of authority within it. From 1642, however, and even more from 1662 and 1689, increasing numbers challenged the very idea of comprehensive membership of a single Church and of a single place of worship in each parish. Inevitably, there was a gradual separation between the secular and the ecclesiastical parish; inevitable, too, was resentment at the effects of their continued overlap. Dissenters were outraged that they should pay for, but have no representation in, the organisation of such vital local matters as poor relief and education.[41] Less foreseen by parliament, probably, was that the legal right to choose a place of worship after 1689 would come to imply the right to choose none: 'churchwardens, reflecting public opinion, assumed that liberty of conscience meant licence to spend Sunday as one pleased. They ceased to present those who did not attend church'.[42]

However, national generalizations of this type can take us only so far. A theoretically uniform system of Church government overlay a variety of local communities and societies, and since much of the origin of and support for the parishes came from below, there was much local variation; several sources of such variety could usefully be explored in future researches. There is the obvious possibility that local regions – whether dioceses, counties, or more likely the more subtly defined regions which Everitt calls *pays* – could have had very differing traditions of lay involvement. There is, in the countryside, the strong probability that 'open' and 'closed' parishes also had very different traditions. Furthermore there is the likely effect of the differing nature and size of the parish, which one can for simplicity's sake categorize in three types.

Of these three, the most stable was the parish of middling size, small enough to be served by a single parish church with resident clergy, yet large enough to have its own lay elite to fill the parish offices. It included many of the Wiltshire parishes delineated by Dr Spaeth, and most of the nucleated villages of the Midland plain, where church, manor and village lay conveniently together in the midst of their fields. It was not, however, confined to nucleated villages; it could also include parishes of dispersed settlement like Gough's Myddle, and town parishes of reasonable size such as the Chester parishes described by Alldridge.

Below this type came the parish which was too small to be really viable, including both rural parishes with a dwindling or vanishing population after 1349, and declining towns with too many parishes created in an earlier period of prosperity. Of the one type, there are numerous cases reported in the returns of the Bishop of Norwich to the Privy Council in 1603, where churches were listed as 'prophaned' and no longer maintained for worship.[43] On the other, one may cite towns like Lincoln, York and Stamford, which took the opportunity of the Reformation to amalgamate parishes and pull down superfluous churches, either by taking advantage of a general statute of 1545 or by securing their own local acts.[44] It was an acute problem; one poor York church was, as has been seen, spared suppression in 1547 at the request of a rich landowner born in the parish, but fourteen years later, despite having another church united to it, it was still 'ofte tymes destitute of a curate', and forty-two years later it could be repaired only by cannibalizing yet another suppressed church.[45]

At the other extreme were the over-large parishes, either because they covered too large an area, or had a huge population, or both. They included the scattered settlements of the Yorkshire and Lancashire Pennines where dependent townships were growing into textile towns, and large and growing towns with too few parishes. Where there were no dependent chapels to act as churches or to be upgraded to parish churches, there was after 1662 a natural breeding-ground for indifference to the Church or for adherence to alternatives. The population of Plymouth, for instance, including its industrial suburb of Devonport, grew from perhaps 4000 around 1550 to 13,000 or more in the 1740s,[46] yet it had only one parish church until the 1640s when a second was added. Their inadequacy for such a growing population may be one of the reasons for the success of Plymouth's Dissent described by Triffitt. There were some attempts in the 1640s and 1650s to divide large parishes and put everyone within easy reach of a parish church, but these foundered on vested interests.[47]

The thriving Dissenting churches of Bristol or Plymouth were not numerically representative of the nation as a whole. Although religious pluralism can be said to have been reluctantly legalized in 1662, and strengthened in 1689 and 1714, the Established Church long remained dominant. The Compton Census of 1676 confirms this, and as late as 1715 fewer than one in ten of the population were Catholics or Dissenters.[48] There is, therefore, a great need for investigations of the conforming Anglican majority, as Spaeth provides here for Wiltshire. Yet perhaps the most important questions are not how many attended which churches, but how many attended church at all, and whether church attendance even by a large majority implied what we may suppose it did. These are crucial problems for any examination of popular religion and for the entire four centuries under consideration.

More than twenty years ago Hill launched an assault on the belief that church attendance was universal in the sixteenth and seventeenth centuries, and since then evidence to support him has proliferated. Peter Clark suggests a regular 80 per cent attendance in Kent in the late sixteenth century, while Alldridge here suggests, from a range of sources, lower levels than this in some Chester parishes. However, Dr Spufford has pointed out that the bishops' returns of 1603, for the very different dioceses of Ely and London, suggest that at most 1 or 2 per cent of the population were noncommunicants or recusants.[49] It may well be that church-going was declining in the very long term, but it is doubtful whether there was ever an 'age of faith' with universal attendance, despite the ecclesiastical obligation to weekly attendance from

1215, and it is very possible that historians finding a declining church attendance after the Reformation are simply finding more records of a long-established pattern. There are isolated cases of presentments for non-attendance well before the Reformation,[50] but there seems to have been no systematic drive to enforce attendance before 1559. Indeed, Scarisbrick suggests that weekly attendance was 'very imperfectly achieved' before the Reformation and was enforced 'more effectively than ever before' after 1559.[51]

There are, however, many indications of layfolk staying away from church in considerable numbers after 1559, as had perhaps long been the case, and not only because of theological differences. 'Manie of the parishioners of Wheldrake' in Yorkshire were in 1580 'verie slacke in coming to devine service and sermons, delighting more in ther owne ease', while the York city council complained more than once of many of the 'inferior sorte' or 'meaner sort of people' preferring alehouses to the church.[52] There were influential voices in the reigns of Elizabeth and James I asserting that the law was simply not enforced,[53] and it may be, as Spaeth suggests for Wiltshire, that church services were often inconvenient interruptions in a busy agricultural routine. An Oxfordshire minister in the early eighteenth century excused low attendance by parishioners on holy days because 'they are all poor labouring people, and I cannot expect them without a breach of charity'.[54]

Church and state, in any case, may have thought in terms of households, rather than all individuals, being represented at services. In fifteenth-century London Sunday work was forbidden because apprentices were trusted to carry on work in the absence of their masters at church.[55] By 1551, if the Venetian ambassador can be trusted, the opposite was the case: Londoners were choosing one in each family to communicate every Sunday, 'so certain merchants treat it as a joke, and are in the habit of sending one of their servants'.[56] In 1571, however, Archbishop Grindal of York enjoined all lay people to attend church, 'especially householders', implying perhaps that servants and the poor were another matter.[57] Nor is it clear, as Wright points out, whether all children were expected to attend, or whether their attendance fluctuated over time. They may well have found services less congenial after the Reformation, with the suppression of 'childish observances' in 1541.[58] There are haphazard post-Reformation indications of children and youths in church, such as a girl of 10 or

11 attending church with her mother, and a lad of 14 assaulted in a dispute over pews,[59] but it is impossible to draw general conclusions from these.

Even where most of a community was present in church for at least one service each Sunday, that of course does not have to imply that they understood the worship in the same way as the clergy expected; and non-participation at communion certainly need not have implied disrespect for the sacrament. In both these respects Spaeth has drawn attention to important differences in perception in late-Stuart Wiltshire which may well have applied to other areas and periods. On the other hand, it would be naive to suppose that differences in perception were invariably between a learned clergy and an uninformed laity; there could be problems the other way round, as puritan surveys of scandalous ministers often alleged in the century after the Reformation. And even before the Reformation there may well have been layfolk well able to comprehend the services better than an ill-educated priest. A fascinating case from the city of York in Mary's reign reveals parishioners pointing out defects in the Latin liturgy of their vicar.[60]

There is also much work to be done on the relative participation in local church communities by different social and age groups, and by men and women. It is clear that, as in Myddle, post-Reformation seating normally reflected the social hierarchy of the parish, whether measured by wealth, ancestry or office. At Normanton, in Yorkshire, in 1584 the gentry were 'convenientlie placed neare the quere and the husbande men removed and set lower'; at Dover a few years later the corporation officers were given special seats at the east end;[61] and many urban parish churches still possess mayoral standards marking the site of the mayor's pew. This is often linked with a new emphasis after the Reformation, as 'parish notables' participated in 'a regenerated and extended system of social control'.[62] I must confess to remaining a sceptic, not about social precedence but about its novelty. Seating disputes and arbitrations were new in the sixteenth century simply because seating for the congregation was new. Parish elites, even parish elites concerned with social control, were not new, and can be discerned well before the Reformation.[63]

What is more interesting is not the broad existence of rank and wealth as dictating precedence in church, but the qualifications to it. Age was as respected as birth and wealth: at the basic level of full church membership this can be seen in the rising age of confirmation and first communion, and age could also be a means of differentiating between adults. The Gloucestershire parish which made parishioners' precedence in church dependent on the date of their weddings was indirectly acknowledging this principle.[64] Young people, even apprentices – who could be in their early twenties – were treated as subordinate inside church as well as outside. One York church in the 1520s kept four pews reserved for householders and their apprentices, 'to the entent that the sayd masteres myght se the conversacon of the sayd prentises'.[65]

Sex was, of course, another source of discrimination, but though laymen almost always monopolized influence at the expense of women, it was not always so. Quite a few women are recorded holding office as churchwardens in the sixteenth and seventeenth centuries, and it would be interesting to see a study of them as a group. At St Budeaux in Devon one male and one female warden were regularly chosen in the early seventeenth century, while at Staplegrove in Somerset two widows were elected in 1645.[66] Ecclesiastical office was, of course, not open to women, but some of the voluntary churches of the 1640s and 1650s did accept female leadership.

Furthermore, it should be remembered that any precedence within the parish community was subject to limitations. Between the sixteenth and eighteenth centuries it was not uncommon for public penance to be enforced against all ranks, whether for offences deemed to be against God and the whole community, like adultery or heresy, or equally significantly for offences against social and sexual inferiors. A York freeman, for instance, was compelled to make public apology in church for slandering a female servant.[67]

Change and continuity

The parish was and remains a communal focus capable of adaptation over many centuries. Its history has been unjustly belittled, and 'parochial' is a popular term of abuse; but it was the parish which mattered most, both in ecclesiastical and secular terms, to the majority of the population from the tenth or eleventh century to the eighteenth or nineteenth. Its importance, and that of its nonconformist equivalents, is demonstrated by the essays which follow. The Reformation, often viewed as a decisive stage in the process of change from compulsory and corporate to voluntary religious practice, is here seen in a different light. There was voluntary as well as compulsory religious practice both before and after it; and if the sixteenth and seventeenth centuries saw the end of some parish-centred activities, they also witnessed the creation or strengthening of others. *The Parish Chest* is the apt title of Dr Tate's study of local records from the sixteenth to the nineteenth centuries, while the parish registers form the indispensable basis for the massive recent analysis of English population changes between 1541 and 1871.[68]

Of course there were substantial changes as an ancient ecclesiastical unit was adapted to new purposes; and it cannot be denied that the Reformation, by making possible – in the long run – religious pluralism and the end of compulsory worship, ultimately led to the decline of the parish as the chief or sole religious focus at the local level, just as the growth of central and local government in the nineteenth century reduced its secular importance. Yet much needless confusion is caused by blurring the problems inherent in the parochial system itself with those created by its anomalies. The long-term problem was that, from the thirteenth century onwards, the conservative nature of ecclesiastical government made it very difficult to modify the parish system. Shifts in population and prosperity made the parish structure less and less suitable in some areas, while leaving it viable in others. The whole system came under immense strain with rapid industrialization and population growth in the eighteenth and early nineteenth centuries, and by the time that parochial geography was seriously overhauled, from the 1830s onwards, the parish was already an irrelevance in many urban and industrial areas.

Yet it would be wrong to overlook the degree of strength and continuity in the system in many other areas that remained until very recent times, and even to the present day. At Clyro, Radnorshire, in the 1870s Francis Kilvert still found in some respects a church-centred community in the medieval sense. On Easter Eve 1870 many parishioners flocked into the churchyard while the graves were being 'dressed' with flowers, 'for the Churchyard on Easter Eve is a place where a great many people meet'. Next morning Kilvert found only twenty-nine communicants but 'a very large congregation . . . for they have here an immense reverence for Easter Sunday'.[69] Nearly a century later, Williams' classic survey of the Cumberland parish of Gosforth found it 'a social unit as well as an administrative unit' with a strong 'feeling of belonging to a community which is different from, and independent of, the outside world'. Although the great majority did not attend church services, 'the secular aspects of church life' were still 'matters which concern every parishioner'.[70] Today any secular powers once enjoyed by the parish vestries – the parochial church councils of today – have been transferred to civil parish councils and other secular authorities, but these civil parishes often preserve the old boundaries of the ecclesiastical parishes and are in many aspects their heirs. Taking the parishes of both kinds together, they are by no means at the end of a long and adaptable life.

Notes and references

1   R. Gough, *The History of Myddle*, ed. W. G. Hoskins (1968); ed. D. G. Hey (1981).

2   W. G. Hoskins, *Local History in England*, 3rd edn (1984), p. 29.

3   K. Wrightson, *English Society 1580–1680* (1982), p. 41.

4   *The Oxford English Dictionary* (1933). See also the discussions of dues by Burgess, Alldridge and Wright in this volume.

5   K. von Greyerz (ed.), *Religion and Society in Early Modern Europe 1500–1800* (1984), pp. 254–5, cited by J. H. Edwards in *European History Quarterly*, **17** (1987), p. 88.

6   R. Hooker, *Of the Laws of Ecclesiastical Policy*, ed. C. Morris, 2 vols. (1958), vol. 2, pp. 42, 44.

7   See also J. R. Kent, *The English Village Constable 1580–1642: a Social and Administrative Study* (1986).

8   J. H. Edwards, *European History Quarterly*, **17** (1987), p. 89.

9   J. Blair, 'Secular minster churches in Domesday Book', in P. Sawyer (ed.), *Domesday Book: a Reassessment* (1985), p. 104.

10 C. Taylor, *Village and Farmstead: a History of Rural Settlement in England* (1983), pp. 104–5, 120, 124, 148. But see also D. Roffe, 'Pre-Conquest estates and parish boundaries', in M. L. Faull (ed.), *Studies in Late Anglo-Saxon Settlement* (1984), pp. 115–22.

11 R. K. Morris, 'The church in the countryside: two lines of inquiry', in D. Hooke (ed.), *Medieval Villages* (1985), pp. 50–1.

12 P. Heath, *English Parish Clergy on the Eve of the Reformation* (1969), p. 68. See also C. Drew, *Early Parochial Organisation in England* (Borthwick Paper 7, 1954).

13 W. A. Pantin, *The English Church in the Fourteenth Century* (1955), p. 199.

14 J. J. Wilkinson (ed.), 'Receipts and expenses in the building of

Bodmin Church', in *The Camden Miscellany*, **VII** (Camden Society, new series, 14, 1875), separately paginated; Scarisbrick, *Reformation*, p. 14.

15 D. M. Palliser, *Tudor York* (1979), p. 231.

16 R. Morris, *Cathedrals and Abbeys of England and Wales: the Building Church, 600–1540* (1979), p. 227.

17 Palliser, *Tudor York*, p. 228.

18 For example, Scarisbrick, *Reformation*, pp. 19–39.

19 P. E. S. Routh, 'A gift and its giver: John Walker and the east window of Holy Trinity, Goodramgate, York', *Yorkshire Archaeological Journal* **58** (1986), pp. 109–21.

20 Dickens, *Reformation*, p. 336.

21 P. Collinson, *The Religion of Protestants: the Church in English Society 1559–1625* (1982), p. 282.

22 A. F. Pollard, *The History of England from the Accession of Edward VI to the Death of Elizabeth, 1547–1603* (1910), p. 462.

23 W. K. Jordan, *Philanthropy in England 1480–1660* (1959), pp. 297–322.

24 Collinson, *Religion of Protestants*, pp. 169–70.

25 Hill, *Society*, pp. 408–11; O. Chadwick, *The Reformation* (1964), p. 427.

26 Wrightson, *English Society 1580–1680*, pp. 181, 227.

27 See below, pp. 152–72 *passim*, 179–96 *passim*.

28 C. W. Chalklin, 'The financing of church building in the provincial towns of eighteenth-century England', in P. Clark (ed.), *The Transformation of English Provincial Towns* (1984), p. 285.

29 See below.

30 D. M. Palliser, *The Staffordshire Landscape* (1976), p. 53; R. E. Moreau, *The Departed Village: Berrick Salome at the Turn of the Century* (1968), pp. 105–8.

31 See below, pp. 29, 32; compare also Heath, *English Parish Clergy*, pp. 68–9.

32 M. W. Beresford and J. K. St Joseph, *Medieval England: an Aerial Survey*, 2nd edn (1979), p. 220; M. K. McIntosh, *Autonomy and Community: the Royal Manor of Havering, 1200–1500* (1986), pp. 235–40.

33 Good examples include Ipswich, Coventry, Leeds and Plymouth. C. Hill, *Economic Problems of the Church from Archbishop Whitgift to the Long Parliament* (1956), p. 57 etc.; P. S. Seaver, *The Puritan Lectureships: the Politics of Religious Dissent, 1560–1640* (Stanford, California, 1970); W. J. Sheils, 'Religion in provincial towns: innovation and tradition', in F. Heal and R. O'Day (eds), *Church and Society in England: Henry VIII to James I* (1977), pp. 159–60; C. Cross, *The Royal Supremacy in the Elizabethan Church* (1969), pp. 95–9.

34 For example, C. Cross, *Church and People 1450–1660: the Triumph of the Laity in the English Church* (1976), chs. 1, 2.

35 Sheils, 'Religion in provincial towns', p. 175.

36 See below, p. 45.

37 R. Houlbrooke, *Church Courts and the People during the English Reformation 1520–1570* (1979), pp. 263, 271–2.

38 G. H. Cook, *The English Mediaeval Parish Church* (1970), pp. 265–6.

39 For example, the many cases in J. S. Purvis, *Tudor Parish Documents of the Diocese of York* (1948).

40 P. Clark, *English Provincial Society from the Reformation to the Revolution: Religion, Politics and Society in Kent 1500–1640* (1977), p. 176.

41 See below, p. 168.

42 M. G. Smith, *Pastoral Discipline and the Church Courts: the Hexham Court 1680–1730* (Borthwick Paper 62, 1982), p. 31.

43 BL, Ms Harley 595, ffs. 139v, 141v, 149v, etc.

44 D. M. Palliser, 'The unions of parishes at York 1547–1586', *Yorkshire Archaeological Journal* **46** (1974), pp. 87–102; Sheils, 'Religion in provincial towns', p. 160. See also N. L. Jones, *Faith by Statute: Parliament and the Settlement of Religion 1559* (1982), pp. 178–9, for another bill to unite parishes.

45 Palliser, 'Unions of parishes', p. 99.

46 Palliser, *Age of Elizabeth*, p. 203; C. W. Chalklin, *The Provincial Towns of Georgian England* (1974), pp. 23–4.

47 R. O'Day and F. Heal (eds), *Princes and Paupers in the English Church 1500–1800* (1981), pp. 9, 182–4.

48 E. A. Whiteman, *The Compton Census: a Critical Edition* (British Academy, 1986); W. A. Speck, *Stability and Strife: England 1714–1760* (1977), pp. 100–3.

49 Hill, *Society*, pp. 457–8; Clark, *English Provincial Society*, pp. 156, 437; Palliser, *Age of Elizabeth*, pp. 337–8. M. Spufford, 'Can we count the "godly" and the "conformable" in the seventeenth century?', *Journal of Ecclesiastical History*, **36** (1985), pp. 435–6.

50 For example, J. S. Purvis, *A Mediaeval Act Book, with some Account of Ecclesiastical Juristiction at York* (c. 1943), pp. 24–5.

51 Scarisbrick, *Reformation*, p. 173.

52 Purvis, *Tudor Parish Documents*, pp. 76–7; York City Archives, B32, fo. 2v (1599: pr. in Palliser, *Tudor Yorks*, p. 259); B34, fo. 58r (1615).

53 Collinson, *Religion of Protestants*, p. 203; Thomas, *Magic* (1973), pp. 190–1.

54 Thomas, *Magic*, p. 190.

55 H. T. Riley, *Memorials of London and London Life, in the 13th, 14th, and 15th Centuries . . .* (1868), p. 218.

56 *Calendar of State Papers Venetian 1534–1554*, p. 348.

57 Thomas, *Magic*, pp. 189–90.

58 P. L. Hughes and J. F. Larkin (eds), *Tudor Royal Proclamations*, vol. I (Yale University Press, 1964), p. 302.

59 W. G. Hoskins, *The Midland Peasant* (1957), p 183; Purvis, *Tudor Parish Documents*, p. 89.

60 C. Cross, 'Lay literacy and clerical misconduct in a York parish during the reign of Mary Tudor', *York Historian*, 3 (1980), pp. 10–15.

61 Purvis, *Tudor Parish Documents*, p. 88; Clark, *English Provincial Society*, p. 176.

62 Wrightson, *English Society 1580–1680*, pp. 226–8.

63 M. Spufford, 'Puritanism and social control', in A. Fletcher and J. Stevenson (eds), *Order and Disorder in Early Modern England* (1985), pp. 41–57.

64 K. Thomas, 'Age and authority in early modern England', *Proceedings of the British Academy*, 62 (1976), pp. 22–4.

65 Palliser, *Tudor York*, p. 149.

66 W. Hunt, *Diocesan Histories: Bath and Wells* (1880), p. 171; A. T. Hart, *The Man in the Pew* (1966), p. 60; *Archives*, 9 (1969–70), p. 213; P. Hogrefe, *Tudor Women* (1975), p. 27.

67 A. Raine (ed.), *York Civic Records* vol. VII (Yorks. Archaeological Society Record Series cxv, 1950), p. 164.

68 W. E. Tate, *The Parish Chest: a Study of the Records of Parochial Administration in England* (3rd edn, 1969); E. A. Wrigley and R. S. Schofield, *The Population History of England 1541–1871: a Reconstruction* (1981).

69 W. Plomer (ed.), *Kilvert's Diary 1870–1871* (1938), pp. 95, 98.

70 W. M. Williams, *The Sociology of an English Village: Gosforth* (1956), pp. 162, 167, 176.

2 Communities of parish and guild in the late Middle Ages

Gervase Rosser

When the twelfth-century founders of a new town in Hertfordshire eulogistically named their creation after the city of Baghdad, their optimism may, even to contemporaries, have seemed hubristic. Yet Baldock had its day, flourishing for a while on the modest scale of a provincial market town.[1] By the late Middle Ages, however, this limited prosperity had failed. In response to the decline, the parishioners of Baldock in 1462 acquired papal licence to found a fraternity, to be known as the Guild of the Name of Jesus. The local population having contracted, the late fifteenth-century rector was unable to support himself or maintain hospitality as of old, while the parishioners could not keep their parish church in repair. The new association was established with the declared purpose of raising funds to redeem this situation; it was promoted by the attraction of an indulgence offered to contributors to the work of the guild.[2] The changing fortunes of Baldock are doubly instructive. They serve as a reminder that the medieval parish was not static. In addition, they illustrate the relationship, within the context of a particular changing society, between two fundamental medieval forms of social and religious organization: the parish and the guild.

Despite growing awareness of major fluctuations in medieval settlement, the notion dies hard that the medieval community presented a scene of unaltering calm, firmly anchored in the immutable institutions of the parish. This image has been made to serve a modern myth, according to which such a supposed parochial stability was, in the post-medieval period, shattered by an alleged growth of individualism.[3] Thus it has been suggested that the sixteenth and seventeenth centuries saw a radical change from a condition of static, natural community to one of voluntaristic pursuit of individual concerns in both economics and religion:

The transition from parish to sect is from a geographical unit which brings the members of a community together for cultural, social and ceremonial purposes, to a voluntary unit to which men belong in order to hear the preacher of their choice.[4]

Closer scrutiny suggests a modification of this formula. Late medieval society was not contained, immobile, within a fixed framework of parochial blocs; nor did it preclude a significant element of personal choice in the responses made by individuals to the opportunities which changing circumstances presented. Such choice, however, might issue in communal as well as in individual-istic behaviour. The Baldock experience may suggest that, in actuality, the potential for collective action in a perceived common cause may best be realized not (as the myth would have it) in places and periods of unbroken calm, but precisely in the response to social transformations. To recognize the reality of change in medieval society is not, therefore, to reject the possibility of community in that context, but to acknowledge the need for more careful definition and analysis of collective behaviour.[5]

Late medieval society was shaped to a large degree by the institutions already encountered in Baldock: parish and guild. The present essay is an attempt to compare these organizations; to assess their respective capacities to adapt to and indeed to facilitate change, in respect both of social relations and of religious attitudes; and to arrive at a conclusion as to the relationship between the two. In so far as their mutual relationship has received serious attention from historians,[6] the guild and the parish of the later Middle Ages have hitherto been identified as representing essentially incompatible and even conflicting forms of association.[7] Whereas the parish is usually understood as an agency of the institutional church, membership of which was compulsory for the laity, the guild has been perceived as a 'little, extra-parochial church' or as a 'consensual parish', a subversive, 'alternative model of the church', closer to the social needs of the people.[8] In regions (such as England) where parishes were well defined, relations between the two are assumed to have taken the form of 'a struggle'.[9] Before considering the implications and the truth of this alleged discord, it will be well to review the qualities of each of these two types of collectivity in the context of late medieval society.

Lest the parish itself be taken for granted, let it be recalled that the parochial divisions of the later Middle Ages were the immediate creation not of some abstract or remote historical force ('the church triumphant') but of the inhabitants of a myriad human settlements, within each of which decisions had been taken, between the eleventh and the thirteenth centuries, to acquire rights of burial, to erect a church and to appoint a minister. These decisions were made, not by lords only, but by groups of local residents anxious to make ecclesiastical provision for growing populations. This process reflected closely the demographic increase, the extension of settlement and the establishment of villages which characterized the high Middle Ages. Social change was itself the stimulus to the formation of new parishes by local communities.[10] After c.1300 the jealousy of established mother churches and the constraints of ecclesiastical bureaucracy set limits on new parochial creations; the tally of approximately 9000 English parishes formed by 1300 was not to be substantially altered before the nineteenth century.[11] The repressive effect of these limitations was, however, partially alleviated in the later Middle Ages, when demographic contraction reduced the overall demand for religious services. Moreover, setting aside a few frustrated late claimants to parochial independence, many adjustments to the system continued to be made by particular communities in the last medieval centuries.[12] Where the demand persisted, chapelries continued to be able to acquire at least partial parochial privileges (usually beginning with that of burial, always so precious to human settlements).[13] When the collapse of demographic growth created redundant churches, parishioners themselves petitioned for the amalgamation of parishes while they refurbished a reduced total of church buildings.[14] Where the focus of a settlement shifted, the parishioners as a body might even dismantle their church to re-erect it on a more convenient site.[15] Apart from such dramatic alterations, ubiquitous rebuildings of churches and adornments of ritual by late medieval parishioners testify to a commitment which, although hard to quantify, showed no sign of diminution before the religious changes of the mid sixteenth century.[16] The parochial system, although in ecclesiastical theory absolute and inescapable, depended for its survival on the voluntary involvement of its members. The readiness of the laity to take collective responsibility for parochial affairs is epitomized in a lease of the Oxford city parish of All Saints, acquired in 1538 from the rector by the parishioners as a fellowship. The lease carried the duties of upkeep of the church fabric, election (and if necessary, dismissal) of a curate and supervision of all services.[17] Lay influence on parochial affairs, including ecclesiastical appointments,[18] may have increased during the later sixteenth and early seventeenth centuries.[19] But the contrast with the preceding period should not be exaggerated. As at Baldock in 1462 and at Oxford in 1538, so in very many English parishes in the later Middle Ages, parishioners were not slow to shoulder responsibility for their parishes, and were able, up to a point, to adapt existing institutions to suit altered social circumstances.

Yet the medieval parish was an unwieldy institution in the face of social change. The limited flexibility of its geographical bounds sometimes failed conspicuously to accommodate shifts in settlement. By the early sixteenth century uneven demographic developments had created such anomalies as a metropolitan suburban parish of 3500 souls[20] and, in rural Kent, a parish containing only a single parishioner.[21] The definite topographical boundaries of the parish had the further drawback that they ignored the fact of geographical mobility. Commerce drew Christian souls to and fro across parish limits, creating supplementary and overlapping associations. The specific institution which, unlike the parish, was able to give expression to these changing and multifarious groupings was the guild. The guild or fraternity was a form of voluntary association, bound by oath. Extremely widespread in medieval Europe, the guilds were universally characterized, on the one hand, by a concern for the swift salvation from purgatory of the souls of dead members through rites of intercession and, on the other, by some form of commensality among the living. The vast majority of the European guilds, at any rate before 1500, were initiated and run by laity. Each, meanwhile, had as its focus a Christian altar, and it was common, where funds permitted, for a guild to employ one or more chaplains to celebrate intercessory masses on behalf of the society. Although infinitely various in detail, the guilds were essentially very simple organisms, easily formed and readily adaptable to changing needs. This, indeed, was one of their strengths.

Research on the particular forms and distribution of the guilds has not yet been systematically carried out;[22] but a hypothesis may be advanced concerning their formation. Although their continuous history runs back into pre-Christian antiquity,[23] the fourteenth and fifteenth centuries stand out as the period of maximum proliferation of new fraternities.[24] This late medieval growth has sometimes been ascribed to intimations of mortality induced by the Black Death.[25] But the plague, although undoubtedly a grim stimulus in specific cases,[26] is inadequate to account for a general movement which began before 1348 and continued into the early sixteenth century. A more compelling explanation may be provided by a circumstance already noted: the virtual cessation of new parochial creations after 1300. Whereas in the twelfth and thirteenth centuries a local society could realize its identity in the parish, in the fourteenth and fifteenth centuries official constraints upon parish formation forced new and shifting communities to adopt an alternative framework, the fraternity. As a general hypothesis this observation could be formulated as follows: in all periods, a common impetus to form fraternities was a desire (conscious or not) to transcend the limitations, geographical or institutional, of the parish. A concomitant of this proposition would be that guilds were most likely to be found in social contexts characterized by a relatively high degree of mobility, such as the parish could not accommodate.

In fact the occurrence of guilds in the later Middle Ages does conform to this pattern. This is particularly clear in the many cases of guilds, the geographical catchment area for whose membership was wider than the parish within which the society was focused. The intercourse, for example, between a busy market town and its surrounding region was commonly given formal expression in the meetings of an urban-based fraternity. The Holy Cross guild of Stratford-upon-Avon, the bulk of whose membership was drawn from the town and its immediate hinterland, comprised in addition adherents from a wide scatter of market villages.[27] Prominent among these were local centres of the butchering, leather and textile trades which were important in Stratford's own economy: Chipping Campden and Shipston-on-Stour to the south, Bromsgrove, Redditch, King's Norton and Feckenham to the north.[28] Guild membership gave these outsiders an identity and a role within Stratford when they came there to trade. The association thus created was not merely passive; in addition to four 'mornspeches' or general meetings each year, all members attended the

annual guild mass and dinner after Easter. On this occasion the
active unity of the guild was demonstrated by the common livery
worn by the brothers and sisters as they processed via the master's
house to the service and the feast.[29] The importance of regular
assembly of the entire membership was underlined, in this as in
other fraternities, by the imposition of a fine upon absentees.[30]

Not only individuals but entire families and even villages were
incorporated within the fraternity. Pebworth and Broad Marston,
adjacent villages situated five miles southwest of Stratford,
contributed thirteen new members in a single year, 1470–1. As
was usual, husbands, wives and other kin joined the guild
together; the ties which bound the society were by no means solely
economic. This particular group included the vicar of Pebworth,
whose recruitment may have influenced some of his parishioners.[31]
A single individual could participate concurrently in various orders
of fellowship according to circumstance: a later vicar of Pebworth
left bequests in 1510 to the churchwardens of his parish (two
cows), to the guild of St Mary at the village of Aston Cantlow,
northwest of Stratford (2s.), and to the Holy Cross guild in
Stratford itself (6s. 8d.).[32] Such short-range contacts (over five, ten
or fifteen miles) were the most characteristic of the fraternity; but
the town's wider connections are evinced by the Droitwich salters
who compounded for their admission fee with the commodity in
which they trafficked, and the Bristol merchant who paid in
wine.[33] Indeed, the ties created by trade could be extensive. The
guild of young merchants of King's Lynn, founded in 1362, soon
recruited junior merchants from other towns; while another guild
there, dedicated to St Edmund, was probably born of trading
connections with Bury St Edmunds.[34]

Less obviously but no less significantly, a guild whose membership was drawn from within a relatively restricted area might also
represent a response to developments which rendered the parish
itself inadequate as a social framework. Once again this is most
clearly instanced in towns. Town society precipitated such associations among incoming residents, the first phase of whose
assimilation to the new urban world could be the formation of a
newcomers' guild, such as those maintained by the immigrant
Flemish and German communities in late medieval London.[35] In
the countryside, a secondary village or urban settlement growing
up within a parish at an inconvenient distance from the church
might give rise to a fraternity able to construct a chapel for the

local community. When Weymouth in Dorset became established inside the older parish of Wyke Regis, a guild of St George maintained a chapel in the new town, explaining to the chantry commissioners in 1548 that 'Weymouth is a haven town and lies very dangerous for enemies to invade the same', so that were the inhabitants to attend services at Wyke, the French might come and seize the port while it was unoccupied.[36] In yet another configuration, a scattered band of shepherds in a district of Lincolnshire, prevented by the nature of their work from regular attendance at the parish church, could form a guild to ensure that candles burned for them there, both before the image of the Virgin Mary and, on feast days, at the elevation of the host in the mass.[37] Late medieval society was diverse and in some respects highly mobile. To this extent it was in tension with a system of parishes defined geographically. The guilds, often created in explicit response to social change, served to ease this tension.

If the parish depended in part on the voluntary support of its members, the guild was voluntary by definition. Active personal commitment was of the essence of guild membership, bringing adherents, however widely dispersed, regularly into direct contact with one another. The solidarity of the guild was the more vital for being the creation, not of the accident of geographical proximity but of the sum of conscious decisions of its participants. This critical element of choice in participation set the guild, like the dissenting church of a later period, apart from the undiscriminating, all-inclusive parish. Entry to the exclusive club that was the guild was, however, conditional upon enjoyment of a degree of economic independence. Those so poor as to lack any resources surplus to subsistence may have formed different solidarities (barely recorded and as little studied) of their own; but they were debarred from the guilds, which (as their Germanic names, relatives of 'geld', clearly stipulated) demanded a material contribution from their members. Here is another parallel with later nonconformist churches, supported by members' offerings. The annual subscription to a medieval guild, commonly 1s., might be as little as 4d.[38] It might even be rendered in service or kind, as it was by a clockmaker admitted in 1419 to the Stratford Holy Cross guild upon his agreeing to make a public clock at the guildhall.[39] But all exacted a levy of some kind. Even so self-consciously lowly a society as the 'poor people's guild' in the humble Norwich parish of St Austin was not open to all.[40] Had it been so, it would have forfeited the quality of exlusiveness which, like all the others, it prized. The specialized minority of trade guilds excepted, by far the greater number of these associations welcomed recruits from virtually all occupations, of both sexes and of most social degrees. Yet each guild, when drawing up its constitution, carefully stipulated the considered criteria for admission. A guild at Heacham in Norfolk, founded in 1359, explicitly excluded villeins from its ranks.[41] The Corpus Christi Guild of St Michael-on-the-Hill in Lincoln, on the other hand, declared that

whereas this guild was founded [in 1350] by people of common and middling rank, it is ordained that no-one of the rank of mayor or bailiff shall become a brother of the guild, unless he is found to be of humble, good and honest conversation.[42]

The self-selecting character of these societies was again underlined by the Hull Corpus Christi guild, which charged an inflated rate of admission to those who were not related to existing members.[43]

These examples point to the profounder truth that the financial requirement for membership was an adjunct to a more general qualification: social respectability. Propriety was monitored both by the procedure for admissions and by a system of discipline within the guild. An aspirant initiate required the favour of the society's officers or even of the entire membership.[44] Blackballing was a possibility, and when this occurred in a Leicester guild the case was debated and decided on a majority vote.[45] Admission achieved, a member's behaviour was subject to regular review at guild meetings.[46] Guild ordinances relating to conduct are characterized by a mixture of spiritual holiness and social probity. Stipulating fines and ultimately expulsion as the punishment for notorious sinfulness, the authors of these ordinances evinced almost as great a concern with the public notoriety as with the religious nature of the offence. Drunkenness, the casting of insults and scandalous modes of dress were repudiated by guilds at Lynn;[47] the unacceptability of gambling was specified in 1384 by a Wisbech guild;[48] while another at Lancaster, in statutes dated 1377, detailed its hostility to adultery, whether the party concerned were an active participant or played 'the brazen role of pander'.[49] The veritably priggish emphasis on public decency is summed up in the condemnation by a guild at Lichfield of any brother or sister 'convicted of adultery or some other infamous (*notabili*) crime,

and publicly defamed on this account': the name of the persistent
offender was to be struck from the register ('even as that of the
malefactor from the Book of Life') without possibility of readmit-
tance.[50] The attention which the guilds devoted to the public
reputation of their members meant that guild membership was
itself a manifest guarantee of respectability. The 'certificate of
moral qualification' which affiliation to a fraternity conferred bears
close comparison with the social credit accruing to the member of
a sect in the centuries after the Reformation.[51] Membership of a
medieval guild, whether powerful or humble in economic and
political terms, bestowed a status in society which was not enjoyed
by the mere parishioner.

The collectivity of the guild was held together, therefore, by the
voluntary and active involvement of its individual members, and
by their shared, self-conscious desire to distinguish themselves in
some way or other, as a group, from the wider mass of humanity.
A third binding factor was the mutual support which the brothers
and sisters of a guild rendered to one another. This mutual
support was emblemized in the kiss of charity exchanged between
a new initiate and the entire fellowship of the fraternity of St
Fabian and St Sebastian in the church of St Botolph Aldersgate,
London.[52] In practice it took three forms, broadly defined: the
assistance of the society to an individual member in his or her
worldly dealings; charitable aid in poverty of sickness; and spiritual
intercession through masses and prayer. It was characteristic of the
first of these forms of help that the Lincoln guild of St Margaret
resolved to 'stand by a brother or sister charged with any offence
(except for theft or homicide) in fairs or markets, with counsel and
help, as if they were all children of the same father and mother'.[53]
At the same time the guilds set themselves up as independent
forums for the resolution of disputes. It was a common provision
in guild statutes that members should bring their quarrels to the
officers of the society for settlement, thus obviating the need for
costly resort to the courts: 'for there should be no need for any
besides fraternity members to intervene between the quarrelling
parties'.[54] Guild membership could also offer insurance against
times of indigence or ill-health. A member who (through no
blameworthy cause: a proviso naturally stressed by these respectable organizations) had fallen into poverty could expect variable
relief, depending on the society. The guild of St Catherine in the
church of Holy Trinity, Cambridge, in the early sixteenth century

made financial loans at interest to its members, the profits from which were allocated to brothers or sisters in need.[55] Elsewhere impoverished brethren were offered a dole of ¼d. a day and ½d. on Sundays; a gift of ½d. or 2d. from each other member; basic clothing; or hospitality in the house of one of the others of the fraternity.[56] Like assistance was provided in the event of sickness, when healthy members might also pay bedside visits on the unwell;[57] and many guilds offered the additional security of an almshouse run by the society.[58] Finally came the benefits held out to a member *in extremis* – and beyond. All guilds made provision for the decent burial of a deceased member, usually attended by the entire company, and for posthumous intercession on his or her behalf. To the majority of the late medieval population for whom the foundation of a personal chantry was beyond private means, association with a guild guaranteed the necessary remembrance after death. For this reason every guild kept a careful and cumulative tally of its membership. By a typical arrangement, a priest of the guild of St Botolph Aldersgate in London read aloud the names of present and deceased members on the day of the annual obit.[59] Because each fraternity comprised the accumulated total of dead as well as living members (indeed it was even possible to join after death), the guild register containing every name was a symbol of the active unity of the society, bound by a mutual concern.

These were the salient characteristics of the guild. It should be evident by this point that the form of association which they defined was different in essence from that of the parish. The same basis of doctrinal belief underlay both parish and guild. As social groupings, however, they differed fundamentally.[60] The parish had the potential to gather all its members at the compulsory Easter service. It further obliged its members to pay tithe for the support of the church: this contribution was quite unlike the subscription to a guild, since the layman retained no control over the way in which the tithe was spent. These two duties apart, the parish had no formal conditions of membership. Parishioners *might* recognize and act upon common interests in addition to that of attending the mass. But whereas these were possible conjunctures in the parish, in the guild they were defining and essential qualities. Occasional honorary members apart, the guild demanded regular attendance of its subscribers; and with the partial exception of craft guilds, the relatively wide range of membership in most cases ensured that the brothers and sisters of a particular fraternity interacted in a variety of ways, professional, social and ritual. The distinction is also clear with regard to benefits. The late medieval parish did not, *qua* parish, serve its members as an agency of mutual assistance; the absence from medieval church-wardens' accounts of any reference to such aid shows that any parochial distribution of charitable relief must have been informal and incidental to the recognized functions of the parish. Conversely, it has been seen that this was a role central to any guild. The social standing accorded to a guild member, sanctioned by the approval of the rest of the fellowship; the material aid doled out in times of hardship; the spiritual support of one another's prayers; these were among the valuable rewards of subscription to such a society, rewards which simple membership of a parish was inadequate to convey. By making the guild attractive, these benefits helped to make it work. Naturally, the attractions generated a problem endemic in aspiring communities: the problem of the freeloader. Because remissions of dues had been conceded to too many members of the Assumption guild at Leicester in the late fourteenth century, the remainder declared themselves overburdened; thenceforth each was to contribute 'faithfully according to his resources'.[61] Doubtless, too, over-generous hand-outs to indigent brethren proved fatal to individual societies. Such explanations probably go far to account for the transience of many guilds, dissolved within a generation or two of their beginning.[62] Nevertheless, the structural difference between the guild and the parish remains. In contrast to the latter, the former was a clearly defined solidarity, whose strength was derived from the active personal commitment of its individual members.

It is now possible to address the charge, cited earlier, that the relation between guild and parish in the later Middle Ages was essentially one of conflict.[63] A potential for disharmony in the relationship was certainly revealed on occasion, when guild services threatened to siphon offerings away from the parish priest. This was probably the context, for example, of a quarrel at Kidderminster in 1401 over a fraternity's right to organize a dawn mass.[64] A related source of friction, which sometimes erupted into violence, was the anomalous legal position of the guild chaplain within the parochial ecclesiastical hierarchy.[65] At Henley-on-Thames in 1444 a composition was drawn up to settle disputes arising between the parson and the clergy of the town guild. By this accord the guild priests agreed to assist the incumbent whenever he should have need:

> and also they shall keep rest and peace between themselves and all their fellows, and principally in the choir and in the church; and also if there shall [be] any dissension, strife or debate between them any time, as God forbid, that then they shall abide the rule, the word and the redressing of the parson, [the] warden [of the guild] and the bridgemen [or church-wardens].[66]

Ructions, therefore, were not unknown. But a hypothesis of fundamental opposition between the fraternities and the parochial clergy cannot be substantiated. The clearest evidence counter to such a hypothesis is the inclusion in almost all guilds for which membership lists survive of parish priests alongside the laity. In the Stratford Holy Cross guild, throughout the century from 1443, clergy comprised some 7 per cent of the total membership, over half of the group being vicars.[67] The vicar of the parish of Pillerton in 1425 was rewarded with a hood by that society, in recognition of his efforts in recruiting new members to the guild.[68] At the same time it was only in very rare instances that an English guild came under the actual control of a parish priest.[69] The latter was in general a welcome member of the guilds, which, however, he did not direct.[70] Yet it does not appear that this degree of lay control was resented by the clergy. In this respect the experience of England differed somewhat (in terms of chronology at least) from that of other parts of Catholic Europe. In Florence after *c*.1500, a security-conscious civil government combined with an increasingly authoritarian Church hierarchy to discourage the city-wide guilds of the later Middle Ages and to promote guilds confined to the parishes, within which parish priests played a novel and dominant role; these clerics now kept a supervisory eye on the lay members.[71] The English guilds, on the other hand, do not appear to have been subject to such clerical interference before their dissolution by the state in 1547. That dissolution should perhaps be seen, in one of its aspects, as a radical version of the controls imposed upon private associations by the governors of a central-izing polity such as Florence in the same period;[72] while the fact that, before 1547, the English ecclesiastical establishment had not yet assumed the intrusively protective and monitory role in the guilds which was adopted by some elements of the continental clergy may have left the English fraternities, when challenged by the state, the weaker for the lack of a strong clerical vested interest.

Nevertheless the English parochial clergy had many causes to lament the suppression of the lay-run guilds. Parochial institutions sometimes owed their very survival to fraternities, by which a parish church was rebuilt or a rector salaried.[73] Effective collaboration, albeit on a relatively modest scale, was instanced at Croscombe in Somerset, where in the later Middle Ages each of half a dozen guilds was issued annually by the parochial churchwardens with a 'stock' of about 1s.; this small fund was invested in guild candles and masses and in social events. Collections made at feast-day celebrations, plays, dances and church ales enabled the guilds to return to the parish church at the end of the year, in addition to their stock, an 'increase' which might amount to as much as one pound; the 'maidens' guild' was particularly successful in raising such contributions to the parish.[74] Very commonly, parochial services were enriched by a guild's provision of ornaments, like the candle provided by a Great Yarmouth fraternity to be carried before the parish priest whenever he went bearing the host to visit the sick.[75] Moreover, guild chaplains were far more often a help than a hindrance to parish priests. In 1546 it was credibly asserted of the Stratford Holy Cross guild that so large a parish as Stratford, ten miles broad and containing 1500 communicants, simply could not be served by the sole offices of the parson, without the assistance he received from the five full-time priests employed by the fraternity.[76] Co-operation seems to have prevailed at Stratford, even though the guild's erection of a freestanding chapel at some distance from the parish church might otherwise have been read as an expression of rebellious independence. In general, whether the guild chapel was a separate structure[77] or was incorporated within the parish church, the two organizations complemented one another. Fraternities founded in mendicant houses in preference to parish churches were never characteristic of England (nor, apparently, of northern France) as they were of the cities of southern Europe;[78] but this distinction is less revealing of northern and southern attitudes towards the parish than it is of the vitality and popularity of the mendicant, and especially the Dominican, convents of Italy and southern France. It has been suggested that the creation of four guilds attached to friaries in London around 1500 might reflect 'dissatisfaction' with the parochial framework;

but these four are hardly conclusive indicators when set against twenty fraternities affiliated to parish churches which first appear in London records of the later half of the fifteenth century and a further thirty, first mentioned in the years 1500–48.[79] The organizational frameworks of parish and guild respectively were, as has been shown, distinct; but the argument that these two structures expressed a mutual hostility, or a rooted divergence of interests, does not stand up to examination.

Yet the idea that guild and parish were antipathetic runs deeper. It is based on a conviction that both the institutions and the doctrine of the official church were remote from or at odds with the actual behaviour and beliefs of the mass of the population; as though institutional religion (represented in one form by the parish) and popular religion (instanced in the guild) were distinct, and led separate lives. According to at least one modern observer, the teachings of the medieval church made no impact whatever upon a persistently pagan people.[80] Other commentators infer that the Christian message penetrated the populace only in so far as it was translatable, at worst into superstitious magic, at best into comfortable maxims subordinated to social needs.[81] These contentions, although in part compelling, arguably do insufficient justice to the integrity of medieval churchmen (by no means invariably prepared to compromise with unchristian behaviour, however socially congenial, among the laity) and to the ability and readiness of lay audiences to assimilate the complexities of doctrine. Certainly, the guilds were social clubs. They were also, however, concerned with salvation. The preoccupation, prominent in all fraternities, with the decent burial and commemoration of dead members was no doubt in part an expression of that 'natural religion of kinship and friendship' which John Bossy has identified at the heart of medieval attitudes to death.[82] Yet to describe the liturgy of intercession as a 'bare skeleton', effectively snubbed by a virtually pagan celebration of social community, is to ignore the dense elaboration of masses for the dead introduced by the guilds.[83] The priest of St Peter's guild in the church of that dedication on Cornhill in London was kept busy almost hourly throughout the year upon the task of offering a plethora of memorial masses and prayers for the brothers and sisters of the fraternity, living and dead; his duties were hardly more onerous than those of many another guild chaplain.[84] The lay memberships of the fraternities not only exercised the power to elect priests of their choice to serve the guild chantries; they played an influential part in determining the character of liturgical practice.[85] Guilds often funded additional masses at particular hours – dawn, midday or dusk – to meet the needs of merchants, travellers and labourers.[86] Certain fraternities undertook the specific role of expounding elements of Christian teaching. Such was the Pater Noster guild of York, founded before 1389, whose primary declared aim was the explication to others of the Lord's Prayer. The guild designed a board on which were displayed, presumably through the medium of texts, 'the whole meaning and use' of the prayer; this board was hung up in the minster for all who could read to peruse. The illiterate, meanwhile, were edified by the regular performance by the guild of 'a play setting forth the goodness of the Lord's Prayer'. The drama showed the triumph of virtues over vices; for each phrase of the prayer was held to countervail against a particular deadly sin.[87] Other guilds took up and promoted newly sanctioned doctrines and patterns of devotion. The cult of Corpus Christi, declared a feast of the church in 1264, owed its wide dissemination in the fourteenth and fifteenth centuries very largely to the efforts of lay fraternities.[88] These bodies organized processions surrounding the liturgy of the festal day and fostered understanding of the doctrine; the early fifteenth century text of the ordinances of the York guild of Corpus Christi is preceded by a sermon on '*Hoc est corpus meum*'.[89] The growth in the fourteenth century of devotion to the Wounds of Christ is reflected in the contemporary practice of a guild at Great Yarmouth of meeting on a Friday after vespers to say together repeatedly five Pater Nosters and five Ave Marias, 'in honour of the wounds of Our Lord'.[90] In the second half of the following century increasing enthusiasm for the name of Jesus found expression in a proliferation of guilds of this dedication. Jesus guilds normally organized a weekly mass on Friday; that at Salisbury additionally arranged choral services on the Fridays in Lent.[91] The intellectual and educational activities of the guilds included the retention of preachers; a fraternity at Charing Cross in the early sixteenth century invited a different speaker each year to give a sermon on the occasion of the principal feast.[92] The didactic efforts of the diocesan and parochial clergy were further complemented by a variety of plays and other imagery supplied by the guilds. The story of St Helen's discovery of the True Cross, for example, was related both in a dramatic procession presented by a guild at Beverley and in a cycle of wall-paintings in the chapel of the Holy Cross guild at Stratford-upon-Avon.[93] The latter association, in common with others, employed a schoolmaster, through whom the ideals of the fraternity might be imparted to the children of the town.[94] In many of the extant guild registers children are recorded as joining the societies together with their parents, giving a domestic dimension to the life of the fraternities.[95]

Some guilds actively encouraged private as well as collective devotion, fostering thereby that personal religious life which was so marked a feature of spiritual writing in the later Middle Ages. Each brother and sister of the Virgin Mary's guild at Maldon in Essex was bound to say three times a year the psalter of the Virgin for the living and dead members of the fraternity and for all Christian souls.[96] While in its most obvious manifestations the guild operated as a group, its activities at many points bore upon the internal spiritual life of the individual member. The medieval guilds have been charged by some modern critics (imbued with the expectations and the language of a later age) with shallowness in this respect.[97] The private side of guild membership is the hardest dimension of all to penetrate. Nevertheless the examples which have been cited show that contemporaries recognized in the guild a potential to foster, within the supportive framework of collective observance, a reflective devotion at a personal level. Late medieval Christianity was not merely the dogma of a clerical elite, foisted with greater or less success upon a passive and uncomprehending laity. On the contrary, doctrine was not alien to the members of the guilds, nor was the liturgy a remote irrelevance. Doctrine and liturgy themselves owed much to changing forms of lay piety, which found expression most readily in the activities of the guilds. To claim so much for the fraternities is not to allege universal comprehension of Christian dogma, but to re-assert the perceived relevance and the active role of that dogma in the lives of medieval communities.

The degree of personal choice accommodated within late medieval religion has not always been fully appreciated. The voluntaristic element in lay piety in this period, however, was expressed only very rarely in anarchic individualism, whether heretical or merely antisocial. Instead, the laity evinced an overwhelming preference for collective forms of religious activity, conceived and directed by themselves. The guild – and this was its decisive advantage over the parish – was the ideal medium for the

realization of this desire. Within a partially standardized constitution, the guilds exhibited enormous variety in the details of their
collective religious rites, while at the same time they helped foster
a richer internal spiritual life for the individual member. The
satisfaction within a voluntary structure of this dual need,
collective and individual, was the distinctive function of the pre-
Reformation guild.

After 1547 the English guilds could no longer perform this role,
being outlawed from that year by the secular authority for
'devising and phantasinge vayne opynions of Purgatorye'.[98] The
official abolition of purgatory removed one *raison d'être* of the
guilds. Yet the other demands which they had met, apart from that
for intercession, remained. It need occasion no surprise, therefore,
to discover patterns of Protestant behaviour bearing a close
similarity to the configurations of the guilds. The doctrinal break
in 1547 was crucial, and there is obviously no question of a simple
continuity of theological position from guild to Protestant sect.
Specific aspects of guild activity – for example, listening to
sermons and the participation of family groups – anticipated
practices of the godlier sort of Protestants. But no late medieval
guild is known to have been charged with heresy; the main roots of
the doctrinal reformation lay elsewhere. At another level, however, the assembly of zealous Protestants takes its place in the
same tradition as the medieval guild meeting. Each was a
voluntary expression of collective interests which transcended the
simple requirement of parochial conformity. The period immediately following the dissolution of the guilds was one of active
official hostility, on both religious and political grounds, to private
associations. These years saw local communities forced back upon
the parish as the sole legitimate focus of collective activity. The
statutory imposition upon the parish of charitable responsibilities
formerly undertaken by the guilds is characteristic of this period.[99]
Nevertheless by the end of the century, notwithstanding the
emphasis given to the parish in Reformation statutes, parochial
boundaries were being crossed as readily by the godly eager to
hear a noted preacher as they had been by the brothers and sisters
of a guild hurrying to take part in the fraternity procession.[100] In
each case, individual religious voluntaryism was channelled into
collective rites and assemblies which were carefully governed by
the lay participants themselves. Both of these voluntary move-
ments, while not normally committed to confrontation with

authority, refused to be constrained by the ministers and institutions of the parish. Patrick Collinson defines 'the significance and the near uniqueness of English puritanism' as follows:

> Nowhere else in early modern Europe within a legally established Church was so much collective religious consciousness and behaviour conditioned not by regulation but by a more or less spontaneous consensus of private men, the religious public themselves.[101]

Omitting the exclusive focus on England, the same observation could be made of the late medieval guilds. Doctrinally divided in England by the Act of 1547, the two forms of association nevertheless shared common ground in the psychological and social needs, unanswered by the parish, to which they responded. In the guild also, private men and women realized a consensus of religious opinion founded upon a voluntary commitment.

Acknowledgements

I wish to thank Jane Garnett, of Lincoln College, Oxford, for many helpful discussions on this subject. I am also grateful to the other contributors for their comments.

Notes and references

1   E. Ekwall, *The Concise Oxford Dictionary of English Place-Names* (4th edn, 1960), p. 24; M. W. Beresford, *New Towns of the Middle Ages* (1967), pp. 452–3.

2   For the Baldock guild of Jesus, see *Calendar of Entries in the Papal Registers relating to Great Britain and Ireland: Papal Letters* (1893–), **xi,** pp. 618–19; *Chantry Certificates for Hertfordshire*, ed. J. E. Brown (1920), pp. 17–20.

3   A. Macfarlane, *Reconstructing Historical Communities* (1977); idem, *The Origins of English Individualism* (1978).

4   Hill, *Society*, pp. 492–4 and *passim* (quotation from p. 492). The age of sects, in Hill's chronology, follows upon an intermediate phase in which the late Tudor national church is seen as playing its own part in dismantling the traditional community.

5   See C. J. Calhoun, 'Community: toward a variable conceptualization for comparative research', *Social History*, **v** (1980), pp. 105–29.

6   See Bossy, *Christianity*, p. 62: 'The relation between fraternities and

parishes in the later medieval Church does not seem to have attracted historians.'

7   The assumption of prevailing harmony with the parish, made by some modern commentators on the guilds, has hitherto been no more than that. For the considered view of the guild as semi-independent of or distinct from the official church, see J. Bossy, 'The Counter-Reformation and the people of Catholic Europe', *Past and Present*, **47** (1970), pp. 51–70, at pp. 58–9; J. Lortz, cited in S. E. Ozment, *The Reformation in the Cities* (1975), p. 17; N. Z. Davis, *Society and Culture in Early Modern France* (1975), p. 75; and references cited in notes 8 and 9 below.

8   J. Toussaert, *Le Sentiment Religieux en Flandre à la Fin du Moyen Age* (Paris, 1963), p. 478; F. Lot and R. Fawtier (eds), *Histoire des Institutions Françaises au Moyen Age*, **iii** (Paris, 1962), p. 291.

9   Bossy, *Christianity*, p. 63.

10 E. Miller and J. Hatcher, *Medieval England: Rural Society and Economic Change 1086–1348* (1978), pp. 106–10; S. Reynolds, *Kingdoms and Communities in Western Europe 900–1300* (1984) ch. 4; J. Blair (ed.), *Minsters and Parish Churches: The Local Church in Transition 900–1200* (1988).

11 Figures for England and Wales are set out in R. K. Morris, 'The church in the countryside: two lines of inquiry', in D. Hooke (ed.), *Medieval Villages. A Review of Current Work*, Oxford University Committee for Archaeology, Monograph no. 5 (1985), pp. 47–60, at pp. 50–1 and table 5.1.

12 See also the continuing, intermittent process of adjustment of parochial bounds, in accord with shifts in the geographical focus of solidarities, in Ancien Régime France: P. M. Jones, 'Parish, seigneurie and the community of inhabitants in southern central France during the eighteenth and nineteenth centuries', *Past and Present*, **91** (1981), pp. 74–108.

13 For example, D. M. Owen, *Church and Society in Medieval Lincolnshire*, Society for Lincolnshire History and Archaeology, History of Lincolnshire, **v** (1981), pp. 17–18; and *Cal. Papal Letters*, **iv**, p. 392; **v**, pp. 94, 265, 317, 320, 390, 405, 443, 486–87, 587, 609. In some instances, however, refusal by the mother church to concede rights of sepulture gave rise to protracted and inconclusive wrangles. For example, C. Lutgens, 'The case of Waghen vs. Sutton: conflict over burial rights in late medieval England', *Mediaeval Studies*, **xxxviii** (1976), pp. 145–84.

14 D. J. Keene, *Survey of Medieval Winchester*, Winchester Studies, **ii** (1985), vol. 1, pp. 116–18, 126–8; see also N. P. Tanner, *The Church in Late Medieval Norwich, 1370–1532*, Pontifical Institute of Mediaeval Studies, Studies and Texts, **66** (Toronto, 1984), pp. 3–5. The problem of excessively numerous, and consequently impov-

erished, parishes in cities persisted, however, into the sixteenth century, when sporadic but inadequate local attempts were made to adjust parochial divisions in relation to resources. See D. M. Palliser, 'The union of parishes at York, 1547–1586', *Yorkshire Archaeological Journal*, **xlvi** (1974), pp. 87–102.

15   In 1402 the inhabitants of Peterborough (Northants) transferred their parish church to a new and more convenient site in the market place. This was approved by the abbot and convent of Peterborough, as rector, in a composition with the *communitas parochie. Peterborough Local Administration: Parochial Government before the Reformation*, ed. W. T. Mellows, Northamptonshire Record Society, **ix** (1939), pp. 219ff. See also Morris, 'Church in the countryside', p. 58 and fig. 5.5 on p. 56.

16   Summarized in C. Platt, *The Parish Churches of Medieval England* (1981), ch. 5; and Scarisbrick, *Reformation*, ch. 1. Derek Keene suggests that substantial investment in their churches by parishioners within the shrunken economy of fifteenth-century Winchester represents a positive increase in commitment to the parish at this period. See *Medieval Winchester*, vol. 1, pp. 116–18, 126–8.

17   *Lincoln Diocese Documents, 1450–1544*, ed. A. Clarke, Early English Text Society, original ser., **cxlix** (1914), pp. 224–30.

18   The practice noted at All Saints, Oxford, in 1538 was continued later in the sixteenth century by town corporations which acquired parochial advowsons: see W. J. Sheils, 'Religion in provincial towns: innovation and tradition', in F. Heal and R. O'Day (eds), *Church and Society in England: Henry VIII to James I* (1977), pp. 156–76, at pp. 159–60.

19   This widely held view has been propounded by, among others, C. Hill, *Economic Problems of the Church from Archbishop Whitgift to the Long Parliament* (1956), p. 54 and *passim*.

20   The parish of St Margaret, Westminster, in 1548 comprised 2500 communicants; addition of the two-fifths probably represented by children aged under 14 years gives the figure of 3500. *London and Middlesex Chantry Certificate 1548*, ed. C. J. Kitching, London Record Society, **xvi** (1980), no. 139. By 1600 (and in the case just cited, long before that date) rapid demographic expansion (the reverse of the problem faced earlier; see note 14 above) was creating insurmountable difficulties for parochial provision, above all in the towns. See P. Collinson, *The Religion of Protestants. The Church in English Society 1559–1625* (1982), p. 210.

21   *Kentish Visitations of Archbishop William Warham and his Deputies, 1511–1512*, ed. K. L. Wood-Legh, Kent Archaeological Society, Kent Records, **xxiv** (1984), pp. 96–7 (Knowlton parish).

22   The present writer is engaged on a broad study of the medieval English guilds.

23 See E. Coornaert, 'Les ghildes médiévales', *Revue Historique*, **cxcix** (1948), pp. 22–55, 208–43.

24 This seems clear, even allowing for the distorting effect of better documentation from these than from preceding centuries. See, for example, the date of their respective foundations (albeit some are certainly dates of *re*-foundation) given by many of the English guilds which replied to a royal inquest of 1389: summaries printed in H. F. Westlake, *The Parish Gilds of Mediaeval England* (1919), Appendix. Further sources indicating a late medieval floriation of fraternities are cited in Scarisbrick, *Reformation*, ch. 2.

25 See C. M. Barron, 'The parish fraternities of medieval London', in C. M. Barron and C. Harper-Bill (eds), *The Church in Pre-Reformation Society* (1985), pp. 13–37, at pp. 24–5. Barron adds the suggestion that the improved economic circumstances of artisans and craftsmen after 1348 enabled such people to subscribe to fraternities (p. 24).

26 For a fifteenth-century example, see *Cal. Papal Letters*, **xii**, p. 644.

27 Stratford-upon-Avon, Shakespeare Birthplace Trust, MSS 1/1; 1/3/1–119. Editions (of uneven completeness and accuracy) of these records have been published: *The Register of the Gild of the Holy Cross, the Blessed Mary and St John the Baptist, of Stratford-upon-Avon*, ed. J. H. Bloom (1907); and *Stratford-on-Avon Corporation Records: The Guild Accounts* (ed. W. J. Hardy, *c.* 1886). See also R. H. Hilton, *The English Peasantry in the Later Middle Ages* (1975), pp. 93–4; and S. J. Wright, 'A Study of the Gild of the Holy Cross, the Blessed Mary and St John the Baptist of Stratford-upon-Avon from 1406 to 1545' (unpublished MA thesis, University of Leicester, 1978).

28 *Stratford Register*, *passim*. Occasional recruitment drives took in these and similar places: *Stratford Accounts*, pp. 27, 29.

29 *Stratford Accounts*, *passim*. Guild ordinances relating to the feast are printed in *English Gilds*, ed. J. Toulmin Smith and L. Toulmin Smith, Early English Text Society, original ser., **xl** (1870) (hereafter Toulmin Smith), p. 217 (1389); and in *Stratford Register*, pp. 1–6, (1443).

30 Toulmin Smith, pp. 217–18.

31 *Stratford Register*, pp. 148–51. Evidently parochial loyalty did not conflict, in this case at least, with support for the extra-parochial guild. On this point, see further below.

32 HWRO, MS. 008.7/BA 3585/1a. For the Aston Cantlow guild see *Calendar of Patent Rolls, 1467–77*, pp. 175–6.

33 *Stratford Register*, pp. 71, 73, 110. Londoners also occur in the register. On London merchants who belonged to provincial fraternities see S. L. Thrupp, *The Merchant Class of Medieval London* (Chicago, 1948), p. 228 and note 64.

34   PRO, C47/43/255; *The Making of King's Lynn. A Documentary Survey*, ed. D. M. Owen, Records of Social and Economic History, new ser., **ix** (1984), pp. 60–3, 295ff.; see also the bequest of a Norwich merchant to a guild at York: Tanner, *Norwich*, p. 75. The category of records in the PRO classified as C47, cited here and frequently below, comprises the surviving returns made by the fraternities to the Royal Commission of Inquiry into such societies in 1389.

35   For guilds formed by *Doche* in London see S. L. Thrupp, 'Aliens in and around London in the fifteenth century', in A. E. J. Hollaender and W. Kellaway (eds), *Studies in London History presented to P. E. Jones* (1969), pp. 251–72, at pp. 263–4; A. G. Rosser, 'Medieval Westminster: The Vill and the Urban Community 1200–1540' (unpublished Ph.D. thesis, University of London, 1984), pp. 228–9, 310–11, 353.

36   *Proceedings of the Dorset Natural History and Antiquarian Field Club*, **xxix** (1908), pp. 42–4. The melodramatic justification was characteristic. A more common explanation of the need for a guild of this kind was that given by the fraternity of Deritend, a hamlet by Birmingham, in 1546: 'They be two miles distant from their parish church, so that, in winter season, the said parishioners could not go to their parish church without great danger of perishing.' Toulmin Smith, p. 260.

37   PRO, C47/40/120: Holbeach (Lincs), 1389.

38   For some examples see *Parish Fraternity Register, Fraternity of the Holy Trinity and SS. Fabian and Sebastian in the Parish Church of St Botolph without Aldersgate*, ed. P. Basing, London Record Society, **xviii** (1982), p. xvii.

39   *Stratford Register*, pp. 22, 30, 40, 46, etc.

40   PRO, C47/43/292; printed in Toulmin Smith, pp. 40–1.

41   PRO, C47/42/234.

42   PRO, C47/40/135; printed in Toulmin Smith, pp. 178–9.

43   PRO, C47/46/449; printed in Toulmin Smith, pp. 160–1.

44   For example, see Toulmin Smith, p. 8.

45   PRO, C47/39/71; the guild of Corpus Christi, St Mary and All Saints in St Martin's Church, Leicester, founded in 1343.

46   Thus, for example, the thrice-yearly assemblies of a Wisbech (Cambs) guild, apart from its annual feast, were said to be 'for the correction and amending of members' behaviour'. PRO, C47/38/39.

47   Toulmin Smith, pp. 81, 87, 107. See also the stipulation by guilds at Lynn that brothers and sisters should not come to meetings with bare legs or feet; military tabards were also proscribed as improper dress (pp. 87, 95, 98).

48   PRO, C47/38/39.

49   PRO, C47/39/69 ('. . . *temerarium officium de baudestrotes*').

50 LJRO, MS. D.77/1, ff. 3v–4; printed in A. G. Rosser (ed.), 'The guild of St Mary and St John the Baptist, Lichfield: ordinances of the late fourteenth century', *Staffordshire Record Society* (forthcoming, 1988). Emphasis added. For the citation likening the guild register to the Book of Life see Psalms 69:28.

51 See also M. Weber, 'The protestant sects and the spirit of capitalism':

It is crucial that sect membership meant a certificate of moral qualification and especially of business morals for the individual. This stands in contrast to membership in a 'church' into which one is 'born' and which lets grace shine over the righteous and the unrighteous alike. . . . Affiliation with the church is, in principle, obligatory and hence proves nothing with regard to the member's qualities. A sect, however, is a voluntary association of only those who, according to the principle, are religiously and morally qualified (*From Max Weber: Essays in Sociology*, trans. and ed. H. H. Gerth and C. Wright Mills (1948), pp. 305–6).

Although in this passage Weber was particularly concerned with the basis of *commercial* trust, his differentiation between voluntary sect and all-embracing national or international church is relevant, in a more general sense, to the distinction drawn here between guild and parish in the Middle Ages.

52 PRO, C47/41/198; printed in Toulmin Smith, p. 9; see also p. 6.

53 PRO, C47/41/143.

54 PRO, C47/38/39 (guild of St John the Baptist, Wisbech). Further examples: PRO, C47/44/339 (guild of All Saints, Upwell [Norfolk]); C47/46/45, printed in Toulmin Smith, pp. 158–9 (guild of the Virgin Mary, Hull).

55 M. Siraut, 'Accounts of Saint Katherine's guild at Holy Trinity church, Cambridge: 1514–1537', *Proceedings of the Cambridge Antiquarian Society*, **lxvii** (1977), pp. 111–21. Here, incidentally, was at least one guild not religiously averse to usury. See Bossy, *Christianity*, p. 61.

56 PRO, C47/38/45; C47/38/47; C47/38/48; C47/44/315; C47/45/373.

57 PRO, C47/39/71; C47/46/448.

58 At the moment of joining the Holy Cross guild at Stratford-upon-Avon in 1425–6, Thomas Elmys and his wife made a fine 'in case the said Thomas and Alice (become) weak and infirm, then they shall have a dwelling in the [guild] almshouses within the manor during their lives; and after their decease all their goods shall remain to the profit of the guild'. *Stratford Register*, p. 43.

59 *Parish Fraternity Register*, p. 4.

60 In the attempt to provide definitions, I have found useful M. Taylor, *Community, Anarchy and Liberty* (1982).

61 PRO, C47/39/70.

62 For example, a small guild in Bridport (Dorset), founded in 1406,

whose register of meetings and membership runs for a few decades before it peters out in 1455. DCRO, MS. B3/CD 56.

63 See above, p. 30.

64 *Cal. Papal Letters*, **v**, p. 411.

65 Assistant chaplains hired by the incumbent of a parish would be required to swear an oath of obedience to him as their superior (see P. Heath, *The English Parish Clergy on the Eve of the Reformation* [1969], pp. 25–6); but the situation of guild priests was not so defined.

66 OCRO, Henley Borough Records, MS. A.II/1, last folio, *dors*.

67 Wright, 'A Study of the Gild', p. 65. In the guild of St Mary and St John the Baptist, Lichfield, the proportion of clerical members over a similar documented period was exactly the same: A. J. Kettle, 'City and close: Lichfield in the century before the Reformation', *Church in Pre-Reformation Society*, pp. 158–69, at p. 161.

68 *Stratford Accounts*, p. 16; see also *Statford Register*, pp. 36, 38.

69 A small minority of guilds comprising lay members were founded by clerics: for example, PRO, C47/46/415.

70 Fraternities in small towns in late medieval Tuscany likewise included clerical members without being subject to clerical direction. C. M. de la Roncière, 'La place des confréries dans l'encadrement religieux du contado florentin: l'exemple de la Val d'Elsa', *Mélanges de l'Ecole Française de Rome: Moyen Age, Temps Modernes*, **lxxxv** (1973), pp. 31–77, esp. p. 42. For similar remarks on parish clergy in French guilds in the fourteenth century, see P. Adam, *La Vie Paroissiale en France au XIVe siècle* (Paris, 1964), pp. 69–71.

71 R. Weissman, *Ritual Brotherhood in Renaissance Florence* (New York, 1982), p. 207; J. Henderson, 'Confraternities and the church in late medieval Florence', in W. J. Sheils and D. Wood (eds), *Voluntary Religion*, Studies in Church History, **xxiii** (1986), pp. 69–83. A similar shift of authority within the guilds has been observed in Counter-Reformation France. See P. T. Hoffman, *Church and Community in the Diocese of Lyon 1500–1789* (1984), pp. 105–14; and J.-P. Gutton, 'Confraternities, *curés* and communities in rural areas of the diocese of Lyons under the Ancien Régime', in K. von Greyerz (ed.), *Religion and Society in Early Modern Europe 1500–1800* (1986), pp. 202–11.

72 The writings of G. R. Elton on early Tudor government suggest this view. See also R. Hutton, 'The local impact of the Tudor Reformation', in C. Haigh (ed.), *The English Reformation Revised* (1987), pp. 114–38.

73 See, for example, *English Historical Documents 1327–1485*, ed. A. R. Myers (1969), pp. 741–4 (guild contributions to the rebuilding of Bodmin church); PRO, C47/41/175 (maintenance by a guild of the impoverished rector of Holy Trinity church, Stamford [Lincs]); and

further instances in Owen, *Church and Society*, p. 114.

74 *Church-Wardens' Accounts of Croscombe, &c.*, ed. Bishop Hobhouse, Somerset Record Society, **iv** (1890), pp. 1–48.

75 PRO, C47/45/367.

76 Toulmin Smith, p. 222.

77 A category of guilds noted above, pp. 34–5.

78 For Dominican-inspired fraternities in southern Europe in general, see G. G. Meersseman, *Ordo Fraternitatis: Confraternite e Pietà dei Laici nel Medioevo*, 3 vols, Italia Sacra, **xxiv–xxvi** (Rome, 1977); and for Florence in particular J. S. Henderson, 'Piety and Charity in Late Medieval Florence. Religious Confraternities from the middle of the thirteenth century to the late fifteenth century', (unpublished Ph.D. thesis, University of London, 1983), p. 24, table on p. 39 and *passim*. For the contrast in this respect between north and south, see M. Venard, 'Les confréries dans l'espace urbain: l'exemple de Rouen', *Annales de Bretagne*, **xc** (1983), pp. 321–32.

79 S. Brigden, 'Religion and social obligation in early sixteenth-century London', *Past and Present*, **103** (1984), p. 67–112, at pp. 96, 97; see also Barron, 'Fraternities of London', p. 27. At the same time it should be noted that guilds based in mendicant houses were not unknown in England from a period well before 1500. For an earlier Franciscan example at Beverley see PRO, C47/46/446 (ordinances of St Helen's guild, Beverley, 1378).

80 Toussaert, *Sentiment Religieux*, *passim*.

81 This is a bald summary of the distinguished arguments, respectively, of Thomas, *Magic*, ch. 2; and of Bossy, *Christianity*, part 1.

82 Bossy, *Christianity*, p. 27.

83 Bossy, p. 27. For many examples of the liturgical activities of the guilds see Westlake, *Parish Gilds*, *passim*.

84 London, Guildhall Library, MS. 4158, ff. 135v–137, 147v–152v; printed in *Historical Manuscripts Commission, 6th Report: Appendix* (1877), pp. 411–14.

85 For a detailed instance of lay control of guild priests see 'Lichfield ordinances', esp. ordinances 12–19.

86 For example, the guild of the Virgin Mary, Northampton, which provided daily a dawn mass ('*pro oportunitate et utilitate extraneorum et aliorum qui mane in negociis suis devillare voluerunt*'), another at eleven o'clock ('*quam extranei laborantes et tarde villam venientes poterunt audire quando omnes alie misse in eadem villa finiuntur*') and a third at one o'clock. PRO, C47/45/383. See also C47/39/87 (Boston).

87 Toulmin Smith, pp. 137–40; E. K. Chambers, *The Mediaeval Stage*, **ii** (1903), pp. 154–5; H. Craig, *English Religious Drama of the Middle Ages* (1955), pp. 37–41; A. F. Johnson, 'The plays of the religious guilds of York – the Creed Play and the Pater Noster Play',

Speculum, **1** (1975), pp. 55–90. The Pater Noster play was last performed at York in 1572.

88   M. Rubin, 'Corpus Christi fraternities and late medieval piety', in *Voluntary Religion*, pp. 97–109.

89   *The Register of the Guild of Corpus Christi in the City of York*, ed. R. H. Skaife, Surtees Society, **lvii** (1871), pp. 1–6.

90   PRO, C47/45/368. For the cult, see F. L. Cross, *The Oxford Dictionary of the Christian Church* (1958), p. 1478 (with references).

91   For the feast, see R. W. Pfaff, *New Liturgical Feasts in Later Medieval England* (1970), pp. 62–83. For Jesus guilds see, for example, Barron, 'Fraternities of London', p. 32; Tanner, *Norwich*, pp. 94, 103, 216, 219; *Calendar of Patent Rolls, 1476–85*, p. 259; and *The Churchwardens' Accounts of St Edmund and St Thomas [of Salisbury]*, *1443–1702*, ed. H. J. F. Swayne (1896), pp. 248–72, *passim*.

92   Accounts of the guild of St Mary Rounceval at Charing Cross, 1520–4, 1538–40 (bound with records of another guild) in Westminster Abbey Muniment room, unnumbered.

93   Toulmin Smith, p. 148; T. Fisher, *Paintings in Fresco, discovered in 1804, on the Walls of the Chapel of the Trinity, belonging to the Gild of the Holy Cross at Stratford-upon-Avon* (1838).

94   Toulmin Smith, pp. 221, 223; and see *Stratford Accounts*, p. 18, for the construction of a schoolhouse in 1427–8.

95   For example, *Stratford Register*; LJRO, MS. D.77/1 (register of the guild of St Mary and St John the Baptist, Lichfield).

96   PRO, C47/39/55. On the fostering of private prayer among fraternity members see also the remarks of de la Roncière, 'La place des confréries', p. 48; and of Adam, *Vie Paroissiale*, pp. 49–50.

97   It is important to be aware of the enormous subsequent influence of the Tridentine (no less than the Protestant) critique of late medieval religion. The Catholic clerical reformers of the late sixteenth century were less than sympathetic to lay religious activity which was virtually independent of ecclesiastical supervision. The attitudes of Trent certainly colour the critical remarks in E. Delaruelle, E.-R. Labande and P. Ourliac, *L'Eglise au Temps du Grand Schisme et de la Crise Conciliaire (1378–1449)*, 2 vols (Paris, 1962–4), **ii**, p. 688; and of Adam, *Vie Paroissiale*, p. 50. See also N. Z. Davis, 'Some tasks and themes in the study of popular religion', in C. Trinkaus and H. A. Oberman (eds), *The Pursuit of Holiness in Late Medieval and Renaissance Religion*, Studies in Medieval and Reformation Thought, **x** (Leiden 1974), pp. 307–36, at p. 317.

98   1 Edw. VI c.14.

99   The climax of this legislation was the imposition throughout the realm of a compulsory parochial poor rate in 1572: 14 Eliz. c.5. The parish had in the Middle Ages been used on occasion as an

instrument and unit of secular government, notably for taxation purposes.

100 On the regional organization of rural nonconformity in the seventeenth century and later, see A. Everitt, *The Pattern of Rural Dissent: The Nineteenth Century*, Leicester University Department of English Local History, Occasional Papers, 2nd series, no. 4 (1972), p. 8 n. 1.

101 Collinson, *Religion of Protestants*, p. 247. On the tendency of 'religious individualism' in Protestant England to manifest itself in collective forms, see further in Collinson, pp. 249–52. And on the tension, noted above, between the requirement of the Act of Uniformity that each person should attend his own parish church and the desire to attend sermons and lectures elsewhere, see also p. 246. Other activities of the guilds (notably in the sphere of local politics, which has been excluded from the present discussion but which I intend to treat elsewhere) also found substitute forms of expression after 1547.

3 'A fond thing vainly invented': an essay on Purgatory and pious motive in later medieval England

Clive Burgess

In the two centuries prior to the Reformation the English laity devoted considerable energy and means to managing their parishes, embellishing their churches and enriching the liturgy from which each sought to benefit.[1] This observation is not novel and, as a day spent looking at late medieval church buildings, fixtures and furniture will disclose, is easy to verify. It has, however, fallen on stony ground. Few historians of the post-Reformation period have shown any inclination to add perspective to assessments of the laity's role in the late sixteenth- and seventeenth-century parish by comparison with earlier practice. Far fewer in number, their pre-Reformation colleagues are still occupied with the primary topics of Church government, hierarchy and heresy, and have by and large refused to linger in the 'faire felde ful of folke'. In that the late medieval pious response was prodigious, arguably exceeding that of any other period, it is extraordinary how little attention has been devoted to the question of what prompted the laity to act as they did.

Why have historians been loath to confront this problem? The answer could be that the late medieval Church and the beliefs and practice of its members have been perceived as more the province of antiquarians. But while acting as a disincentive, this reputation is a symptom of a more fundamental problem. Late medieval Catholicism itself elicits responses militating against close interpretative study. Historians in the Protestant tradition muster little understanding and less sympathy for the principles and practices against which they consider their forebears to have reacted. Few have felt any inclination to explore. Contending with this frequently critical response, Catholics appear to have judged discretion the better course and have preferred to skirt the minefield. More generally, many historians presently exhibit distaste for sympathetic analysis of religious belief and fervour: the subject offends them and, as it defies objectivity, threatens their credibility. So, for those who seek to understand precisely why late medieval men and women acted in so distinctive a fashion very little guidance is available. Colin Platt in *The Parish Churches of Medieval England*, for instance, dwells on parishioners' abundant provision for building, liturgical equipment and intercession, but touches on motive only fleetingly: parishioners were 'easing their way through Purgatory', 'ensuring fitting commemorations', or were influenced by 'competitive gift-giving'.[2] In another survey, J. C. Dickinson reveals himself willing to consider contemporaries' concern about life after death, mentioning the far-reaching repercussions contingent on their precautions to ensure that in due course they would be 'ranked with the blessed'.[3] But, having whetted the appetite, he fails to elaborate and only occasionally integrates such observation with analysis of commonplace devotional activity.[4] Neither historian isolates or expounds adequate motive or aspiration to explain the commitment and generosity elicited from ordinary men and women in the late medieval period.

Historians who have undertaken more specialist investigation of late medieval pious provision ascribe motives which are far from attractive. Alan Kreider, contemplating the reasons for the numbers of perpetual chantries established in the fifteenth and early sixteenth centuries, cites fear – 'fear that an excruciating posthumous purgation was in store'.[5] Kathleen Wood-Legh is similarly forthright. Her diagnosis is that in appearing to give a high, almost mystical, value to mere repetition of formulae, that is to the repeated celebration of the Mass, the chantry was 'hardly reconcilable with the message of the Gospel'.[6] She, too, implies that fear was contemporaries' motive:

Still more daunting is the conception [implicit in chantry foundation] of God – a being of infinite severity in whose dealings with men there are few signs of love, who prefers the endless repetition of the sacrifice to any manifestation of Christian character, and who, for all his majesty, has so little magnanimity that he will allow the souls in Purgatory to suffer, if, despite all the precautions a pious founder could devise, the services of his chantry, long after he and all his friends were dead, should be discontinued.[7]

Wood-Legh's conspicuous lack of any approbation for her

subject renders her achievement all the more remarkable. Others have yet to emulate her in the detailed examination of late medieval devotional practice.

But Wood-Legh's censures pinpoint the conundrum which best explains why the achievement of the late medieval laity has received scant analysis or recognition. The aesthetics of the laity's architectural enterprise or, for chantries, the ingenuity of their financial endowment, may commend close attention; but the motives which prompted building, no less than more personal arrangements, seem repellent. If motive has emerged at all from study of late medieval pious provision, then the mainspring is said to be Purgatory, a doctrine now popularly projected as at odds with the fundamentals of Christianity. Unable to sympathize with this doctrine, historians have turned a blind eye both to it and to what it implies, which is effectively to forfeit proper understanding of the role that the laity played in the parishes of later medieval England. Consider the specialist appraisals of the chantry, perhaps the most distinctive response to the doctrine of Purgatory: neither Kreider nor Wood-Legh makes any serious attempt to plumb the beliefs of men and women. Each assumes that the chantry's proliferation bore a direct relationship to fear. And consider more general historical writing: virtually the only attention paid to common motives and belief are paragraphs on Purgatory in works by A. G. Dickens, C. S. L. Davies and F. Oakley.[8] Significantly, each author lights on the same passage in Thomas More's *The Supplication of Souls* to cite the harrowing description of the dead in Purgatory suffering pains barely distinguishable from those of Hell. Dickens comments, in keeping with Kreider and Wood-Legh's assumptions, that 'medieval men were faced by quite terrifying views of punishment in the life to come'.

Allowing for the time being that contemporaries may have been spurred to activity by a wider range of motives than historians have so far cared to elucidate, it is certainly admissible to question Purgatory's unequivocal reputation. As Dickens, Davies and Oakley all depend on the same source to summarize contemporary attitudes, scrutiny may start there. The results are salutary. For when More wrote *The Supplication of Souls*, he was anything but the urbane humanist of popular legend.[9] According to one commentator, the work was the product of a mind experiencing increasing horror as a profound and growing hatred of heresy was compounded by fear that the King's dalliance with anti-clerical sentiment would lead to a breach with Rome which 'would cut England off from the evolution of God's purpose in history and rupture the unity of Christendom'.[10] More's tract was the product of a complex combination of political events and, equally specifically, was produced to counter the arguments of Simon Fish's *A Supplication for the Beggars* and to turn Henry against the faction which endorsed it – for 'if Englishmen allowed Lutheranism to prosper God would "withdraw his grace and let all run to ruin"'.[11] More parried Fish's call to disavow Purgatory by first attempting to justify the doctrine and then, in the passage commonly cited, by dramatizing it. He sought both to strengthen Henry's sense of duty toward the faithful dead, his own family included, and to exploit Henry's fears by evoking the pains to which his own unprotected soul would be subject – the more so had he betrayed his responsibilities towards God and the Church. More's portrayal of Purgatory in *The Supplication of Souls* is, simply, the climax of a vehement polemic. It is misguided to dragoon quotation from its text so unquestioningly in the exposition of popular belief. Added to which, the authors citing the tract emasculate the real point of More's argument – to which I shall return.[12] But if Dickens, Davies and Oakley can be challenged, how much trust may be placed in the assumptions, in substance very similar, that other historians have been prepared to make when characterizing Purgatory? – for it is these which have impeded proper appreciation of the contribution that the laity made to church life in the period preceding the Reformation. Clearly a fuller understanding of the redemptive process as popularly conceived in the fifteenth and early sixteenth centuries, and of Purgatory's place within it, is long overdue. What follows is at best a pioneering effort, paving the way to more perceptive appraisal of the priorities and aspirations which prompted the late medieval laity's remarkable generosity and achievement.

In the following I work on the assumptions that by the fifteenth century Christian teaching was, at however basic a level, pervasive in England, and that the common people shared a desire for salvation. I would also assert that while interpreters of the period have attached considerable significance to the influence exercised by the sacrament of the Mass, of which the cult of Corpus Christi is but one sign,[13] the sacrament of penance played, if anything, a more formative role in shaping men's priorities and actions. As the process by which the Church mediates the mercy of God to fallen mankind and by which sinful individuals are able to annul the otherwise inevitable consequences of their predisposition in order to gain either readmission to the community of the faithful or, ultimately, salvation, the sacrament of penance has always been of prime importance.[14] It depends upon four essential responses. Sinners must feel sorrow for having lapsed. They must make explicit confession of their sins or sinfulness and, next, should discharge penitential exercises to expiate their sins. Finally, they must participate in a ritual performed with the aid of priests who pronounce penitents absolved from sin and reconciled with the body of the faithful. Over the course of Christian history varying emphases have been applied to these procedures. The earliest formal system for forgiveness and reconciliation, known as 'canonical' penance, held sway until the seventh century. Its most striking features were the severity of the penances it imposed and its very public quality. The penitent was, for instance, publicly excluded from the body of the faithful, and the disavowal of sin, penitential exercises and formal reconciliation were all to be public actions – and could be allowed once only. Supplanting this, in frequency of use at least, was a system evolved in Ireland by the end of the sixth century and based on penitentials, short manuals which classified sins and guided priests in the imposition of specified penances for particular offences. The concept of a penitential tariff was probably this system's most influential feature as far as later practice was concerned, but its contrasts with 'canonical' penance best explain its relative popularity. It was a private system: penance was privately imposed by a priest and required neither admission to an order of penitents nor a solemn public reconciliation. It was, moreover, reiterable for grave sins no less than for minor misdemeanours. But, contrasts apart, it is to be emphasized that each of these systems shared the fundamental premise that absolution had to be earned in this life. This necessarily involved the penitent in years of strict asceticism, worship and charity.[15] By performing the arduous requirements demanded by the Church, a man might derive the consolation of knowing that he was forgiven and that there was hope for his soul. Nevertheless, the severity of the prescribed regimes rendered the effective discharge of penance unlikely for anyone who was not a monk and thereby devoted to a life of prayer and obedience. Deathbed penance was one way round the problem of impossibly high standards, but, unable to overcome the consequences of guilt in this life, for most the prospect was bleak. St Anselm, for instance, was of the opinion that 'Few will be saved and most of these will be monks', a sentiment which sheds at least some light on the development of substitutive penance whereby monks, in return for massive landed endowments, worked off the penances incurred by their benefactors.[16] The lower orders, by contrast, could do very little to escape the wages of sin until such time as the penitential emphasis could be recast.

From the eleventh century, growth in both population and productivity in Western Europe paved the way for changes in government and social organization.[17] The Church certainly experienced profound jurisdictional and financial upheaval as it tried to establish independence from, and even superiority over, the lay magistracy. This was accompanied and rendered feasible by its exploitation of a source of income, the tithe, which soon came to exceed all its other revenues. R. W. Southern observes that

This was a major factor in changing the pastoral aims of the Church. It was no longer dependent upon the huge benefactions and good will of the top aristocracy, but increasingly dependent on, and concerned with, the good will and co-operation of the whole population.

The creation of 'a workable scheme of religious discipline for everyone' was clearly a priority and its fulfilment in large part the achievement of scholastic theologians at the universities, men and institutions largely owing their existence to the new reserves of accessible wealth. The essentials of the sacrament of penance remained inviolate but were subjected to significant shifts in emphasis. As a preliminary, the functions implicit in the penitential process repay careful analysis. In the early systems, forgiveness for the guilt, or *culpa*, of mortal sin and remission for due punishment, or *poena*, were both dependent upon the successful discharge of protracted penitential effort. Contrition prompted confession which in turn led to the imposition and endurance of prescribed rigorous penances. When these were completed absolution for the *culpa* had been earned and, also, satisfaction made for the *poena*. But, as suggested above, for the laity this led in practice to penitential regimes which, while unavoidable, were unendurable. So, to render penance feasible, absolution and satisfaction were split and could be effected in two stages. Each may be dealt with in turn.

Culpa was still to be absolved in life, so that in death the soul would surely be saved. Contrition was to lead to confession and priests hearing confession were still to impose a penance to be completed before pronounced absolution could become fully effective. But the emphasis was changed: in that less was now to be achieved by it, lenience was increasingly advocated where the imposition of penance was concerned. Penances became arbitrary, decided by the priest rather than dictated by a fixed tariff, and they became less severe. Alain of Lille (*c.*1128–1203), to take one example, argued that in the primitive Church penances had been harsh to dissuade people from sin, but that lighter penances had become apposite to ensure that the process was medicinal rather than harmful.[18] In the later Middle Ages this trend developed to the point where, in Tentler's words, 'the most prudent authorities urged confessors to impose a penance that could be done immediately, such as one Our Father, before the penitent left the church, returned to his sins, and fell from the state of grace'.[19] The twelfth century also witnessed an increasing – perhaps a compensatory – emphasis on the importance of contrition. The answer to the question 'How do I know I am forgiven?' no longer consisted of a willingness to submit to arduous penitential exercise, but was located in the emotion of sorrow and intention of amendment. Abelard, Gratian, Peter Lombard and others argued that pardon came from sorrow elicited by the love of God.[20] But internal emotion was not allowed to render the sacramental and sacerdotal elements of penance redundant: far from it. In 1215, the Fourth Lateran Council emphasized the necessity of both by the imposition of obligatory confession at least once a year. The formal requirement of confession to a priest emphasized the sacramental character of penance and this in turn led to more careful definition of the powers of the priest pronouncing absolution on the penitent.[21] Thus, while it was maintained that contrition was 'the most important and effective part of the sacrament of Penance', sacramental confession was also held to be obligatory, divinely instituted and necessary. Emphases changed. In the mid thirteenth century St Thomas Aquinas and his followers insisted that contrition could not produce forgiveness apart from the sacramental absolution of a priest. By the early fourteenth century Duns Scotus had moved so far as to advance a position which, admitting that contrition, confession and satisfaction were necessary for the forgiveness of sins, nevertheless attached a more profound significance to the words of absolution pronounced by the priest. For Duns Scotus, the essence of the sacrament of penance was the absolution of the priest: 'In sum, the Scotist doctrine made forgiveness easier. And . . . it made it easier to know you were forgiven.' In theory at least, the power and significance of the words of absolution as spoken by the priest were progressively enhanced.[22]

But absolution might not grant immediate admission to Heaven, for, as indicated above, sin also incurred a debt of temporal punishment. This had also to be satisfied in accordance with harsh tariffs laid down in the early medieval penitentials and never rescinded.[23] Of course, it was always admissible – even desirable – to perform the requisite penances in life, but this proved unreasonable for those outside the cloister. Resolution of this impasse was perhaps the theologians' most significant achievement: they projected the process of satisfaction into the next life and with greater clarity than ever before defined the place and purpose of Purgatory where, as necessary, *poena* could be expiated. Southern comments that in the early period

It was certain that some kind of purgatorial process existed for some souls for minor sins – so much seemed clear from St. Paul's words about a man's works in wood, hay and stubble being burnt, while the man himself was saved. But which souls and what sins were capable of being purged were all in doubt. It was only safe to say that purgation was for the few, probably mainly monks who had been guilty of minor lapses. For ordinary mortals the choice lay starkly open between Heaven and Hell, with a strong likelihood of the latter.[24]

The recasting of religious discipline, however, meant that 'the vague and emaciated idea of Purgatory . . . was enlarged and shaped towards new ends . . . entirely in keeping with other theological developments and with the general expansive tendencies of the period after about 1050'. Southern describes how Peter Lombard, who died in 1160, the last great theologian of the formative period, was able to declare that *any* sin truly repented is remitted by purgatorial pains after death and that minor venial sins are purged even if they have not been repented. The new idea of Purgatory would have 'immense elaborations of practice added to it over the next three hundred years', but was in essence simple: 'any reasonably repentant, reasonably obedient sinner could hope to go to Heaven via Purgatory'. It is, then, fundamentally important when attempting to come to any understanding of Purgatory that its development as a doctrine, especially when taken with developments in other aspects of the sacrament of penance, marked a liberation for the people of Western Christendom:

It played an important part in lifting the cloud of uncertainty and gloom about the after-life which lay over the early centuries of European history. It made possible a more relaxed attitude to this world and the next: it turned the straight and narrow way of salvation into a highway trodden by a multitude of feet.

So in view of the difference that Purgatory wrought in the lives of ordinary men and women, the response that the doctrine elicits from most historians appears at the very least misconceived. But is this response no more than an aspect of denominational prejudice, or were the later 'immense elaborations of practice', to which Southern alludes, so vulgar as to explain historians' almost routine condemnation? Clearly, to answer this question we need to know what the 'elaborations of practice' were and may ask, first, how the doctrine spread from the universities to Western Christendom at large. Southern asserts that the task of broadcasting this, and other crucial doctrines and procedures defined at about the same time, began in earnest *circa* 1170.[25] Textbooks were compiled and employed which 'gave the whole body of society a single set of rules'. Legislation at universal and provincial councils was also promulgated which 'gave legal effect to this body of teaching at a parochial and individual level'. Englishmen of or bound for the governing classes who were trained at the European universities often returned home deeply committed to the new religious disciplines and their enforcement. Men like Robert Curzon and Stephen Langton are cited by Southern as the active agents, advocates and, when necessary, pulpiteers of the new religious ordering.[26] Robert Grosseteste, too, while probably not having attended any of the European centres of study, embraced the new ideals and attempted, when bishop, to use episcopal visitation as a means of instructing the laity. Describing his own first visitation as Bishop of Lincoln in 1235, Grosseteste later wrote

So I began to perambulate my bishopric, archdeaconry by archdeaconry, and rural deanery by rural deanery, requiring the clergy of each deanery to bring their people with their children together at a fixed place and time in order to have their children confirmed, to hear the Word of God, and to make their confessions. When the clergy and people were assembed, I myself frequently preached to the clergy, a Friar Preacher or Minor preached to the people, and four friars heard confessions and imposed penances. Then, having confirmed the children on two days, I and my clerks gave our attention to enquiring into things which needed correction or reform so far as they lay within our power.[27]

Clearly the established hierarchy might exercise a forceful presence for instructing the lower clergy and the laity which, if intermittent, would have left some mark. But the other personnel to whom Grosseteste refers were in a position to exercise a more durable influence, and a good measure of the responsibility for having popularized Purgatory is usually assigned to the mendicant orders.[28] The friars' inception in the first quarter of the thirteenth century, their quickly acquired scholastic eminence, their proficiency as preachers, and their advocacy of the benefits of confession and notorious readiness to hear it are factors which, when taken together, certainly suggest that they played a formative role in altering popular perceptions of penance. This achievement may not have been entirely altruistic, however, for while friars could not have survived without the support of prospering urban environments,[29] the laity would hardly have been amenable to support them so generously had they not been taught that small-scale almsgiving would profit their souls.[30] In that it could be made to open men's purses, the friars had a vested interest in the doctrine of Purgatory, and while the speed and scale of their success permits an understanding of many aspects of the contemporary condition, one of the most interesting of these is the potency of the appeal of Purgatory. But the doctrine was of wider moment; its promulgation was of fundamental importance for Western Christendom as a whole since it enabled the Church Militant to function – and, at a parochial level, flourish – free of undue financial dependence on kings and magnates, and indeed in spite of the continuing depredations of the governing classes. For it must be emphasized that Purgatory's main effect was to re-habilitate and encourage widespread penitential practice – to the immense financial benefit of the Church, the local church particularly. The early penitential systems failed in practice because they demanded too much to make them worth attempting. Purgatory's success and the gravity of its consequences were, by comparison, the result of a halfway-house mentality which reassured men and women that while they may not have been able to make complete satisfaction for all their *poena*, to ease its completion in the hereafter it was well worth making a start in the here and now. Penances, be they prayers, almsgiving, financial bequests to clergy and churches, or the commission of pious acts and services – good works, in short – became well worthwhile and immensely popular. The reasons for this development deserve to be considered in more detail.

Two points must be made. First, while some conceived of the purgatorial process as blissful since it implied the progressive reduction of the barriers between soul and creator,[31] it seems clear that most were taught and certainly conceived that the process was painful, its torment exceeding that suffered by penitents satisfying the *poena* in life.[32] As a transitory stage Purgatory was infinitely less awful than Hell. Nevertheless, men and women still wished to minimize its rigours. The second point is that they were able to. Implicit in the Church's teaching was the possibility of remitting purgatorial suffering on a basis proportionate to merit accrued by works performed in life, or by others after death. For, as mentioned earlier, the tariff mentality associated with sin and remission was never abandoned: this on the one hand inculcated a conviction that the duration of the soul's sojourn in Purgatory was determined by the gravity of sins committed, and on the other perpetuated the notion that penances would inexorably earn remission.[33] The notion that certain actions benefited the soul obviously underpins the tenet of the efficacy of penance, and was, quite simply, adapted to promote the precept that works might expedite the progress of the soul through Purgatory. Individuals were now encouraged to amass a store of merit, as a result of which they might reduce the *poena* that awaited them. Interestingly, the substitutive principle – fostering good works for and by others – resurfaced with a broader application. For it was held that suffrages could be of benefit only to those who, in this world, showed themselves worthy of benefiting from them after death.[34] Dovetailing closely with the ideal of Christian altruism, a simple dictum like this became a potent force stimulating the commission and provision of suffrages for others, the dead in particular, in order to qualify for benefit from one's own works and also, when the time came, for assistance from the works of those still living. In shaping one of the later medieval period's most distinctive *mentalités*, termed by Le Goff as the solidarity of the living and the dead, the precept that greater merit accrued from assisting others' souls was fundamental.[35]

This *mentalité* manifested itself in a variety of ways. Late medieval wills, for instance, certainly presupposed the living would make painstaking provision for dead forebears and acquaintances.[36] *Post obit* services, like the chantry and anniversary, provided for constant interplay between the living and the dead. Founders of the former invariably specified that their Masses were to be for the profit of all the faithful departed and, of course, depended upon the living both to celebrate the Masses and maintain the service.[37] Those who paid for the latter sought to stimulate the continual intercession of the living by the careful repetition of their own funeral service at least once a year.[38] The founders of hospitals and almshouses, and colleges too, committed beneficiaries to intercede for benefactors. Churches were equipped and priests provided with the wherewithal to administer the sacraments on the premise that the living beneficiaries, the parishioners, would be prompted to intercede for their forebears and benefactors.[39] This *mentalité* is similarly of central importance in explaining the widespread success of confraternities whose living members were obliged, *inter alia*, to provide intercession and Masses for the benefit of dead forebears, and did so in the firm expectation that in time each would benefit from the perpetuation of these services.[40] Ultimately, self-interest and altruism became hopelessly entangled: without doubt, men and women were mindful of their own needs, but these were well served by assisting others' and, particularly, by attending to the needs of the dead. 'The system of solidarity between the living and the dead instituted an unending circular flow, a full circuit of reciprocity.'[41] The abundance of pious provision in late medieval England suggests that the dead were, by their design no less than by the calculation of the living, a very real presence in everyday life. 'The two extremes were knit together.'[42]

Before proceeding to consider just how abundant pious provision was in late medieval England and how important for the Church its consequences were, it is worth tidying up some of the questions prompted by what has gone before. First, the question inevitably arising from discussion of the evolution of penance: did such change really affect the common people and, if so, how far were they aware of the implications of doctrinal innovation? Our ignorance of the workings of men's minds means that a satisfying answer to the latter part of the question may never be possible, so caution is necessary. It would certainly be unwise to insist that accurate understanding of the sacrament was ever widespread. Nevertheless, via schools and universities the Church instructed an influential proportion of the clergy; and the regular, secular and mendicant clergy, via schools, the pulpit, the written word, iconography, and even by instruction at confession itself, propounded the basic message, and could doubtless rest assured that pious lay people would continue the work by admonishing their peers. The conviction of sin, on which the operation of the sacrament ultimately depended, could be heightened. Equally, the efficacy of the available remedies could be extolled. Sufficient evidence survives to indicate that by the later Middle Ages the common people were certainly aware of the dictates of the sacrament of penance. We may not tell what proportion of the population confessed at least annually as bound, but it is plain that confession was recognized as an important obligation.[43] Moreover, to judge from wills, among many other indicators, the generosity and abundance of pious provision certainly suggests that a significant section of the population unreservedly exploited good works.[44]

The second question has a direct bearing on a point just made. In effecting the changes contingent on recasting the sacrament of penance the Church exploited the channels at its disposal to heighten the sense of sin and to extol the efficacy of its twofold remedy. Thus, to foster contrition and penitential activity the Church exploited the threat either of damnation or an extended purgation, as well as extending the promise of salvation and its assured attainment. It thus diagnosed man's malaise and offered a cure. So, when assessing the efforts made by the Church and the lay response to these, are historians justified in judging that fear explains the fervent pious activity and abundant provision which is so distinctive an aspect of late medieval life? I would contend that they are not. Their argument apparently proceeds on the premise that, be it confession or penitential activity to make satisfaction, the remedies may be discounted as specious. It follows that the late medieval laity were denied effective treatment for their predicament and that the relatively outlandish remedies that they embraced thus rested on and were expressive of fear. This undoubtedly misinterprets contemporary aspiration. While being conscious of sin and its wages – regular contemplation of Doom paintings and similar motifs would have left few in much doubt on this score – people nevertheless took the promise of an eased salvation to heart. This they strove to secure using all the means at their disposal. They were, in other words, much more positive: they sought to avoid the avoidable by invoking a self-help salvation. Indeed to survey the laity's achievements – supporting clergy, embellishing liturgy and, most strikingly, embarking on an almost unequalled enterprise of church building, decoration and furnishing – does not to my mind suggest men and women flinching from the Almighty in abject fear of what, inevitably, was to come. For the wealthy, punishment was to be feared only if they steadfastly turned away from diagnosis and remedy, unrepentently using their money solely for their own increase. From the honest poor less was demanded. While the other six sacraments might operate for their benefit as for anyone else, where penance was concerned the intrinsic blessedness of their state gave them slightly different responsibilities.[45] If they had an obligation it was to intercede the more effectively for the wealthy and the dead. In making satisfaction for other less spiritually advantaged souls they might prove their own charity, and it is clear from testamentary provision that their services were assiduously sought. Again, a 'circular flow' operated, uniting classes of men and in this instance having the important effect of mitigating social tension.

In practice the emphases of the redemptive process were constructive rather than punitive. But the reputation of the pre-Reformation Church, from which Luther broke because, *inter alia*, he found its emphasis on works insufficient to allay his fears, will die hard – even though Luther was hardly a man to be labelled typical.[46] In hindsight historians have found the charges of fear and anxiety irresistible, offering both an explanation for change and, in so far as the late medieval 'remedy' is now found wanting, a justification for what was to happen. But this interpretation is possible only if the sacrament of Penance and its implications are left unexplored which, as indicated above, is precisely what has happened. Denominational prejudice is, in Britain at least, inextricably combined with the perception of national identity. Revision will make slow progress. To illustrate how pre-Reformation mores have been misrepresented, reference may again be made to Thomas More's *The Supplication of Souls* – one extract from which has entered into the canon of received historical wisdom marking the tyranny of fear under which those living in pre-Reformation times commonly laboured. Apart from neglecting the highly charged political manoeuvring which produced and shaped the tract, historians have ignored the full range of More's argument. His point was that the pains of Purgatory would be unendurable only if his opponents' arguments prevailed.[47] More himself extolled the efficacy of suffrages:

And therefore as we say, passing over such jesting and railing of those uncharitable heretics mortal enemies unto us, and to themself both: consider you our pains, and pity them in your hearts, and help us with your prayers, pilgrimages, and other almsdeeds; and of all thing in special procure us the suffrages and blessed oblation of the holy mass, whereof no man living so well can tell the fruit, as we that here feel it. The comfort that we have here, except our continual hope in our lord god, cometh at seasons from our lady, with such glorious saints, as either our self with our own devotion while we lived or you with yours for us since our decease and departing have made intercessors for us.[48]

He repeatedly stressed the benefits accruing from the prayers of those in Purgatory to those who show themselves worthy of them on earth:

They [the good angels] carry up our prayers to god and good saints for us, and they bring down from them the comfort and consolation to us: only god and we know what joy it is to our hearts and how heartily we pray for you. . . . Our prayer must need be profitable, for we stand sure of his grace. And our prayer for you is so fervent that you can nowhere find any such affection on earth. . . . Remember what kin you and we be together: what familiar friendship has ere this been between us: what sweet words you have spoken, and what promises you have made us. Let now your words appear and your fair promise be kept. . . . So God keep you hence, or not long here, but bring you shortly to that bliss, to which for our lord's love help you to bring us, and we shall set hand to help you thither to us.[49]

More sought to safeguard the 'circular flow' of grace which he perceived as essential in expediting Everyman's salvation. Hope for and attainment of Heaven are his priorities, and if we turn to examine the principles and actions of ordinary people it is clear that More, albeit passionately, was simply defending a common aspiration which had inspired considerable investment and which could not be denied, nor its effects dismantled, without far reaching dislocation.[50]

Among dogmas demanding a response from the faithful, the

penitential scheme was perhaps the most positive spur to action. But were they to respond, how might the faithful act? While some may have been called to monastic or more solitary lives, in general the lay response was channelled through the parish. The development of the parish system, as outlined above, meant that for the majority of English people the means of salvation were within relatively easy reach. The parish provided a priest to convert, instruct and administer the sacraments, and also afforded access to a building facilitating these processes.[51] Existing to stimulate and satisfy 'spiritual' aspiration, the local church was bound in return to benefit from parishioners' devotion, and, in particular, their penitential response. In certain circumstances, of course, other institutions or organizations commanded loyalty. Monastic communities, with shrines and relics, exercised a pull that paid no respect to parish boundaries.[52] In towns perhaps more than the countryside, friars offered alternative services with better preaching and easier confession that similarly undermined parish loyalties.[53] Confraternities, too, were organizations offering additional, more flexible rallying points for lay devotion.[54] Alternatives existed, but none superseded the parish in influence or competence. For the great majority of English men and women, the parish remained the hub of spiritual life and focus of religious expression. The penitential mentality merged with and found expression through parish loyalty with notably constructive results.

Contrary to expectations, discord was far from endemic where relations between laity and clergy were concerned. Circumstances predisposed rapport between the two orders. For the laity, the sacramental emphasis of late medieval Catholicism meant that salvation, if not impossible, was very difficult without the ministrations of the priesthood. This, when coupled with the obligation of sacerdotal confession, meant that it was in the interests of all to maintain the priest or priests in their midst and keep on good terms with them. Parishioners paid for their clergy in order both to satisfy their desire for salvation and also, in all likelihood, to mark their own penitence. Evidence is scarce, but tithe was an obligation apparently taken seriously. Non-payment was an omission against which almost every testator chose to make a gesture;[55] and while tithe disputes occurred in some centres – such as London – because of the problems implicit in adapting payments formulated for agrarian communities to a mercantile environment, such disputes were infrequent.[56] In his study of late medieval Norwich, Norman Tanner discovered no evidence for widespread or organized resistance to tithe. Such disputes as there were arose from doubt as to the parish in which titheable property lay and to whom the payment was due.[57] Generally, the principle of paying the tithe was well established,[58] and A. G. Little's finding that the 'small' or 'vicar's' tithe was both generally paid in town parishes in the fourteenth and fifteenth centuries and that it was well worth having, acts as a useful corrective to received opinion.[59]

The late medieval laity's predisposition to support the clergy went considerably farther than payment of tithe, particularly in some urban areas. Bearing in mind that some of its citizens had means far in excess of those available to the majority of other town and country dwellers, Bristol appears to have supported a strong clerical presence. Testators envisaged no difficulty in assembling large numbers of supplementary priests at short notice to attend funeral services. In 1404, John Bannebury left a shilling to each of the five chaplains celebrating in his parish church, St Werburgh, on condition that they diligently occupied themselves in the rites on the day of his burial. Nineteen other priests were also paid to attend his exequies and Mass.[60] Walter Seymour left similar instructions that twenty-four chaplains be paid 6d. each to attend his exequies and Requiem in St Werburgh's in 1409.[61] In some instances, the pious generosity of the rich sustained these priests and clerks. Before he died, William Canynges of Bristol left £340 to shore up an endowment – probably inaugurated by his grandfather, another William Canynges – to perpetuate the presence and services of two chaplains and three clerks in St Mary Redcliffe.[62] The clerks, however, were to receive only relatively small sums from this endowment, implying that other parishioners found the remainder of their maintenance. Records from St Ewen's, Bristol, indicate that lesser clergy were indeed supported by a rate collected from parishioners. In 1459, its rector petitioned the Mayor and Commonalty of Bristol complaining of the 'right great hurt and impoverishing' resulting when one of the most important buildings in the parish had been taken into the hands of the town authorities. Formerly, its inhabitants had contributed 'right worshipfully and notably' towards the parson's tithe and offerings, the church cake and lights, and 'to the parish clerk his quartrages' – that is, his quarterly stipend.[63] Significantly, John Mathew of St Ewen's bequeathed 6s. 8d. annually to the clerk's wages in 1521, to ensure that the 'poorest householders of the parish might thereby be eased of his wages'.[64] The rate never appears in the churchwardens' accounts, which were concerned with managing the church and its fabric and contents rather than with the livelihood of the parish and auxiliary clergy. Nevertheless, the wardens were prepared to make up shortfalls, and the accounts occasionally record debits such as '11d. to fulfil the clerk's wages' or '6d. for half the year's wages to the clerk'.[65]

Parishes were staffed as a result of lay provision, as men and women sought both to succour their souls and garner merit. In Bristol, many priests – probably the greater number of the chaplains referred to in testamentary provisions like those cited – were chantry priests, and were in one sense undeniably the 'creatures' of lay penitential motive. But chantry founders were not content simply to profit from their priest's daily Mass. Had this been all they wanted, much cheaper expedients were available.[66] Founders shouldered the expense to ensure that, in addition to grace derived from the Masses celebrated, their generosity would secure a supplementary priest within their parish church, embellishing its liturgy and enhancing its prestige. The benefit of the parish was itself desirable and its promotion further profited the benefactor's soul. Chantry foundation neatly satisfied a desire to assist the soul at the same time as advancing the efficacy of the parish as a centre of worship, ministry and instruction – as a centre, in short, facilitating salvation. Parishes certainly regarded chantry foundation as benefaction since it guaranteed the presence of priests 'to the increase of Divine Service', whose cost was defrayed by their founders. Chantry foundation was a common recourse, but it was not simply a self-centred exercise whereby the rich allayed their anxieties in a surfeit of Masses.[67] Rather it demonstrates how the penitential motive in action ensured considerable practical benefits for parish and parishioners alike.

Individual largesse which profited the parish community and prompted intercession for the benefactor was a 'circular flow' in which the clergy also joined. Maintained priests, be they parish incumbents or chantry chaplains, were no doubt mindful of their own duties and needs. To seek to satisfy both was simple prudence, as failure to do so would have imperilled their souls no less than those of parishioners or patrons. Consequently, parish priests played a prominent role in pursuing parish interests. The archives of All Saints', Bristol, reveal how Maurice Hardwick, vicar in the mid fifteenth century, encouraged parishioners to make donations to the parish – in part, of course, satisfying their own penitential needs. He 'procured, moved and stirred' Agnes Fylour to devise her dwelling house to All Saints' in return for certain services.[68] When her son, Thomas, a London merchant, opposed this plan and sought to affirm his rights to the property, Hardwick acted with the wardens of All Saints' to defend the parish's interests. They forced a compromise whereby the house reverted to the church. A vicar might also seek to ensure that parish properties were safely kept and their revenues maintained. Hardwick went so far as to provide for a chest, with locks and keys, for parish muniments, remedying the situation whereby documents 'lay abroad likely to be embezzled or mischiefed'. Similarly he laboured to make and compile the All Saints' Church Book 'to be a memorial and remembrance for ever for the curates and churchwardens'; without such record, benefactions could the more easily have been forfeit had the parish by oversight omitted to fulfil benefactors' stipulations.

Priests and members of the auxiliary clergy also made donations to their church. Hardwick was particularly generous.[69] His gifts included silver clasps for All Saints' best suit of vestments, a wooden image of St Ursula, several sets of altar linen, a pair of red velvet vestments, and a new antiphoner. He contributed towards the new parish organs, paid for gilding the parish's image of All Saints and a crucifix, and gave ornately decorated cloths to hang in the church at the principal feasts of the year. William Warens, chantry priest in All Saints', gave a pair of red baudkin vestments for his successors. To the church itself he gave four books of pricksong 'to the laud of God and the increase of Divine Service', and a breviary to be chained in the church 'to the ease of all manner of priests to say their service when they did not have their own books with them'.[70] Finally Thomas Haxby gave 20s. to the church to be remembered among its benefactors, and 6s. 8d. to the high altar to be 'spent on necessities'. The Church Book discloses that Haxby 'was a well-willed man in all his days, and a profitable unto this church and specially when he was common servant in this parish, that is to say parish clerk', a position which he is said to have held for twenty-eight years.[71] Harmonious co-existence between clergy and laity was in the interests of both. The penitential urge prompted the clergy to generosity no less than the laity and offers some explanation for the latter's willingness to support so many clergy.[72]

If the supposition that before the Reformation clergy and laity were at obligatory loggerheads is not surprisingly found wanting, similarly the premise that parishioners were at best resentful participants in church life or, worse, were coerced by fear, must be questioned. The indications are that pious motive – the urge to devote an appreciable portion of one's estate to good works – was strong and indulged for positive reasons. Men and women took the Church's promise to heart that the way to Heaven might be greatly eased by good works, for self and others, in life and after. Essentially, the penitent forged contracts, seeking as material benefactors to become spiritual beneficiaries. Ignorant as we are of everyday acts of charity, late medieval sources unequivocally reveal the poor as the material beneficiaries of a common intent among the wealthy to benefit their own souls. In return for the prayers of the poor, almshouses were built, property devised, and doles of cash or clothes or food bequeathed.[73] In the context of the parish similar transactions were endlessly repeated. Men and women gave to the clergy to profit from their prayers.[74] They also gave liturgical equipment – chalices, candlesticks, vestments and many other items, each of which might be inscribed with the name of the donor and the exhortation to pray for his, her or their souls – to ensure that clergy and parishioners would constantly be reminded of their reciprocal duties. Parishioners of substance also gave property, the income from which could be devoted to maintaining lights, services or commemorations, or, as recently suggested, a priest to celebrate Masses and add to the liturgical 'battery' of the parish. In short, in late medieval England, wills, deeds and inventories reveal that where there were wealthy parishioners there were also generous benefactors, giving to redeem their success by demonstrating their piety, benefiting others to ensure that contemporaries and successors would intercede for them.

This had many consequences. Contrary to the long-established orthodoxy, tailored to explain and justify the Reformation, of a church in neglect and local disarray, the penitential motive made a considerable contribution towards parish income, services and equipment in a period when, admittedly, other forces exploited the landed revenues of local churches for their own interest.[75] Men and women were prepared to fund and provide for their religion. As a further consequence this first fostered and subsequently occupied churchwardens in English parishes, and it is to this process and these officers that I turn.

The new religious disciplines elicited donations of both money and property to parish churches. Much of this was managed in the short term by widows, heirs and executors. If, however, revenues were to be raised from endowments in perpetuity, other agents had to be found to maintain property and distribute revenues according to benefactors' wishes. Similarly, if items were bequeathed to parish churches, agents were needed to safeguard the goods. Moreover, in the thirteenth century legislation was enacted which formally transferred the responsibility for the upkeep of the nave in each parish church to those who used it; that is, to the congregation.[76] Later in the century, parishioners were also assigned the responsibility for providing and maintaining the requisite complement of liturgical equipment within their church.[77] The first of these obligations meant that congregations were obliged to raise and dispose of appreciable sums of money; the second, that valuable utensils and equipment, if not donated, had to be purchased, kept and, as necessary, replaced by parishioners. The coincidence is tantalizing. The imposition of penitential disciplines applicable to all and eliciting a prodigious response, coincided with synodal legislation devolving responsibility for church fabric and equipment upon the laity. Simultaneously, in response to the obvious need for permanent – or at least permanently renewable – lay superintendants, churchwardens emerged to assume an increasingly responsible role in parish life.[78] Involvement in the scheme of redemption elicited responses as well as imposing responsibilities, and churchwardens facilitated the effective discharge and management of the lay response in each parish. Drew summarizes their brief as follows:

They were in the first place the representatives through whom the parishioners fulfilled certain 'collective' responsibilities; it was their duty to hold and administer any form of property with which the parishioners might be endowed for the discharge of such responsibilities; should such endowments not exist or suffice, it was their business to provide for the raising of the funds required to meet a particular need; they were responsible for the safe custody of the ornaments and utensils to be provided by the parishioners for the services of the church; and, finally, they were the acknowledged representatives of the parishioners in any collective action they might wish or be compelled to undertake.[79]

Churchwardens' responsibilities were serious and wide-ranging: they comprised the maintenance, or even enhancement, of the parish church as property, property-holder and liturgical centre, and encompassed the duty of perpetuating the 'presence' of dead parishioners by observing their wishes and enforcing their plans. Surviving late medieval churchwardens' accounts illustrate the dedication and diligence with which many discharged their duties, although they do not reflect the full range of wardens' responsibilities. Rather they record the monies involved in the discharge of parishioners' liabilities for the fabric and contents of the parish church. The accounts surviving for St Ewen's, Bristol, for instance, did not record the rates levied to sustain the parish clerk, although the churchwardens ensured that he was properly paid, and may have supervised his conduct.[80] He was a supernumerary and his stipend merited no place in accounts devoted to the fulfilment of obligations. It is the chance survival of separate accounts for the Halleways' chantry in All Saints', Bristol, and of some of the Spicers' chantry in St James', documents which are in both cases fully as painstaking as parish accounts, which reveals just how much care churchwardens lavished on intercessory services established by parishioners.[81] Each set of accounts also itemizes expenditure on the founders' anniversary celebrations, observances which co-ordinated masses, prayer, bell-ringing and the distribution of alms. These, too, are eloquent as to the time and energy churchwardens devoted to the elaborate commemorative rites from which many sought benefit in death. Defective as our detailed knowledge of late medieval churchwardens' duties may be, there is no doubt that parishioner after parishioner shouldered a particularly onerous commission in undertaking the office.

A number of observations follow. First, that the men (and occasionally women) who fulfilled these duties played a pivotal role in sustaining the life, business and identity of the parish – be it in discharging lay obligations, protecting property, safeguarding pious gifts or guaranteeing full observance of *post obit* arrangements – in short, in maintaining all services associated with and enriching the parish church. More than any others, churchwardens were responsible for perpetuating the 'circular flow' of intercession and grace between benefactors and beneficiaries, dead and living, poor and rich, laity and clergy, which the parish fostered. Consequently, some answer may be offered to the question of why busy and successful citizens became churchwardens, even if only for a year or two at a time. Parish pride apart, their reasons were doubtless directly related to the penitential motive. The effort and sacrifice involved in discharging the task was itself a good work, the profit accruing to all further benefiting their own souls. Service as warden would redeem worldly success in much the same way as almsgiving, whereas refusal to serve would have tokened unrepentant indifference to the needs of close neighbours and deprived the individual from any right to depend on or gain from others' ministrations. Participation brought rewards. Finally, by the eve of the Reformation the discipline imposed on and participation elicited from parishioners had transformed the parish into an administrative unit of much more than spiritual competence. Interestingly, the most telling testimony to the transformation was a post-Reformation development. As a result of the late sixteenth-century Poor Laws, provision for the indigent was co-ordinated as an activity exploiting the traditions and expertise of parish government.[82] If the problems of poverty and vagabondage were conceivably exacerbated by the Reformation, with doctrinal change altering the habit and practice of charity and much else, it is at the very least ironic that the attempted solution perforce rested on agencies which owed their existence and competence to other aspects of the medieval penitential response. After the Reformation the 'circular flow' was sustained by legislation; late medieval Catholics were stimulated to action by the assurance of future benefits.

Should the preceding observations seem unconvincing, one final category of evidence may be adduced to demonstrate the strength of the late medieval parish and that men and women were remarkably generous as they strove to benefit their souls by glorifying God. It flatly contradicts much written about the late medieval church, and is structural rather than documentary. Late medieval English church building, interior furnishing and decoration witness the positive participatory character of pre-Reformation penitential practice. In the fourteenth century men and women were prepared to add aisles or towers or windows to their parish churches. By the fifteenth century, complete demolition, rebuilding and furnishing on a grand scale was frequently undertaken throughout England.[83] 'There is no period at which money was lavished so freely [on the fabric of parish churches] as in the fifteenth century.'[84] The proof that such munificence was intimately related to the penitential system and was, I would argue, largely its result, was that the imposition of a new redemptive discipline so obviously arrested church building in England after the Reformation.[85] The disjunction is eloquent testimony to the positive potential of the earlier system, and to the reduction in the role allowed the laity thereafter. The churchwardens of St James', Louth, Lincolnshire, may have the last word.[86] In 1515, after fifteen years of building and the feverish accumulation of as much as possible in money and kind from parishioners, gilds, and richer benefactors, the tower which still dominates the town was finally rebuilt. The whole parish community celebrated:

William Appleby, parish priest, with many of his brother priests there being present, hallowed the weathercock and the stone that it stands upon, and so conveyed upon the said broch [tower]. And then the said priests sang Te Deum Laudamus with organs. And then the church wardens began to ring the bells and caused all the people present to have bread and ale. And all to the loving of God, our lady and all saints.

Acknowledgements

I should like to thank Susan Bennett, Thomas Charles-Edwards, Isobel Harvey and David Moncur for their time and suggestions, and acknowledge a particular debt of gratitude to William McCaffrey for being much more helpful than ever he realized.

Notes and references

1   J. Cox, *Churchwardens' Accounts from the Fourteenth Century to the Close of the Seventeenth Century* (1913); J. Scarisbrick, *The Reformation and the English People* (1984), chap. 1; C. Platt, *The Parish Churches of Medieval England* (1981), chap. 5.
2   Platt, pp. 100–6.
3   J. C. Dickinson, *The Later Middle Ages* (1979), pp. 13–22.
4   J. C. Dickinson, pp. 257–63, 345–60, 376–81.
5   A. Kreider, *English Chantries: The Road to Dissolution* (Cambridge, Mass., 1979), pp. 91–2.
6   K. L. Wood-Legh, *Perpetual Chantries in Britain* (1965), p. 312.

7   Wood-Legh, p. 313 and n. 1.

8   A. G. Dickens, *The English Reformation* (1964), pp. 5–6; C. S. L. Davies, *Peace, Print and Protestantism, 1450–1558* (1976), p. 146; F. Oakley, *The Western Church in the Later Middle Ages* (Ithaca, 1979), p. 121.

9   T. More, *The Works of Sir Thomas More Knyght . . . Wrytten by Hym in the Englysch Tonge* (1557), pp. 288–339; *The Supplication* was published in September 1529.

10   A. Fox, *Thomas More: History and Providence* (1982), pp. 167ff, especially p. 176.

11   Fox, p. 202. For Simon Fish, 'A supplication for the beggars', see F. J. Furnival (ed.), *Four Supplications, 1529–1553 A.D.*, Early English Text Society, Extra Series **XIII** (1871), pp. 1–15.

12   See below, p. 70.

13   See, for instance, M. James, 'Ritual, drama and social body in the late medieval English town', *Past and Present*, **98** (1983), pp. 3–29 and notes.

14   In the following discussion of penance I am much indebted to T. N. Tentler, *Sin and Confession on the Eve of the Reformation* (Princeton, 1977), especially chapters 1 and 5.

15   It should, however, be noted that some Irish penitentials were more lenient than others in the duration of penances imposed for sins, see 'The Penitential of Finnian', L. Bieler (ed.) *The Irish Penitentials*, (Dublin, 1963), pp. 74–95.

16   R. W. Southern, *St Anselm and his Biographer. A Study of Monastic Life and Thought, 1059–c.1130* (1963), p. 101; Southern, *Western Society and the Church in the Middle Ages* (1970), pp. 225–8.

17   In the following I am much indebted to R. W. Southern, 'Between Heaven and Hell', *Times Literary Supplement*, 18 June 1982, pp. 651–2, a review of J. Le Goff, *La Naissance du Pugatoire* (Paris, 1981) (subsequently published in English as *The Birth of Purgatory*, transl. Goldhammer (1984)). See also J. Bossy, *Christianity in the West* (1985), pp. 45–56.

18   Cited by Tentler, p. 17.

19   Tentler, pp. 339–40.

20   Tentler, pp. 18–19, for a fuller exposition of the arguments.

21   Text of Decree *Omnis utriusque sexus* accessible in O. D. Watkins, *A History of Penance* (1920), ii, pp. 733–4, 748–9; and see Tentler, pp. 20–2.

22   Tentler, p. 27; for a fuller summary of the arguments of Lombard, Aquinas and Scotus, see pp. 22–7.

23   Tentler, p. 319ff.

24   This and the following quotations are taken from Southern, *art. cit.*; the reference to St Paul's teaching is 1 Corinthians, 3, v.15.

25   R. W. Southern, *Robert Grosseteste: The Growth of an English Mind*

in *Medieval Europe* (1986), p. 238, and the following quotations are taken from the same page.

26 Southern, *Robert Grosseteste*, pp. 239–42.
27 Cited in Southern, *ibid.*, p. 258.
28 See, for instance, Le Goff, *Purgatory* (1984), pp. 238, 297–8, 310 and 328. See also D. L. D'Avray, *The Preaching of the Friars* (1985), *passim*, but especially pp. 50–1, 56, 149, and 184 and n. 1.
29 Southern, *Western Society and the Church*, pp. 273–7, 286–92.
30 Le Goff, pp. 237–78.
31 A theme developed by St Catherine of Genoa (1447–1510) in her *Treatise on Purgatory*, transl. Balfour and Irvine (1934); see also Thomas More, 'De quatuor novissimus' in *Works*, p. 75c.
32 Tentler, p. 319 and n.22; and see Le Goff, pp. 248–9, 273.
33 Tentler, pp. 319–44; and see Le Goff, pp. 227–9, 262–4 and 274–8.
34 Le Goff, pp. 266, 292–3.
35 Le Goff, pp. 326–8.
36 I do not propose to give detailed examples from wills in this essay as there are many available studies which are based on and describe testamentary provision. The most detailed study is N. P. Tanner, *The Church in Late Medieval Norwich* (Toronto, 1984), especially pp. 91–140; see also Scarisbrick, chap. 1; P. Heath, 'Urban Piety in the Later Middle Ages: the Evidence of Hull Wills', in R. B. Dobson (ed.), *The Church, Politics and Patronage in the Fifteenth Century* (1984), pp. 209–34; J. Kermode, 'The Merchants of Three Northern English Towns', C. H. Clough (ed.) *Profession, Vocation, and Culture in Later Medieval England*, (1982) pp. 7–51; P. W. Fleming, 'Charity, Faith, and the Gentry of Kent, 1422–1529', T. Pollard (ed.), *Property and Politics in Later Medieval English History* (1984), pp. 36–58.
37 Tanner, pp. 105–6. My researches on pious provision in fifteenth-century Bristol certainly corroborate Tanner's observation that 'all the faithful departed' were almost invariably specified as beneficiaries of chantry endowments.
38 On the anniverary, see C. R. Burgess, 'A Service for the Dead: the Anniversary in late medieval Bristol', *Transactions of the Bristol and Gloucestershire Archaeological Society*, **105** (1987), pp. 168–96.
39 Tanner, pp. 126–9; C. R. Burgess, ' "For the Increase of Divine Service": Chantries in the Parish in late medieval Bristol', *Journal of Ecclesiastical History*, **xxxvi** (1985), pp. 46–65.
40 Above pp. 29–46; and see Scarisbrick, chap. 2, and Le Goff, p. 294.
41 Le Goff, pp. 356–7.
42 Le Goff, p. 357.
43 Tentler, *passim*; B. L. Manning, *The People's Faith in the Time of Wyclif* (2nd edn, 1975), chap. 3 and notes; L. G. Duggan, 'Fear and Confession on the Eve of the Reformation', *Archiv fur Reformationsgeschichte*, **75** (1984), pp. 159–62; Bossy, pp. 45–56.

44 See above, n.36.

45 Manning, chap. 10; M. Rubin, *Charity and Community in Medieval Cambridge* (1987), pp. 1–13, 54–98 and notes.

46 S. Ozment, *The Reformation in the Cities* (New Haven, 1975), pp. 12, 20–8, 118–19, 176–7; Ozment, *The Age of Reform, 1250–1550* (New Haven, 1980), pp. 209, 216–19; B. Moeller, 'Religious Life in Germany on the Eve of the Reformation', G. Strauss (ed.), *Pre-Reformation Germany* (1972), pp. 13–42. But compare Duggan, *art. cit.*

47 More, p. 338a; see also p. 316b.

48 More, p. 338e and f.

49 More, pp. 338g and h–339a and f.; compare also p. 10d.

50 See also B. Bradshaw, 'The Controversial Thomas More', *Journal of Ecclesiastical History*, **xxxvi** (1985), pp. 566–9 for analysis of More's theological objections to Luther.

51 See above, pp. 29–46.

52 See, for example, R. B. Dobson, *Durham Priory, 1400–1450* (1973), pp. 11–50.

53 A. G. Little, *Studies in English Franciscan History* (1917), pp. 92–122; G. R. Owst, *Preaching in Medieval England* (1926), chaps. 2–5; W. A. Pantin, *The English Church in the Fourteenth Century* (1955), pp. 124–6.

54 See above.

55 Tanner, p. 5 and n.28.

56 J. A. F. Thomson, 'Tithe Disputes in Later Medieval London', *English Historical Review*, **lxxviii** (1963), pp. 1–17.

57 Tanner, pp. 5–7.

58 G. Constable, 'Resistance to Tithes in the Middle Ages', *Journal of Ecclesiastical History*, **xiii** (1962), pp. 172–5, 184–5.

59 A. G. Little, 'Personal Tithes', *English Historical Review*, **lx** (1945), pp. 67–88.

60 BAO: Great Orphan Book, fo. 90–90v.

61 Great Orphan Book, fos. 112v–113.

62 E. E. Williams, *The Chantries of William Canynges in St Mary Redcliffe, Bristol* (1950), pp. 67, 266–8.

63 B. R. Masters and E. Ralph (eds), *The Church Book of St Ewen's, Bristol, 1454–1584*, (Bristol and Gloucestershire Records Section, vi, 1967), pp. xxii–iii, 257–8.

64 PRO: Maynwaring 17 (fo. 131–131v).

65 *Church Book of St Ewen's*, pp. xxiii and n.3; and, for example, pp. 145, 155.

66 I discuss this in more detail in 'By Quick and by Dead: Wills and Pious Provision in a late medieval Bristol', *English Historical Review*, **cii** (1987), pp. 849–50, particularly in reference to provision made by Agnes Gorges and Richard Paans.

67 I argue in the above article that reliance on will-analysis seriously underestimates the scale of chantry provision, certainly in late medieval towns.

68 BAO: All Saints' Church Book, p. 83 (this Church Book, although in manuscript, has been paginated).

69 All Saints Church Book, pp. 82–4.

70 All Saints Church Book, p. 85.

71 All Saints Church Book, p. 85.

72 M. L. Zell, 'The Personnel of the Clergy in Kent in the Reformation Period', *English Historical Review*, **lxxxix** (1974), pp. 517–24; Zell, 'Economic Problems of the parochial clergy in the sixteenth century', R. O'Day and F. Heal (eds.), *Princes and Paupers in the English Church 1500–1800* (1981), pp. 21–9.

73 See above, n.36.

74 See above, n.36.

75 P. Heath, *The English Parish Clergy on the Eve of the Reformation* (1969), pp. 50–6; F. Heal, 'Economic Problems of the Clergy', in F. Heal and R. O'Day (eds.), *Church and Society in England: Henry VIII to James I* (1977), pp. 99–108.

76 F. M. Powicke and C. R. Cheney (eds.), *Councils and Synods II*, (1964), pp. 128, 367; C. Drew, *Early Parochial Organisation in England. The Origin of the Office of Churchwarden* (1954), p. 8 and ns.

77 *Councils and Synods II*, pp. 1006, 1122–3, 1385–8; Drew, p. 9.

78 Drew, pp. 14ff; D. Owen, *Church and Society in Medieval Lincolnshire* (1971), pp. 115ff.

79 Drew, pp. 5–6.

80 The wardens' supervisory role is implicit in Bristol's evidence, for instance, in Canynges' instructions for his clerks, above n.62.

81 BAO: P/AS/C1 and P/St J/ Ca/1.

82 On the Poor Law, see P. Williams, *The Tudor Regime* (1979), pp. 200ff; P. Slack, 'Poverty and Social Regulation in Elizabethan England', in C. Haigh (ed.), *The Reign of Elizabeth I* (1984), pp. 221–41. On its administrative debt to medieval parochial organization, see Drew, pp. 5, 25–6; A. H. Thompson, *The English Clergy and their Organisation in the later Middle Ages* (1947), p. 130.

83 Scarisbrick, p. 13 and n.13; Platt, pp. 90–7; and for lavish illustration see H. M. Cautley, *Suffolk Churches and their Treasures* (5th edn, 1982) and Cautley, *Norfolk Churches* (1949). A particularly vivid record of demolishing and rebuilding a parish church is 'Receipts and Expenses in the Building of Bodmin Church, AD. 1469–72', in J. J. Wilkinson (ed.), *Camden Miscellany VII* (Camden Soc., new series, **xiv**, 1875), separately paginated.

84 Thompson, p. 128.

85 The abundance and quality of later sixteenth-century secular building render economic decline inadequate as an explanation for this striking

change; see D. M. Palliser, *The Age of Elizabeth: England under the later Tudors 1547–1603* (1983), pp. 110–13, and M. Girouard, *Robert Smythson and the Elizabethan Country House* (1983), pp. 4–5 and passim.

86 R. C. Dudding (ed.), *The First Churchwardens' Book of Louth, 1500–1524*, (1941), pp. xviii, 181; see also Owen, p. 115.

4 Loyalty and identity in Chester parishes 1540–1640

Nick Alldridge

This study of the early modern urban parish as a social organism is offered as a contribution both to current revaluation of the grass-roots impact of the English Reformation and to developments in local studies. In common with much recent work it questions the validity of drawing too sharp a contrast between pre- and post-Reformation society. All too often the hundred years between the Dissolution of the Monasteries and the Civil War – 'Tawney's century' – have been presented as a time of overall deterioration in the quality of social relations by comparison with a (probably idealized) 'medieval' past. Historians have written of the break-up of traditional structures, the disappearance of unifying rituals from the public domain, the 'decline of corporate feeling', the 'secularization of the parish', even the 'exhaustion of genuine Christian feeling'.[1] To this bleak picture urban historians have added the possibility that communal dislocation went furthest in cities where political and demographic conditions may have encouraged disorder, godlessness and growing impersonality.[2] Recently, however, some parts of this depressing thesis, what Valerie Pearl has dubbed the 'doom and gloom' view, have been challenged. Peter Burke has questioned whether the process of secularization was headlong. Some local studies, even of the nascent great wen of London, have found social discipline holding up well in the face of religious, economic and political change.[3] Since the central issue here is the fate of communal values, over which late medieval society waxed so eloquent, detailed studies of particular communities are research priorities. At the same time historians working at the local scale are best equipped to illustrate the variety of response within the kingdom to major upheavals, and to explore the realities of the vast mass of ordinary people's social and religious behaviour.

But if grass-roots attitudes and practices are the subject of this case-study, it may seem inconsistent to have chosen to examine *urban* parishes given that such a small fraction of the population of Elizabethan and early Stuart England lived in towns.[4] In fact there are a number of reasons for the choice, not the least of which is that towns generally have more satisfactory archives. In addition, towns were disproportionately significant for the diffusion of Protestant and other ideas.[5] Lastly, for the social historian there is the intrinsic interest which springs from the complexity of urban society. As a unit of local government administration, the town was a single entity, circumscribed by walls and liberties and operating under its own charter or municipal constitution. In the language of medieval lawyers, it formed 'a community', particularly *vis-à-vis* outside authorities.[6] But the social anatomy which functioned beneath this formal legal dress was a complex articulation of associations, jurisdictions, and institutions answering to both local and supra-local needs and subject to both secular and ecclesiastical authorities. From inside, the town could be seen as composed of a mosaic of interlocking and overlapping communities, simultaneously independent and interdependent. Nowhere is this truer than in urban ecclesiastical organization. If this fact complicates the task of historical analysis, it may also be said to enrich the conclusions to be drawn by forcing contrasts and comparisons on the observer.

Chester had nine parishes, varying in size, layout, population density, endowment and social composition (see Figure 1). Four parishes straddled the city walls. The largest of these, St Oswald's to the north and St Mary's to the south, had a densely inhabited urban core containing the church with far-flung rural outliers intermittently served by dependent chapelries. Geography and historical tradition linked St Mary's to the castle, seat of the Chester Palatinate, and thus brought many armigerous and professional people from the county élite into the parish. St John's to the east, an almost wholly extramural parish, was comparatively compact, consisting of a gentrified enclave beneath the walls and a progressively plebeian ribbon development along Foregate Street. To the west, Holy Trinity's bounds extended well beyond the walls thus ensuring that a number of minor gentry in the vicinity were parishioners, although the bulk of its population was properly urban. The remaining parishes were much smaller. St Peter's

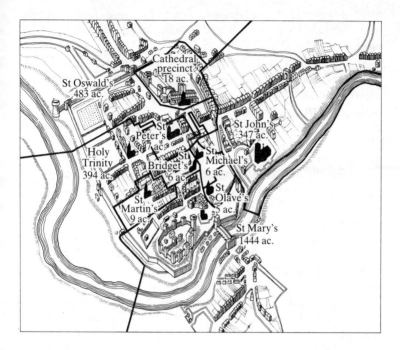

Figure 1　*Parish bounds and churches in seventeenth-century Chester*[7]

dominating the central crossroads and having the mayor's offices
built against the south facade of the church, was closely associated
with municipal government. St Michael's and St Bridget's faced
each other across the major market thoroughfare of Bridge Street.
St Olave's and St Martin's were so small, and in the latter case also
so poor, that they were often obliged to share ministers with
adjacent parishes. On the other hand every parish had its own
administration and lay officials. As well as its nine parishes,
Chester boasted a cathedral within which the bishop and the dean
and chapter operated separate jurisdictions that, naturally, rarely
harmonized. As a further complication, St Oswald's parish church
was located in the south transept of the cathedral, a fertile source
of institutional conflict. To physical and financial differences was
added a degree of particularism in parochial customs, rituals
and lay organization since the canons of the established church

offered only broad guidelines in many 'indifferent' matters, and where opportunities for diversity existed they were eagerly exploited.

This group of parishes provides sufficient information and at the same time sufficient variety of examples to permit a systematic exploration of some important themes relating to the nature of the early modern urban community: popular response to coercive institutions, the impact of church authority on ordinary people, participation in local government, and the coherence and solidarity of social groups. 'Religious' issues cannot of course be cleanly separated from 'secular' ones since at that time they were perceived as inextricably – and desirably – linked. To the parish's pastoral role of spiritual instruction and inspiration the state added administrative and charitable functions. Parish officials were laymen and often also town councillors and magistrates. The parish was thus a rounded social entity impinging on inhabitants at numerous points in their public and private lives and equipped with powerful institutional structures in order to serve clearly formulated aims. In addition, the parish imposed geographical unity on inhabitants who were assigned to a church according to their place of dwelling. Indeed, in the period under review here the parish's territorial identity was more marked than before or since because the Reformation had suppressed alternative places of worship to the parish church and nonconformists had not yet won the right to frequent dissenting chapels. Structurally and *de iure* therefore the parish was a community. How far was it also a community in the sociologist's stricter *de facto* sense of a 'moral' or 'affective' community, sharing attitudes, activities and relationships in sufficient intensity as to form a coherent group distinguishable from surrounding society?[8]

The Book of Common Prayer summed up the communal ideal when it spoke of 'all sorts and conditions of men' gathered at the Lord's table for communion. But this posed a severe challenge to a non-egalitarian society, aggravated in towns where small neighbourhoods were composed of widely different social types. Most Chester parishes had steep social pyramids with well-marked strata (see Table 1). St Oswald's parish, for instance, had a householder population which in 1619 ranged from two knights and eight gentlemen and lawyers at the top, through a middling band of 121 craftsmen and traders, down to 235 parishioners at the

Table 1 *Social structure of three parishes*[9]

Social group (householders)	St Oswald's, 1619		St John's, 1597		St Michael's, 1603	
	n.	*%*	*n.*	*%*	*n.*	*%*
Titled	2 ⎫		1 ⎫		0 ⎫	
Gent/profession	8 ⎭	2.8	11 ⎭	3.7	6 ⎭	7.6
Magistrates/ councillors	7 ⎫		5 ⎫		8 ⎫	
Other freemen	114 ⎭	32	130 ⎭	41.5	33 ⎭	51.3
'Non-free' and widows	235	65.2	178	54.8	33	41.3
Total	356		325		80	

bottom who were either poor widows or who followed obscure or precarious livelihoods as labourers, semi-skilled workers like carters and mariners, or rural cottagers. The social gulf separating the armigerous from commoners needs no urging, but in corporate cities the franchise, meaning full citizen rights and formal membership of the craft and trade companies, put as sharp a distinction between 'freeman', or citizens proper, and the 'non-free', or the urban masses.[10] Violation of this latter distinction could arouse the fury of the privileged. Such was the reaction of the Chester merchant and mayor William Gamull when he learned that parliamentary elections had been infiltrated by 'people who were no free citizens but inhabitants . . . of the suburbs, of the basest sort such as were not capable of voices, . . . among whom the Recorder's tenants and servants'.[11] Gamull lived in St John's which in 1597 had a similar social structure to St Oswald's, going from a handful of titled and gentry persons through a substantial group of enfranchised citizens down to the most numerous group of all, Gamull's 'base multitude'. St Michael's, typical of the small inner-city parishes, had no titled inhabitants and more citizens than non-free, but essentially followed the same social contours. But even the three broad strata tabulated here make only a crude typology. Within the citizen body, for example, contemporaries would have perceived a world of difference between merchants and other prosperous retailers, many of whom attained civic office, and bakers, shoemakers and the proverbially lowly tailor. These socio-economic distinctions, formalized in the trade companies, became the framework of much of Chester's public and ritual life. But the accidents of parish topography cut across them and created not homogeneous milieux but heterogeneous neighbourhoods. What common ground could unite a parish's rich and poor, its learned and illiterate, its privileged citizens and labouring masses?[12]

This miracle was not left to be performed unaided by the evangelical message. Nor did the authorities rely only on communion together in church. A web of secondary cultural and administrative activities was woven to catch all parishioners and permit expression of corporate membership in symbolic terms. This symbolism always stressed hierarchical position. So far from offending the communal spirit, as would be the case in an egalitarian society, it served rather to project a model society in which a special place was reserved for everyone. Care was taken to forge the 'vertical' links of patronage and deference that related people on different levels to each other.[13] Processions and banquets were means of expressing symbolic solidarity. Leading commoners and the parish's gentry were brought together at perambulations of the bounds, often followed by ritual feasts such as 'dinner for the parish . . . the day of the perambulation', 'eating of a salmon sent to the parish from the Lord Crewe', or when '2s. 4d. [was] spent on some of the gentlemen of the parish after we had been with the Lord Bishop at Mrs Ellis' house'.[14] By fêting the gentry in this way, the parish secured their goodwill as patrons. A wider social spectrum was involved in funeral processions, especially at the pompous heraldic funeral which enjoyed such a vogue at Chester in the early decades of the seventeenth century.[15] Although family, friends and aldermen from outside the parish joined the procession, a special role was reserved for a designated number of poor parishioners who were equipped with new black frieze gowns and led the cortège from house to church or churchyard. This rite brought a cross-section of the community into formalized contact but in such a way that the presence of the poor enhanced rather than impaired a family's dignity. 'Look they keep their ranks', wrote the herald-undertaker Randle Holme in a memorandum,[16] and the fact that the poor men kept their gowns and sometimes received a dole of money explicitly established the deceased's status as patron and benefactor of the parish, turning it momentarily into a factitious seigneurie.

If the church building was the physical core of the community, work on its fabric could be organized in age-old fashion to express its economic unity. Repairs and decorations were financed by annual assessments made on 'all men of ability . . . and according to every man's estate'.[17] This system implied graduated contributions, but also a level of means below which nothing was exacted. But funds were used communally so as to create jobs for parishioners of middling to humble rank. There was work for skilled craftsmen such as masons, carpenters, painters and glaziers, and therefore also for their semi-skilled and unskilled assistants such as carters and labourers. More menial tasks still – like washing linen, sweeping out the aisle or street, hanging up holly at Christmas, or even whipping dogs out of the church – gave suitably remunerated employment to a small army of the parish poor, especially women. The ideal aspect of this miniature economy was expressed by George Herbert, the Wiltshire parson, in his hymn:

> Who sweeps a room as for Thy laws
> Makes that and the action fine.

In practical terms it meant that the richer parishioners who bore the brunt of financing the church fabric were rewarded by being permitted to appropriate much of the wall and floor space with family pews and monuments and memorial inscriptions. Conversely the poor were attracted churchwards in order to find relief for their material needs. Without any blurring of social distinctions, indeed by emphasizing them, activities related to maintenance of the building promoted economic interdependence and solidarity. Since a parish's church symbolized its identity, appeal for help outside the parish was a rare and desperate resort. Only one example can be cited in Chester during the period: in 1657 a collection was made 'throughout the city' for the repair of St Mary's steeple, damaged in the Civil War siege, and even then the number and level of contributions raised within the parish exceeded those from the whole of the rest of the city.[18] The independence of different parish economies was in contrast, though not in conflict, with the interdependence of social groups within each parish. The two faces of the economic coin taken together defined communal identity.

The church fabric fund was selective; but simultaneously an 'Easter' rate was levied comprehensively on all parishioners, and as such expressed a rather different communal relationship, less mutual aid than corporative membership, less economic than social. Adapted from pre-Reformation church tithes, which had been legally binding on all communicants, the Easter rate covered the payment of the minister's and clerk's wages. In Chester, it was operating in Holy Trinity by 1547, in St Mary's by 1576 and in St Michael's by 1578, while at least three other parishes made use of it at least from time to time as clerical provision dictated.[19] Among the plethora of other local taxes recorded in ecclesiastical and municipal records of this period, the Easter rate's outstanding feature was its comprehensiveness. Detailed analysis of Chester records suggests that no householders were exempted.[20] This condition called for considerable administrative effort. In order to weave a net fine enough to catch the smallest fry, churchwardens were ready to set the bottom payments at purely nominal levels. In St Michael's, for instance, a note in 1636 specified that 'these poor are to pay but 2d.' a quarter – at a time when an artisan might earn between 5s. and 9s. a week and even church-sweepers were paid 2s. a quarter. Some poor people were not pressed to pay the trivial sums they were assessed at. On the other hand, they were not removed from the list. Being listed was therefore the essential consideration. The lists gave every householder's name as well as his or her assessment (usually calculated from house-rent) and were written out afresh on the basis of a street by street perambulation shortly after Easter when the new wardens came into office. Collections were made quarterly, names being ticked off, or deleted if people moved out or died, or added in the case of new arrivals. On the one hand, the wardens' circuit acquired overtones of ritual; on the other hand, the resulting list had a fundamental social significance. Occupying a prime position in the record of annual business, it acted as a roll-call of parish members. There was no urban anonymity for Chester parishioners! Naturally the identification of the whole community of householders by name and address had its value for the purposes of social control: reference to the Easter rate list could reveal absences from church on Sunday, or the arrival of strangers in the parish, or parishioners' 'rateable value' when more selective assessments were being made. In short, it was an administrative master-list.

As such it might at first sight suggest the unwelcome face of the community, at once inquisitive and exacting, evoked by such deprecating phrases as Jane Austen's 'a neighbourhood of voluntary spies', or Raymond Williams's 'the mutuality of the oppressed'. Christopher Hill has quoted comments from Oxfordshire parishioners who objected to paying a compulsory rate, and has argued that when a rate was spent on things like beautifying the church it was not in the interests of the poor and hence proved socially divisive.[21] In the first place it is necessary to distinguish the purposes of different rates. Only the Easter rate fell on everybody, and the maintenance of a minister could be seen as the *sine qua non* of an Anglican parish. Second, even the Easter rate was not aimed at shifting the burden of parish support from the parish élite on to the masses for it was extended to the latter in only a nominal sense, while the top level of contributions paid by the former was correspondingly raised. In St Michael's the whole lower third of the parish together paid no more than one alderman, 15s. In Holy Trinity in the 1630s, all the 6d.-men paid less than the 30s. at which Thomas Stanley esq., the lay impropriator, was assessed. These examples are typical. Essentially therefore parishes were financed from the pockets of the rich, the very people who through the vestry fixed the level of individual contributions.

This raises the question of why the poor had to pay at all. The answer is found by turning the pages of churchwardens' accounts. On one page the poor pay their token rate, and on the next the same people receive back eight or ten or twelve times as much in alms. The Easter rate was thus one wing of a reciprocal system, like modern social security, where adherence must be maintained by making nominal payments in order that withdrawals can be claimed according to one's needs. It was one of those procedures whereby, as D. H. Pennington has put it, 'authority harassed the poor but also kept them alive'.[22] Private charity too was often funnelled through the administrative machine in order to make use of official information. More than one testator left money to be given to the poor 'at their houses and not otherwise' on the assumption that the authorities knew the whereabouts of deserving cases; and one testator stipulated what others probably took for granted, that his executors should be assisted 'by some honest of the parish best acquainted thereof'.[23] The parochial rating system, though managed by laymen, was the administrative expression of a pastoral purpose and as such achieved a close official acquaintance with the mass of the urban population – a far closer acquaintance than had the parallel municipal network of wards, whose main function nevertheless was the regulation of the poor. Comparison of ward and parish documents from the crisis year of 1631 points up the difference between the two spheres. The ward constables of St Olave's, reporting to the mayor, could name no more than six poor people but referred vaguely to 'a great company more . . . that goes a-begging'. By contrast the churchwardens of St Mary's parish, an area almost exactly coterminous with St Olave's ward, having to make a regular annual distribution of nearly £5's worth of charitable bequests, could instantly identify the needy from 'a roll of their names remaining in the chest'.[24] This roll, if not the Easter rate list, would have been compiled from it. Clearly therefore the comprehensive rate had social uses that raised it above a blunt instrument of taxation, transforming it into both a means of control and an earnest of belonging, both a check-list of communicants and a passport to communal aid.

A final way in which communal membership might be expressed within a stratified and hierarchical society was the order of seating in church. This was not a matter left to chance. Churchwardens were periodically charged with drawing up a 'pew map' or plan showing the allocation of pews 'for to have the parish in good order'.[25] 'Order' might mean supervision and control. In St John's a seat opposite the entrance was regularly reserved for the wardens from which they could check comings and goings. The sidesmen of St Mary's were stationed at strategic points among the congregation to keep an eye on boys and girls who misbehaved during the sermon. In St Peter's, as population grew in the later seventeenth century, people were allowed to sit in the galleries, but by 1681 the wardens were complaining that because of the overhang they could not observe 'above half of the capacity of the church and galleries' from their place by the entrance.[26] But 'order' also meant precedence. The front pews nearest the altar were the most prestigious and so were automatically reserved for the parish élite. This set a target for the rest. But the simple scale of ranks described by Richard Gough in the rural parish of Myddle would have been inadequate to express the complexities of urban society. Disputes were common in all Chester parishes because people cared intensely about placing yet there was no absolute rule. Some claimed precedence 'as by reason of their houses';

others 'according to any fitting degree of magistracy . . . which they should be advanced to within the said city'; others again appealed bluntly to the amount they paid in church rates: 'Henry Harpur hath paid and doth pay more than you, . . . and almost double as much'.[27] In any dispute the churchwardens' discretion was final, but their decisions had to be made with finesse. In St John's the matter was considered so delicate that it was put into the hands of five Commissioners for Placing and Displacing, all of whom were leading members of the parish and holders of city office. No other parish went this far, but each had its own conception of propriety.

Place was never determined by an individual's rank alone, but by a broader concept of respect or 'honour' in which a number of considerations were balanced against each other. In St John's it was the mayor who occupied the central pew in the front row while gentlemen were dotted around him in the central nave and especially in the north aisle. In St Oswald's there was an aisle 'commonly called the merchants' aisle', while in Holy Trinity a bid was made in 1640 to attract the corporation to its services by building 'a convenient seat made fit and handsome for the Forty to sit in along after the north side of the church'.[28] Although titled people were welcome in a burgess congregation for the lustre they could shed on the parish, they were expected to accept the seats they were allocated within the communal plan, and to occupy them regularly on pain of losing them to someone else. No parish quailed from bearding an obstructive knight or esquire.[29]

The ruck of citizens proved less easy to place according to self-evident criteria. In St Michael's, a small parish where social distinctions corresponded broadly to its topography, in 1578 inhabitants of Bridge Street were generally favoured over those from Pepper Lane, while only two of the fourteen cellar-dwellers – the parish's most indigent stratum – could afford pew rents. Perhaps the other twelve cellar-dwellers sat on the 'common seats' at the back (see Table 2). If freemen were slightly favoured over the 'non-free', that was a corollary of their occupying commercial premises on the main street. On the other hand a householder's age was also taken into account and might moderate the importance of his economic circumstances. Freemen in the third row had an average age of about 49, while those in the fifth, sixth and seventh rows were progressively younger. The age gradient is not quite regular, perhaps in part because only freemen's ages are

Table 2   *Some factors determining order in church in St Michael's parish, 1578*[30]

Pew	No. of families	Gent	Free	'Non-free'	Wids	Street	Lane	Cellar	Age (mean years)
			Social rank			Dwelling*			Age
1	1	1				1			
2	1	1				1			
3	8	3	5			8			49
4	8		6	2		8			36
5	9		3	2	4	6	1		45
6	9		6	1	2	7	1	1	37
7	10		6	3	1	6	3	1	29
8	9		5	3	1		9		30
9	6			4	2		3		39
10	4			1	3	1	3		
11	1			1		1			

Note: *Five householders not traced.

susceptible to estimate, but the impression is that older inhabitants could rely on a certain tribute being paid to their seniority. In order to cope with the effect of age-cycles, as of general population turnover, geographical mobility and the tenure of magistracies, pewing must have been periodically reviewed if it were not to lose the distinctive features of a social model that such deliberate arrangement was evidently designed to express.

The pew plan of St John's in 1638 projects a model similar in essentials but with additional refinements permitted by the greater size of the congregation.[31] First, the sexes could be separated. Prominent citizens paid for two pews, one for themselves and another, sometimes on the other side of the church, for their wives. It followed from this that there were some single-sex pews. In addition, young batchelors were regularly segregated from women; but upon marriage – unless they could afford two pews – they moved with their wives to mixed pews. On the 1638 plan, three separate changes were noted in the course of twelve months to accommodate batchelors who had just married. Second, kin were conspicuous by their dispersal. While households usually sat together, blood relatives tended to sit far apart. At least six sets of kin were split up in this way in contrast to only two cases where fathers and married sons sat together. This strengthens the inference that placement in church was an order consciously devised to project an artificially conceived social image corresponding to the local community's particular conceptions of status, just as the wardens' powers to regulate position suggest the importance attributed to communal assent before the marks of status could be displayed.

Rituals, parish rates and pewing show how the inequalities of contemporary society were carried over from secular to religious life but so far from proving divisive actually provided the framework on which communal unity could be constructed. It was not a *de facto* unity between equals, but an institutionalized unity based on corporate activities. This unity, conceived and ordained by officialdom, expressed an ideal order. But how far were the official attitudes shared by the body of parishioners? How far did the parish consent and conform to the social prescription? How far was the ideal realized? Some objective test must be found of the parish's real cohesiveness. Contribution to the Easter rate was obligatory and might even be enforced in the mayor's courts if the wardens insisted.[32] But in areas where more voluntary attitudes are known to have prevailed, such as in the crucial matter of attendance at church, the parish's *raison d'être*, it may be possible to estimate the degree of real popular involvement. Given the impact of the church as an institution in sixteenth- and seventeenth-century society, there are few more basic questions for the social historian than what proportion of communicants actively conformed, but to judge from the sparse and varied estimates that historians have proposed this question is also one of the most elusive.[33] As a recent article by Margaret Spufford has reminded us, the problem is essentially that of finding suitable documentary evidence.[34] For a quantitative approach, the Chester historian may well start with records of numbers of householders paying pew rents.

Since payment was involved, this source contains a degree of bias, but, as with Easter rates, pew rents were scaled according to individual resources and ranged from £1 to 1s. a year. In view of the social pressures towards public display, only the very poor or strangers and transients would have wished to occupy the anonymous benches at the back. On the assumption that no one would pay for a seat he had no intention of using at least for the

minimum number of communions and services that would maintain his right to occupy it and keep him from presentation in the
church courts, a pew-holder was a conformable parishioner. This
hypothesis has been tested by the behaviour of recusants, the most
obvious example of non-attenders. Two parishioners of St Michael's,
John Whitehead, a baker, and Henry Primrose, a tailor, both
presented before the Metropolitan courts or the Quarter Sessions
for actions that smelt of popery, were traced in the Easter list for
1578 (so incidentally confirming the comprehensiveness of this
rate) yet were missing from the same year's pew plan.[35] In
contemporary St Oswald's, all five parishioners convicted of
recusant acts were missing from the pew plan of 1575. They
included the gentleman Ralph Worseley junior whose position in
society would normally have earned him a prominent place in
church and whose bequests to the poor bespeak a conscientious
member of the community.[36] Recusants are an extreme case, but
their behaviour suggests that there should be a general correlation
between renting pews and attendance at church. Of course, the
frequency of attendance cannot be established statistically. On the
other hand, once a parishioner figured on a pew plan his
attendances could be checked all the more easily, adding a further
incentive to conform to the local norms, according to the number
of services and communions provided in a given parish.

On the basis of this argument, Table 3 indicates the dimensions
of conformity in three parishes at different dates when a
convergence of suitable records makes it possible to compare pew
rents with the total household population. St Michael's had a high

Table 3   *Estimated church attendance rates in three parishes*[37]

Parish	Year	Householders paying rates	Housholders renting pews	Attendance rate	Area of parish
St Michael's	1578	80	66	83%	8.5 ac.
St Oswald's	1563	184*			
	1575		113	61%	483.5 ac.
St John's	1638		208		
	1642	409**		51%	347.5 ac.

Notes
* 'Population' figure from diocesan returns.
** 'Population' figures from tithe rolls.

attendance rate. Only fourteen householders did not pay for pews, twelve of whom were poor cellar-dwellers who may have sat on the common bench, leaving two known recusants as the only certain absentees. Therefore at least 83 per cent of householders attended, perhaps more. Neither of the other sample parishes approached this level of attendance. The population figure for St Oswald's has been taken from the Diocesan Returns, a source inferior to the Easter rates. If it understates numbers of householders, then the real attendance rate would be even lower than the 61 per cent calculated here. Adopting St Paul's language, we may characterize the parishioners of St Michael's as 'hot' and those of St Oswald's as 'lukewarm'. The churchwardens of St Oswald's seem to have recognized the problem of non-attendance and to have attempted to remedy it for an item in their accounts for 1583 records their 'going about the parish to take the names of those that want [i.e. lack] kneeling places'.[38] St John's, however, was positively 'cold'. Barely half the householders attended. The variety of practice between neighbouring parishes in the same city calls for explanation. Evidently factors peculiar to each community were at work. St Michael's was no doubt advantaged by its small size, but the impact of geography should not be exaggerated because the majority of St Oswald's and St John's parishioners would not have had to walk more than a mile to church, no further in fact than their distance to market. Social factors were probably more influential. Freemen were disproportionately numerous as pew-renters in the big parishes, suggesting that the prestige conferred by this type of social display meant more to them than to the mass of non-free parishioners. Social rank had its topographical dimension. In St John's the better houses and commercial premises tended to cluster at the centre of the parish near the church. If a circle were drawn at a radius of 500 yards around St John's church, the parishioners living inside it, amounting to three-fifths of all householders, rented four-fifths of the pews. This has the feel of a whole neighbourhood sensitive to the prestige of attending church together.

Institutional factors, in particular the calibre of the local minister and the parish's lay officers, probably also entered the equation. Their impact is best examined in relation to another source, the Protestation of 1642, from which an alternative measure of conformity may be derived. The Protestation was an oath to which Parliament required all adult males to swear, pledging themselves to defend 'the true reformed Protestant religion, . . . His Majesty's royal person, . . . the power and privileges of Parliaments, [and] the lawful rights and liberties of the subjects'. Any who refused the oath would be deemed unfit to hold office in church or commonwealth. Although the Protestation was inspired in part by political motives, its foremost object has been seen as a call to religious conformity and a means of unmasking papists. In this spirit it was administered to the population parish by parish at the hands of ministers and parochial officers; sometimes actually in the church building.[39] Some historians have assumed that the population's response was virtually universal, giving the Protestation returns the value of a census. In fact, detailed checks tend to reveal omissions, but this increases the document's significance as a measure of popular attitudes and allegiances since some degree of individual choice was involved.[40] In the eight Chester parishes for which returns survive, the returns name 1295 jurors, but as between 1600 and 1700 adult males were liable, anything from a fifth to a quarter slipped through the net.[41] Some men may have been absent from the city on business, but the greater part of the shortfall is most plausibly attributed to the occasional pocket of recusant of nonconformist resistance and a good deal of indifference. Moreover, as with church attendance, if some parishes were 'hot', others were 'lukewarm' or 'cold', suggesting that indifference was bred in the institutional heart of some communities.

In St Michael's, response to the Protestation seems to have been high, recalling its high attendance rate in the 1570s. As Table 4

Table 4   *Estimated rates of response to the Protestation in four parishes*

| Parish | Protestation | | Easter lists | | Ratio of male house-holders to jurors |
	Date	Jurors (males 18+)	Date	Male house-holders	
St Peter's	May 1642	169	Mar. 1642	98	1.73
St Michael's	July 1642	123	Mar. 1640	75	1.64
Holy Trinity	Aug. 1642	133	April 1643	109	1.22
St Oswald's	Mar. 1642	187	1608–20*	198	0.94

Note: *Mean of male householders between these dates.

shows, 123 men of 18 or over took the oath in July 1642. The male householder population was seventy-five in March 1640, the nearest date for which an Easter list survives. The remaining forty-eight jurors would have been other adult males who did not yet head families: sons, servants, journeymen, apprentices and lodgers. These numbers indicate a ratio of 1.64 jurors per household. At this time the ratio of males per household throughout the whole city was 1.75.[42] If this ratio represents what a full turnout would have produced, St Michael's came very close to it. By the same statistical tests, St Peter's can scarcely have had any absentees at all. Holy Trinity, by contrast, with a population half as big again as St Michael's only mobilized ten more jurors. There must have been widespread evasion in Holy Trinity. In social structure it was similar to St Michael's and St Peter's, but nevertheless differed in communal discipline. Lastly St Oswald's, with a ratio of male householders to jurors about half that of St Peter's, must have suffered from massive abstention. If this parish's poor record in provision of pews is recalled, this conclusion will come as no surprise. Over the whole city, one Cestrian in four or five failed to take the oath, but non-jurors were unevenly distributed among the various communities. Moreover, the individual characters of communities could be persistent. For three generations St Michael's upheld a tradition of discipline which St Oswald's equally consistently lacked.

Closer insight into the nature of interparochial differences of response is possible because of a lucky combination of sources covering one area of the city centre. Eastgate Street and Fleshmongers Lane formed a ward whose exact social structure in July 1641 is revealed in a Poll Tax return of all inhabitants, even almsmen, of 16 years or over. At the same time the ward was split between parts of two parishes, St Peter's and St Oswald's. By name-linkage with Protestation returns made in March and May 1642 it is possible to analyse the social and topographical pattern of response and evasion. The two parishes' social homogeneity only serves to emphasize the contrast in their communal attitudes.

During the lapse of eight to ten months between the Poll Tax and the Protestation returns, changes will have occurred in the population through death and mobility,[43] so one should not expect to find all those present in July 1641 swearing in March or May 1642. The significance of the percentages calculated in Table 5 lies in their variation according to place and category. The response

Table 5 *Contrasting rates of response to the Protestation: St Peter's and St Oswald's*[44]

Category (adult males)	St Peter's			St Oswald's		
	Poll Tax 24 July 1641 assessed	Protestation 3 May 1642 jurors	%	Poll Tax 24 July 1641 assessed	Protestation 8 March 1642 jurors	%
Householder	45	35	78	41	21	51
Sons with fathers	2	2 ⎫		3	0 ⎫	
Sons with widowed mothers	1	1 ⎭	100	3	1 ⎭	17
Apprentices	23	13 ⎫		13	4 ⎫	
Apprentices with widows	1	1 ⎭	58	—	— ⎭	31
Journeymen	6	3 ⎫		4	1 ⎫	
Clerks	3	3 ⎪		2	0 ⎪	
Servants	2	1 ⎬	64	5	0 ⎬	7
Servants with widows	—	— ⎭		4	0 ⎭	
Lodgers	2	1	50	3	2	67
Almsmen	3	3	100	2	1	50
Totals	88	63	76	80	30	38

evoked in the observable part of St Peter's parish was twice as strong as in the neighbouring parish. Among heads of families, respectively three-quarters and one-half took the oath, and their example had a demonstrable influence on the dependent male members of their households. Two-thirds of journeymen, clerks and servants in St Peter's were jurors, compared to a single one out of fifteen in St Oswald's, while among apprentices the rates were three-fifths and one-third. Sons still living at home and apprentices serving female heads of households and even almsmen – the poorest of the poor – showed a distinctly greater readiness to conform in St Peter's than in St Oswald's.

Contrasts as sharp as these must essentially reflect institutional differences between the two parishes, superimposed upon a general tendency for older and more responsible adults to be more conformable. Although the oath was offered to individuals on their own conscience – 'severally and everyone apart openly', as the preamble to St Bridget's returns put it – parishioners cannot have been impervious to the influence of their ministers. The vicar of St Oswald's, John Conney, though a puritan was also a pluralist, holding the divinity lectureship of the cathedral and the vicarage of

St John's alongside the cure of St Oswald's. This would have reduced his activity and 'visibility' in any one parish, which would in turn have undermined parishioners' loyalty. At St Peter's the fervent puritan John Glendale was renowned for his evangelistic energy.[45] The lengths the latter went to in order to procure his flock's assent to the Protestation are shown by the fact that uniquely (and contrary to parliamentary instructions) he wrote down *in his own hand* the names of all the jurors in his congregation. In the seventeenth century as much as nowadays, the quality of a minister, no doubt backed up by like-minded lay officials, could be the decisive factor in his flock's conformity and allegiance.

We have seen that the parish was a territory residence within which automatically entrained membership, and membership implied obligations. For example, even 'strangers who sojourn but for a time in the parish and depart away before Easter' were liable to be assessed for so many quarters' contributions to the rates.[46] But the line of residual membership was drawn very low on the scale of social activity. If the parish were to aspire to establishing a more positive form of corporate identity, a 'community of sentiment' bound by common acts of worship or mutual acts of charity and allegiance, institutional efforts were necessary to promote the co-operative ideal and to encourage or even enforce participation. The sense of belonging was not left to arise spontaneously from the mere fact of living at close quarters: it was underpinned by a conscious social code and discipline whose realization was entrusted to a cadre of officials. Chester parishes exemplify what Keith Wrightson has observed as a general rule in the workings of English local society at this time, that the relative 'success' of a given group as a cohesive entity depended greatly on the specific impact of its power structures.[47] We therefore need to examine in more detail the apparatus of parish administration and politics as the means whereby an active communal identity could be achieved.

   J. J. Scarisbrick has argued that in the post-Reformation parish the suppression of non-parochial *foci* of worship where lay representation and control had predominated 'caused a marked shift in the balance of power in the favour of the clergy'.[48] All the while that guilds and fraternities had multiplied special tasks and the officials necessary to perform them, parishes had customarily made do with two officials, the churchwardens. These, though laymen appointed by laymen, were servants of the bishop whose orders and articles they swore to enforce (hence their alternative names, 'swornmen' and 'sidesmen', originally 'synodsmen'), and as such they would be unlikely to challenge the parson's power, particularly if the latter were backed by a local gentleman who had impropriated the tithes. But if Scarisbrick is right about the years immediately following the Edwardian and Elizabethan settlements, in the course of the following hundred years the balance of forces in many cases, especially in urban parishes, swung back to laymen. In Chester, county gentry and magnates were relegated to the position of figureheads in parish politics. Simultaneously, there was a proliferation of new lay officials drawn from the ranks of urban commoners, suggesting that thwarted lay initiative soon reasserted itself, this time inside the parish and also within the canons of the established church.[49] Tudor local government statutes were an important catalyst in extending parishes' administrative competence, but so equally was local initiative which not infrequently anticipated the passing of a statute. In St Mary's Chester, 1551 was 'the first year of the overseers' of the highways, four years before they were called for by law. The same parish also provided more in charity than the Poor Laws demanded. By 1630 it was administering three private bequests for the highways and eight charities for its poor on top of the statutory rates levied by annual assessments for those purposes. *Pari passu* the number of officers grew. By 1630 the churchwardens and overseers had been joined by two sidesmen (now an office separate from that of the churchwardens), four 'collectors for the poor' and ten 'sessors for the poor', making a tenfold increase in parochial personnel in the course of a hundred years. Central government's desire to devolve administrative tasks was met half-way by rising grassroots enthusiasm for bureaucratic employment. And as ever more laymen were involved in running the parish the power of the minister, who was in many cases appointed and paid by the parishioners, correspondingly declined. It is perhaps no coincidence that the 1620s and 1630s, decades when St Mary's lay officialdom reached its fullest extent, were marked by conflicts with the parson, Francis Edwards, in which the parishioners were invariably victorious. They defended their sole right to appoint churchwardens, they chose and paid a parish clerk to read services, they made a voluntary collection to hire a preacher, they refused Edwards and his curate a rise in salary, and they stopped Edwards enclosing pews in the choir on the grounds that these had been purchased as parish property from the monastic impropriators at the time of the Dissolution. In the face of this lay solidarity Francis Edwards became non-resident, thus leaving the parishioners in complete control of 'their own' affairs.[50] In other Chester parishes relations with the minister were usually smoother, but the trend for offices to multiply and for lay control to strengthen was equally in evidence. By Charles I's reign Holy Trinity had eleven officers, St Peter's had twelve, St Oswald's sixteen, and St John's twenty-three. Well might George Herbert write of the churchwardens that 'the whole order and discipline of the parish is put in their hands':[51] had he been thinking more specifically of urban parishes he would have had to add that the wardens stood at the head of a small cohort of auxiliary representatives.

A greater number of officers not only gave laymen more power but also created new vehicles for communal initiative and representation and made it possible for more people to participate in local government, albeit at a very modest level. The accessibility of parochial office can be roughly quantified. In seventeenth-century St Oswald's, for example, there were six offices to fill annually – churchwardens, sidesmen and swornmen – and a pool of about 100 potential candidates, which in an urban context meant literate adult male householders, whether free or non-free. Other things being equal, they could all have served in the course of seventeen years. Therefore at any given moment over one-third of the parish's 'responsible' population had enjoyed some taste of public authority. In addition, St Oswald's had ten more important 'senior' offices held for several years at a time by candidates from a more restricted social group though recruited in equal numbers from among parishioners living inside and outside the walls: these were the sessors and auditors. In other parishes offices were distributed and filled in similar ways, and indeed were often rather more accessible than in St Oswald's. Taken as a whole, parochial government's relative openness of access to the ordinary towns-man contrasts with the situation in the city's main secular institutions. Chester's twenty-one trade companies made a gesture towards popular participation. Each appointed four officers on a rotational basis with length of service in the company being a leading factor in selection. There was therefore an element of 'Buggin's turn' about appointment. On the other hand, posts might be held for many years successively by the same individual, or an individual might hold the same office for two periods in his lifetime, so that many craftmasters were effectively excluded. And of course none of the non-free population were eligible. Municipal government appointed four constables to twelve wards every year, but this was an unpopular job which was rather avoided than sought.[52] The city corporation, where real power lay, was the most exclusive institution of all. Intake to the Assembly averaged two new men a year, overwhelmingly drawn from the nine most prosperous trade companies, and yet this was a period when the number of those technically eligible – free citizens – nearly doubled.[53] At the same time the effective value of the ordinary Cestrian's franchise became steadily eroded from the powers and privileges accorded in Charter of 1506. Despite pious claims that mayoral elections were 'for the public good' and ought to be free 'according as God shall direct every man's mind', by the early seventeenth century any refusal by the civic body to ratify aldermanic candidates was castigated as 'disobedience' and 'faction'.[54] Increasingly city government became the preserve of a hardening oligarchy based on social rank with a dash of nepotism. The parishes' role in upholding and extending communal ideals of participation in government offers a striking contrast to parallel trends in the secular sphere, and may even have been partly inspired by a conscious desire to compensate middle and lower ranks of society for dwindling political liberties.

However, parish government was far from being egalitarian. Its openness was strictly relative. For instance, while this was the sole institution where the 'non-free' could play an active part alongside freemen, they had many fewer opportunities (see Table 6). Office holding, like seating in church, was hierarchically conceived, so that the churchwardens, nearly always freemen, were superior to swornmen, occasionally non-free, but themselves subordinate to the assessors and auditors. The chain of command, observed link by link, defined official status. Thus the parish's 'bankers' in committee assessed the level of rates, the wardens collected and recorded, and the swornmen delivered the sum raised to the minister and clerk as their wages.[55] The qualifications of franchise, family, company, wealth, address and age required to mount each step on the pyramid were as carefully observed. If the lower slopes were pitched shallow so as to encourage participation, the higher ones were correspondingly steep so as to preserve status. Rees

Table 6 *The social profile of office holding in three parishes*

Parish	Period	Office	Gentlemen, yeomen	Freemen	'Non-free'	Mean age in years
St Mary's	1560–1630	Sidesmen and collectors	25%	75%	—	26.5
		Churchwardens	27%	57%	16%	33.2
		Auditors and sessors	50%	40%	10%	45.5
Holy Trinity	1626–37	Churchwardens	7%	79%	14%	37.9
		Auditors and sessors	—	100%	—	44
St John's	1637–50	Swornmen	—	92%	8%	28.6
		Churchwardens	12%	88%	—	42.6
		Auditors, sessors and commissioners	50%	50%	—	52.3

Cotgreave, one of the 'non-free', became a swornman in St John's in 1637 and a churchwarden in 1650. The latter step was exceptional, perhaps due to a thinning out of citizen ranks following the siege of 1644–6 and a grave epidemic of 1647, and Cotgreave never graduated any further. Between the same years Alexander Bird, a tanner, passed from churchwarden to being a sessor, a post he continued to hold for several years. The advantages of a prosperous trade and family connections (his father was mayor in 1631 and a parish commissioner in 1637) propelled Bird across the all-important divide separating 'minor' posts, those whose tenure was annual and which therefore had a brisk turnover and were relatively open, from 'major' posts which, though more numerous than minor ones, were held for longer and so were less accessible.

This two-tier structure of office gave scope for a variety of social distinctions. The rule of seniority, for instance, was applied quite systematically, as a glance at the last column in Table 6 shows. Minor officials also tended to be junior. In St Mary's, swornmen were typically in their 20s, churchwardens in their 30s and auditors and sessors in their 40s. The more prestigious parish of St John's slowed the whole process down but maintained the intervals, appointing swornmen in their late 20s, churchwardens in their 40s and auditors and sessors in their 50s. Financial means were another consideration. In St John's the 1637–50 cohort of swornmen, traced in the 1660 Poll Tax, were rated at an average of 6s. each, while churchwardens from the same years paid sums ranging between 9s. 6d. and £5.[56] Wealth was so clearly felt to be an attribute of higher office that when a parishioner achieved this rank, willy nilly his rates were doubled. One paid for privilege. William Hignett of Holy Trinity paid 2s. 8d. as a warden in 1626, but 5s. as a sessor three years later. Thomas Hand, following in his wake, saw his rates leap from 2s. to 6s. Major office holders dubbed themselves the 'best men', literally a self-ordained aristocracy. Accounts almost always style them 'Mister'. Some would have been so styled as of prior right, being clergymen, armigerous or senior city magistrates, but others acquired it *ex post facto* like the butcher William Hignett who received the title of respect in his second year as a sessor – no doubt as a corollary of the higher rates he was now paying. As a general rule therefore functions in the community were distributed by rank: in the sociologist's term, they were ascriptive. But this rule could be stood on its head without losing all its force. Exercise of a function could be a way of attaining rank by acquisition of the outward signs by which rank was recognized. Prolonged tenure of higher offices had the effect of making 'new men's' status permanent. In Holy Trinity auditors and sessors stayed in office for an average of three years. In St John's they were still more tenacious. Of ten 'best men' in 1637, five were still in office in 1650, and of the remainder four are known to have died in the interim. Perhaps in this parish major office was held for life. The sense of 'freemasonry' was certainly strong there. The ten 'best men' of 1637 between them occupied seventeen posts, some of them wearing two or three hats. In church they sat in three groups of neighbouring pews, roughly on a level with each other. One of the ten was the minister. The other nine held civic office and included a sheriff, an ex-sheriff and a future sheriff, three ex-mayors (two of whom had served twice) and a future mayor, while two other men held subsidiary posts like sessors for city taxes and auditors to the city treasurer.

The two-tier system of offices complicated the structure of parish government. It contained a paradoxical situation. Semi-permanent committees of older, richer more prestigious citizens, collectively forming the parish vestry, grew in number. But in Chester they did not, as happened in many rural parishes, degenerate into monopolistic 'closed' or 'select' vestries because minor offices also multiplied, widening participation. To judge from their constitution, therefore, Chester parishes combined oligarchic with pluralistic elements, neither of which excluded the other. But how true were appearances? Who really governed? Or rather, since power in the last analysis inevitably came from above, what parts did the various offices play in the total business of parish government and beyond that, how far were genuinely communal interests served?

If the classic signs of closed vestries are restricted attendance at meetings and secrecy about the budget and expenditure, then they were foreign to Chester custom. While accounts of meetings never record exactly how many people were present, contenting themselves with variations on the phrase 'many of the parishioners', it is significant that those convening meetings were obliged to give 'customary warning beforehand' and that meetings were usually held after divine service in the church, the one building that could contain everybody.[57] Of course, these circumstances also put a premium on church attendance. An exception which proves the rule was the action of William Parnell, a troublemaker in St Michael's, who

conspired with the churchwarden James Lingley to procure the minister or curate to read divine service sooner than the accustomed time upon purpose to procure a sudden and secret dispatch of the business when few might be present.

Later in the day when 'the best and choicest men of the parish' held an election of churchwardens, they were kept in ignorance of the pre-emptive meeting. Parnell's plan misfired, for the irregularities it contained rendered the vote he secured null and void. Thus, though political direction was essentially in the hands of the parish elite, it was supposed to be conducted openly and 'with the general consent of the parishioners and upon condition that not any man should be offended at the same'.[58]

Parish finances, though managed by the vestry, were likewise a matter for public discussion. In 1626 in St Oswald's the churchwardens revealed that their predecessors had overspent by £1 17s. 9d., whereupon 'most of the parishioners' agreed to levy a special rate on 'all men of ability' to cover the deficit. There was obviously discussion and disagreement at this meeting, but the majority will was followed and collective responsibility for the communal debt acknowledged. This then bound a minority of richer parishioners to put their hands in their pockets. When St Mary's bells were broken during an unauthorized ring by certain unnamed parishioners who had got carried away by their good spirits, a public meeting was held to condemn their action and to decide how to replace the bells. A mute church was unthinkable. Its distinctive carillon was the public voice by which it summoned parishioners and proudly sang their doings to God and neighbouring parishes. But bells were also expensive, in this case costing far more than the culprits could afford on their own. The parish as a whole therefore assumed the burden by means of a graduated rate which fell proportionately heavier on the richer members. These were the very people who were pressing hardest for replacement, being those most conscious of the prestige value of bells. Their financial sacrifice also secured them an extended control over the use of the bells for a new regulation was introduced requiring that in future permission to ring be granted only by express order of the churchwardens.[59] These two minor but typical incidents are revealing about the complex relations between the many and the few within the community. If the latter held the reins of government, they were at the same time guided by a strong sense of responsibility and accountability to the former.

The formal language in which debates, resolutions and elections were recorded was calculated to reflect the communal ethic. 'Controversy' was a thing to be avoided. This meant the subordination of 'will' to 'custom' or 'consent'. Wilful actions 'upon voluntary occasion' were taken by awkward individuals like William Parnell, or heedless groups like that which broke St Mary's bells, or outright 'factions' like that mobilized by parson Edwards.[60] This terminology stigmatized innovation and the minority. Accordingly the vestry and parish officials ranged themselves on the side of the majority, basing the authority for their actions on precedent and popular approval. 'Consent' and 'agreement' beat like *leit-motifs* through churchwardens' accounts. Philip Mitton of Holy Trinity was 'by general and unanimous consent of the whole parish' chosen clerk. Sessors for St Mary's were appointed 'by the whole parish, . . . being nominated by the two churchwardens . . . and approved by the whole parish'. St Michael's first Easter rate, though an innovation, was nevertheless derived from the old tithe system and received 'common assent'.[61]

These phrases echo to the most ancient ideas of collective interest found in the medieval *communitas*. Although sociology has taught us to mistrust the language of consensus politics on the grounds that a ruling élite's 'ethic of "service"' is but the cynical legitimation of its arbitrary rule, there is reason to believe that in the present case parishioners were genuinely consulted and were not dumbly acquiescent.[62] Should the vestry be challenged, it was capable of demonstrating support, usually by asking for signatures under the order in question. As many as thirty-two signatures 'et alii' ratified the official choice of churchwardens for St Mary's in 1630 against parson Edwards's nominees, and similar lists are found in other parishes' account books. 'Grassroots' opinion could be expressed in the same way. Thirty-four people put their names to a petition about the state of St Peter's churchyard, thirty of them signing and four, presumably illiterate, managing only a mark. The issue was one that touched ordinary people. For years the churchyard had been 'annoyed and abused in loathsome and profaned manner, that few or none will suffer their friends to be buried there'. (Burial in the churchyard, cheaper than a place in the church itself, was essentially a matter that concerned the poorer sort.) Moreover, the churchyard was used as a thoroughfare to three taphouses selling 'wine, beer and ale on Sundays and other days', and prominent among the complainants were several people known to have lived in the same lane as those keeping the taphouses. The previous year's churchwardens were taken to task for neglecting earlier orders to deal with the scandal, and those then in office were told to take immediate steps to restrict access to the churchyard 'at the charges of the whole parish'. This order was to be recorded in the accounts.[63] This was pressure from below with a vengeance, an expression of neighbourhood interests and popular piety and proof that they too could activate the machinery of parochial government. If certain vestrymen were to forget the meaning of service to the community, there were others capable of reminding them. Hearing someone praise Mr William Gamull's 'pains and industry' in rebuilding St John's steeple, Henry Annion, a tanner, described Gamull as 'but a hireling [who] had nothing to do with the matter'. Asked whose hireling Gamull was, Annion replied: 'Mine. I pay his wages.'[64] For Annion, even as exalted a man as William Gamull, an ex-mayor and a parish sessor, could not claim personal credit for tasks performed for the community by virtue of his office. It was rather the body of ratepayers, including Annion himself, which was really in charge and hence deserving of praise.

The fact that minor officers mediated between the parish élite and its rank and file helped prevent a gulf opening between the social poles. Vestries may have formed an exclusive social group, but an unwritten rule of their job was that they acted not directly and unilaterally but in conjunction with and by means of the churchwardens. The latter were always the parish's formal spokesmen and alone had the keeping of its records. It was because they were backed by the 'best men' that wardens could assign or revoke the pews of knights and esquires. The power to confront social superiors in this way in the hands of a tailor or a shoemaker was only conceivable if their office was clearly understood to be titular not personal, and if the title derived ultimately from the communal will. Many a warden quite properly felt diffident about giving orders that might conflict with a higher authority. In 1584 the wardens of St Oswald's, a draper and a yeoman, refused to take responsibility for allowing a special collection to be made in church for a poor labourer, George Massey, even 'by those well disposed to him' till he had armed himself with a licence from the mayor or JPs.[65] The churchwardens' role no doubt often served to mask the vestries' power, but it also had the effect of diffusing it and making it less absolute. On the one hand vestries were curbed by having to work through annually accountable officers, and on the other junior and relatively humble parishioners became involved in the regular exercise of authority. The turnover of recruits into the lower slopes of the hierarchy where they would occupy defined places on a chain of command, deferring to superiors but temporarily deferred to by all around them, gradually spread administrative expertise throughout the community, simultaneously inculcating the appropriate values of respect for authority and order and an appreciation of the need for social solidarity.

Canon law required integration into the parish of residence, and where geographical circumstances made it possible, such as in the large rural parishes of Cheshire, the bishop was able to interpret membership strictly and reject petitions for a transfer of allegiance to a nearer church or one with a more active minister.[66] But in Chester and the villages immediately surrounding it the existence of so many churches within easy walking distance, together with the sheer size and mobility of the population, made it impossible to keep congregations rigidly distinct. Once Easter communion had been attended, church dues paid, a pew rented and church-wardens elected, the motivated layman could scarcely be prevented from frequenting other parishes as well if he chose. Urban parish bounds proved readily permeable, and this had its effect on parish loyalties.

Physical mobility meant that a townsman was likely to inhabit more than one parish in his lifetime. Over two or three generations a family was bound to find itself with branches spreading across several parishes though only a few streets away from each other. William Gamull was a pillar of St John's, but the senior branch of the family was established in St Mary's where the family monument stood.[67] When an individual changed parishes he did not necessarily sever all his old attachments. A case brought before the Consistory Court in 1639 well illustrates how allegiances could accumulate. Two previous parishioners of St Michael's claimed that William Parnell, at that time a new-comer to the parish, had 'usurped' their old pews. Henry Harpur had buried three of his children on that spot and erected a brass memorial to them. Although Harpur had subsequently moved to St Olave's a little further down the street, the memorial remained and betokened a sort of abiding ownership. He occasionally attended services or vestry meetings in St Michael's (which at that time shared a minister with St Olave's), but had to suffer the indignity of sitting at the back on the poor bench. Similarly, John Leche had moved to Holy Trinity but in his old house in St Michael's he had installed a respectable tenant whom he had expected would be able to occupy his old pew: literally keeping Leche's seat warm. Leche's links with his old parish were a mixture of sentiment and vested interests. Not only had he paid 'lays, sessments and church dues' there for many years and maintained a valuable piece of real estate, but he was bound to be conscious of the 'public fame and voice' he enjoyed there as a landlord.[68] Neither Harpur nor Leche felt any clash of loyalties between their new and their old parishes. It was natural to foster existing ties as an extension of their prestige, family connections and general patronage within the city. Local opinion found Leche and Harpur's behaviour equally natural, as is shown by the parade of witnesses they could rally in support of it. On the other hand, the tenacity of old families in retaining hold of honours and affections in a former parish might block the ambitions of new men.

In some cases it is difficult to decide whether an individual's use of more than one church indicates a change of address or simply the exercise of choice. Thomas Higginson, a beerbrewer (1615–63) was baptized in St Bridget's, but his marriage took place in Holy Trinity, his marriage licence describing him as of Holy Trinity and his wife of St Bridget's. He became a churchwarden in Holy Trinity and his first two children were baptized there. But in 1656 he buried a son and his wife in St Olave's. A second marriage was solemnized by the parson of Holy Trinity. We do not know where Thomas was buried, but his widow Anne was recorded as deceased in 1679 in the register of St Oswald's but was buried in St Olave's.[69] Free choice led many people who passed their whole lives in a single parish to develop supplementary attachments elsewhere. Randle Holme II, like his father a stalwart of St Mary's, forged strong links with Holy Trinity, possibly in the pursuit of his antiquarian interests. Holy Trinity's parish chest contained Chester's earliest set of churchwardens' accounts which Holme copied out from the beginning of 1532 to his own day, 1637. He undertook several other antiquarian projects in association with George Bellin, the parish clerk at Holy Trinity.[70] Testamentary bequests give some idea of the frequency of cross-parish allegiances.[71] Whereas most benefactors (48 per cent) left money to the poor of their home parish alone and a generous minority (30 per cent) left money to the poor of the whole city indiscriminately, there were 19 per cent who made bequests to two parishes and 3 per cent who remembered three parishes. This precision must indicate a specific attachment to more than one place. In the same spirit 10 per cent of the sample left money to the poor of a parish outside the city, probably their birthplace, as well as their parish of residence at the time of their death.

Not only did individuals cross parish bounds for personal reasons but whole congregations did so for reasons that the church establishment was forced to accept. Short-comings in pastoral provision meant that St Olave's frequently shared a minister with St Michael's and St Martin's with St Bridget's. The all too common absenteeism of pluralists may have encouraged the pious to attend elsewhere. The shortage of preachers at Chester was even more serious. Educated and talented speakers, whether lay or clerical, cost more than most poor parishes could afford, yet the popularity of preaching over prayers and communion meant that they could draw crowds from all over the city or beyond. Mixed congregations were common at funerals for which visiting preachers were hired. Thomas Benson of St John's left 10s. in his will for a Mr Ashbrook to preach at his funeral. But he also left 20s. to the 'afflicted' Mr Byfield, Friday lecturer at St Peter's, implying that that was where Benson normally went to hear a sermon. Thomas Dewsbury of St Bridget's was another who demanded the services of Mr Ashbrook, while Christopher Barnard of St John's wanted Mr Clark from Tarvin, a nearby village. Perhaps during his life he had gone out of town to hear Mr Clark.[72] Conversely, Chester as a major provincial city increasingly became a centre for travelling speakers such as Henry Newcome, who in 1662 preached at Holy Trinity on Sunday morning and at St Peter's in the afternoon, both centrally placed and fairly large churches.[73]

The pulpit's power to unify the whole city in religious exercise was recognized by both ecclesiastical and secular authorities. Three Chester churches were sufficiently endowed to play a special civic role. The cathedral had six preaching prebendaries and a divinity lecturer, and on great occasions the bishop himself spoke. Naturally, royal visitors to Chester attended services at the cathedral, and the funerals of specially honoured citizens were celebrated there.[74] Bishop Lloyd preached the sermon for Thomas Gamull, the city Recorder, from the cathedral pulpit in memory of a great benefactor of the city although he had lived in St Mary's and would be buried there.[75] Mrs Jane Ratcliffe, 'widow and citizen of Chester', was given a commemorative sermon in the cathedral in 1639 before her fellow Cestrians so that 'though she be now taken out of your sight . . . she may yet remain in your minds'. She had lived in St Oswald's and had died and been buried in London; yet John Ley, a prebendary of the cathedral, argued that a sermon *in memoriam* from the cathedral pulpit was most proper 'as I am your preacher called by you in this place to officiate unto you with society of my bretheren'. As if to substantiate the universality of the occasion, Ley's language was replete with civic allusions. The deceased, 'born in your city and brought up in it', had lived an exemplary life as one of 'the Lord's freemen and freewomen', watching in her chamber and praying to 'the watchmen of Israel to keep the city' just as at time of plague 'watchmen were set to keep out suspected persons'. By her attention to the 'welfare of all, whether civil societies or particular persons', by her charity 'whether it were a pension to a preacher or alms to the poor', and by her presence in church, 'diligently listening with open ears and eyes (for she never slept in the church as too many do use to do)', she had been the fit partner of her husband, twice mayor, in his 'public ministration in this city'.[76] Conscious as much of the elevation of his cathedral pulpit as of the qualities of his subject, Ley addressed the citizens as members of a single congregation transcending narrow parish loyalties. We have here in Chester a reflection of the sort of articulation of Protestant parishes into an 'all-city consistory' which N. Z. Davies has observed in later sixteenth-century Lyon.[77]

The cathedral's broad civic associations were by a natural extension shared by the church of St Oswald's, located as it was in the cathedral building and long enjoying the patronage of the mayor and corporation. Of a Sunday, after hearing matins in their own churches,

the great assembly of the mayor, aldermen, sheriffs-peers and the whole city [came there] to hear sermons, . . . being indeed the most spacious and fit place for it.[78]

They would return to their various parish churches for evensong. From the beginning of the seventeenth century a third church came to the fore as a centre of preaching when Valentine Broughton, a devout Calvinist and ex-mayor, left a bequest for a Friday lecture at St Peter's.[79] From 1605 to 1615 the post was filled by the strict Sabbatarian Nicholas Byfield, and from 1622 till the Civil War by John Ley, who combined it with his job as a prebendary and as vicar of Great Budworth in Cheshire.[80] In addition the parishioners themselves agreed in 1628 to pay their minister John Glendale £20 a year to preach 'once every Sabbath'.[81] These endowments, coming at a time when the Chester corporation was locked in strife with the Cathedral Chapter about their access to St Oswald's, encouraged the corporation to switch its allegiance to St Peter's.[82] The decisive move was made by mayor John Ratcliffe II, the husband of Jane Ratcliffe. In 1612, convinced by Byfield's zeal, he ordered a new mayoral pew to be set up in St Peter's.[83] While Ratcliffe and his wife continued to reside in St Oswald's parish, indeed within the Abbey Court itself as the Chapter's tenants, Chester's mayors henceforth had a titular seat at St Peter's. The choice of church was not haphazard. St Peter's stood at the precise centre of the city, dominating the crossroads formed by its main streets, and had the mayor's offices built against its south face. Its clock and chimes, which had long regulated the city's working day, were appropriately renewed at the close of Ratcliffe's mayoralty.[84]

During his lectureship, Byfield made St Peter's a focus for local theological debate. When he left Chester, he printed 'the substance of near seven years' sermons' as *An Exposition upon the Epistle to the Colossians* (1615). His pronouncements had stirred controversy which in one case reverberated beyond the city walls. Edward Brerewood, a native of Chester but resident in London as Gresham College's first professor of astronomy, had attacked his Sabbatarianism, giving rise to a long exchange in letters, pamphlets and sermons. Byfield's side was published posthumously as *A Learned Treatise upon the Sabbath* (1630). John Ley, too, used the London press to give wider circulation to his work in the pulpit. At least two funeral orations were published: as well as that for Jane Ratcliffe there were those for the wife and daughter of Henry Harpur, the parishioner of St Michael's and St Olave's. Later, at the instigation of fourteen Cheshire and Chester clergymen, he too took up the Sabbatarian question in *Sunday a Sabbath, . . . being the first part of a greater work* (1641). His introduction made reference to a number of local personalities and the dedicatee was James Ussher, Archbishop of Armagh who had close connections with Chester.[85] So for Ley also the urban pulpit had acted as a springboard into the heart of a national debate. When he wrote in *Sunday a Sabbath* that his labour was to 'build up the walls of our Jerusalem . . . with sound doctrine and conversation', the biblical image had behind it the solid experiences of his Chester ministry.

If the case of Chester was typical, the urban parish remained a dynamic institution long after the Reformation, possibly stimulated rather than enfeebled by the climate of religious and social change. From the mid sixteenth to the mid seventeenth centuries its functions multiplied and its concomitant official and financial apparatus grew with the result that more of its members were directly involved in the management of a greater number of activities. These developments gave back to laymen what they had lost by the suppression of guilds and fraternities, but in conditions more conducive to social unity since the parish was an all-embracing, non-voluntaristic community. This fact did not abolish social distinctions but it maintained if it did not intensify interaction and interdependence across ranks which in the society of that day made for cohesion. It is true that not all parishes were equally successful in this direction. In such crucial matters as enforcing church attendance and religious conformity, adjacent parishes in a densely inhabited town might develop contrasting characteristics under the guidance of their lay or clerical leaders. In small communities a few strong personalities could have a decisive impact. The pattern of loyalties was therefore not uniform across the city. For this and other reasons, the primary loyalties to a 'home' parish did not exclude secondary loyalties from being excited elsewhere. But this sort of complexity was in the nature of urban life and does not affect the central conclusion that Chester parishes remained vital communities at least up to the Civil War. Their example tends to bear out the suggestion made long ago by Tawney that the traditional values of corporate life continued to flourish more effectively in 'the lower ranges of ecclesiastical organisation' than in any other institution in post-Reformation society.[86]

Acknowledgements

This essay has benefited from the comments of the editor and other contributors, and of Dr M. J. Power and Dr A. T. Thacker, to all of whom my thanks are due.

Notes and references

1　Christopher Hill, *Society and Puritanism in Pre-Revolutionary England* (1964), ch. 12. Keith Thomas, *Religion and the Decline of Magic* (Penguin edn 1973), p. 74; but cf. pp. 189, 205–6. John Bossy, *Christianity in the West 1400–1700* (1985), p. 86. Cf. Charles · Phythian-Adams, 'Ceremony and the citizen: the communal year at Coventry 1450–1550', in P. Clark and P. Slack (eds.), *Crisis and Order in English Towns 1500–1700* (1972), pp. 57, 78–80.

2　Peter Clark and Paul Slack, *English Towns in Transition 1500–1700* (1976), pp. 64, 69–71, 78–9, 78–9, 146–7.

3　Peter Burke, 'Religion and secularisation', in Peter Burke (ed.), *The New Cambridge Modern History* (1979), vol. 13, pp. 293–5, 297, 305. Valeric Pearl, 'Change and stability in seventeenth-century London', *London Journal*, **5** no. 1 (1979), pp. 3–34. J. P. Boulton, 'The limits of formal religion: the administration of Holy Communion in late

Elizabethan and early Stuart London', *London Journal*, **10** no. 2 (1984), pp. 135–54. Cf. Keith Wrightson, *English Society 1580–1680* (1982), pp. 41, 55–6, 171.

4 Roger Mols, 'Population in Europe 1500–1700', in Carlo M. Cipolla (ed.), *The Fontana Economic History of Europe: the Sixteenth and Seventeenth Centuries* (1974), p. 40. F. V. Emery, 'England *circa* 1600', in H. C. Darby (ed.), *A New Historical Geography of England before 1600* (1976 edn), p. 253. Clark and Slack, *English Towns*, pp. 7–12.

5 Fernand Braudel, *Capitalism and Material Life 1400–1800* (1974), p. 373. Peter Clark, 'The early modern town in the West', in Peter Clark (ed.), *The Early Modern Town* (1976), pp. 6, 12. W. J. Sheils, 'Religion in provincial towns: innovation and tradition', in Felicity Heal and Rosemary O'Day (eds.), *Church and Society in England Henry VIII to James I*, (1977), p. 156.

6 Cf. Susan Reynolds, *An Introduction to the History of English Medieval Towns* (1977), pp. 103–4, 108, 136.

7 The map is Wenceslas Hollar's, printed in Daniel King, *The Vale-Royall of England* [1656], ed. Theodore Besterman (Collegium Graphicum, Portland, Oregon 1972). Parish bounds are as established by N. J. Alldridge, 'Aspects of the topography of early medieval Chester', *Journal of the Chester Archaeological Society*, n.s., **64** (1981), pp. 5–31. Miscellaneous information on Chester parishes is derived from G. Ormerod, *The History of the County Palatine and City of Chester*, (3 vols., Helsby edn 1882), vol. 1; R. H. Morris, *Chester in the Plantagenet and Tudor Reigns*, (1893), ch. 3; S. Cooper-Scott, *Lectures on the History of St John's, Chester* (1892); J. P. Earwaker, *The History of the Church and Parish of St Mary on the Hill, Chester* (1898); F. Simpson, *A History of the Church of St Peter, Chester* (1909); L. M. Farrell, *The Parish Registers of Holy Trinity, Chester* (1914); and M. J. Crossley Evans, 'The clergy of the city of Chester 1630–1672', *Journal of the Chester Archaeological Society*, n.s., **68** (1985), pp. 97–123.

8 A useful survey of this vast field is Colin Bell and Howard Newby, *Community Studies* (1971), ch. 1 and 2. See also Colin Bell and Howard Newby, 'Community, communion, class and community action: the social sources of the new urban politics', in D. T. Herbert and R. J. Johnson (eds.), *Social Areas in Cities: Processes, Patterns and Problems* (1978), pp. 283–301. Among historians, Alan Macfarlane has made extensive use of sociological concepts: see his *Reconstructing Historical Communities* (1977), ch. 1; and *The Origins of English Individualism* (1978), esp. chs. 1 and 2.

9 Sources for Table 1: CDRO, P 29/7/2 f. 283; P 65/8/1 unfolioed (1603). CCRO, CR 65 Bdl. 39 unfol. (1597). *Note*: where MSS are unfolioed, the date is cited to aid location of the reference.

10 Cf. Joan Beck, *Tudor Cheshire* (1969), vol. 7 of A General History of Cheshire, J. J. Bagley (ed.), p. 50; J. T. Evans, *Seventeenth-Century Norwich: Politics, Religion and Government 1620–1690* (1979), p. 7; Pearl, 'Stability', p. 14.

11 Quoted by J. K. Gruenfelder, 'The Parliamentary election at Chester 1621', *Transactions of the Historic Society of Lancashire and Cheshire*, **120** (1968), pp. 41–2. Observance of the distinction of the 'free' and the 'non-free' was a constant preoccupation in city politics in this period: see BL Harleian MS 2125 ff. 60v, 166v; *A Cheshire Sheaf*, 3rd series, **9**, p. 5; P. H. Lawson, 'Family memoranda of the Stanleys of Alderley 1590–1601 and 1621–1627', *Journal of the Chester Archaeological Society*, n.s., **23** (1920), p. 99; M. J. Groombridge (ed.), *A Calendar of the Chester City Council Minutes 1603–1642*, Record Society of Lancashire and Cheshire, **106** (1956), p. 145; R. H. Morris and P. H. Lawson (eds.), 'The siege of Chester 1643–1646', *Journal of the Chester Archaeological Society*, n.s., **25** (1923), p. 208.

12 Cf. N. Z. Davis, 'The sacred and the body social in sixteenth-century Lyon', *Past and Present*, no. 90 (February 1981), pp. 62–5, 68.

13 Cf. Keith Wrightson, 'The social order of early modern England: three approaches', in L. Bonfield, R. Smith and K. Wrightson (eds.), *The World We Have Gained* (1986), pp. 192–3, 198–9; Wrightson, *English Society*, pp. 57–61 and ch. 6. By contrast, in present-day society sociologists have observed that communal bonds tend to be created 'horizontally' between people or groups of like status or class. See, for example, Bell and Newby, *Community Studies*, pp. 27–32; J. Connell, 'Social networks in urban society', *Social Patterns in Cities* (Institute of British Geographers, Special Publication No. 5 1973), esp. 43–5.

14 CDRO, P 1/11 (16 April 1637); P 63/7/1/f. 84.

15 Randle Holme II issued at least 130 funeral certificates in Chester between 1600 and 1639: J. P. Rylands (ed.), *Cheshire and Lancashire Funeral Certificates*, Record Society of Lancashire and Cheshire, **6** (1882).

16 Rylands (ed.), p. xiii.

17 CDRO, P 29/7/1 f. 42.

18 CDRO, P 20/13/1 (July 1657).

19 *Holy Trinity*: BL Harleian MS 1277 f. 19 ff., printed in J. R. Beresford, 'The churchwardens' accounts of Holy Trinity, Chester, 1532 to 1633', *Journal of the Chester Archaeological Society*, n.s., **38** (1951), pp. 95–172; and CDRO, P 1/11 and /12. *St Michael's*: CDRO, P 65/8/1 and /2, *St Oswald's*: CDRO, P 29/7/2. *St Peter's*: CDRO, P 63/7/1. The churchwardens' accounts of *St Mary's* frequently refer to 'Easter Books' from 1576 onwards, although the documents are no longer extant: CDRO, P 20/13/1. In *St John's* reference was made

to a lost 'houseling book', or list of communicants, by the churchwardens in 1644: CDRO, P 51/12/1. In addition, the tithe rolls of St John's survive from 1597 to 1730. These were kept by the lay impropriators' stewards: CCRO, CR 65 Bdls 39–41. No churchwardens' accounts survive from the remaining three parishes but the probability is that they employed the same system.

20 Among contemporary lists of inhabitants, the Easter rating lists are always the longest. For a statistical comparison, see Nick Alldridge, The population profile of an early modern town: Chester 1547–1728', *Annales de Démographie Historique* (Paris, 1986), pp. 115–31. Administrative error may have led to the omission of some names, but the *principle* of the rate did not admit exceptions. In general see S. J. Wright, 'Easter books and parish rate books: a new source for the urban historian', in *Urban History Yearbook* (1985), pp. 30–45. Cf. Susan Brigden, 'Tithe controversy in Reformation London', *Journal of Ecclesiastical History*, **32** no. 3 (July 1981), pp. 285–301.

21 Hill, p. 430.

22 D. H. Pennington, *Seventeenth-Century Europe* (1979), p. 18.

23 G. Piccope (ed.), *Lancashire and Cheshire Wills and Inventories from the Ecclesiastical Court, Chester* (3 vols.), Chetham Society (1893), **54**, pp. 17, 167, CDRO, WS Robert Brerewood, will (1601).

24 CCRO, QSF/75 f. 6. CDRO, P 51/12/1 (1631).

25 Beresford (ed.), p. 159. In 1631 the wardens of St Mary's had 'one roll containing three church maps of the seats': CDRO, P 20/13/1 (20 May 1631).

26 CDRO, P 51/12/1 (1638); P 20/13/1 (9 May 1644); P 63/7/1 f. 136v. Frank Simpson, *A History of the Church of St Peter, Chester* (1909), p. 42.

27 Beresford (ed.), p. 126. CDRO, EDC 5 (1639), File 9, Part A: doc. 7, article 6; unnumbered doc., article 3; Part B, article 1.

28 *A Cheshire Sheaf* (3rd series), **46** (1951), p. 1. CDRO, P 1/11 (23 August 1640).

29 For example, CDRO, P 20/13/1 (14 August 1628), P 63/7/1 f. 5r; P 1/ 11 (23 August 1640).

30 Source for Table 2: CDRO, P 65/8/1 ff. 70v–71r. *Note*: freemens' ages have been estimated from the date of their enfranchisement on the assumption that this took place on average at the age of 22. This in turn rests on the observation that apprentices were indentured at 14, and at Chester served an average of eight years each. J. H. E. Bennett (ed.), *The Rolls of the Freemen of the City of Chester* (2 vols.), Record Society of Lancashire and Cheshire, **51** and **52** (1906, 1908). *A Cheshire Sheaf* (3rd series), **7**, **8** and **26** (1909, 1910, 1929), *passim*. For the method of locating parishioners by street and dwelling, see Nick Alldridge, 'Hearth and home: a three-dimensional

reconstruction', in N. Alldridge (ed.), *The Hearth Tax: Problems and Possibilities* (1984), figures 1 and 2.

31   CDRO, P 51/12/1 (1638).

32   For example, CDRO, P 65/8/1 (1651).

33   See above, D. M. Palliser, 'The parish in perspective', and works cited there. See also Burke, 'Secularisation', p. 305.

34   Margaret Spufford, 'Can we count the "godly" and the "conformable" in the seventeenth century?', *Journal of Ecclesiastical History*, **36** no. 3 (1985), pp. 428–38. The spiritual significance of 'conformity' is an even more elusive question and one which lies beyond the scope of this article.

35   K. R. Wark, *Elizabethan Recusancy in Cheshire*, Chetham Society (3rd series), **19** (1971), appendix.

36   CDRO, P 20/13/1 (6 April 1603).

37   Sources for Table 3: CDRO, P 29/7/1 ff. 1r–3r; P 51/12/1; P65/8/1. CCRO, CR 65 Bdl. 39. BL Harleian MS 594 f. 97. Note that by the Restoration, attendance at St John's had shrunk even further to 37 per cent (113 pews rented in 1665, but 310 householders paying tithes in 1670).

38   CDRO, P 29/7/1 f. 10.

39   C. S. Dobson (ed.), *Oxfordshire Protestation Returns 1641–2*, Oxfordshire Record Society (n.s.) **35** (1955), pp. v–vii. Valerie Pearl, *London and the Outbreak of the Puritan Revolution* (1961), p. 218. Hill, p. 422.

40   W. G. Hoskins, *Local History in England*, (2nd edn, 1972), pp. 172–3, 184. W. B. Stephens, *Sources for English Local History* (1973), p. 38. Joan Thirsk, *Sources of Information on Population 1500–1760* (n.d.), pp. 7–8. Lawrence Stone, 'The educational revolution in England 1560–1640', *Past and Present*, no. 28 (1964), pp. 99–100. A. M. Johnson, 'Some aspects of the political, constitutional, social and economic history of the City of Chester 1550–1662' (unpublished D. Phil. thesis, University of Oxford, 1970), pp. 7–8. Dobson, p. vii.

41   Most of the Protestation Returns are in the House of Lords Record Office, 'Chester City', but part of St Mary's is in BL Harleian MS 2107 f. 118, the latter overlooked by Stone and Johnson. For population estimates and the size of the missing parish, St John's, see Alldridge, 'Profile', pp. 118, 121.

42   In Eastgate in 1641, the ratio of adult males (16+) per household was 1.77; and in St John's parish 1597–1620, the ratio of adult males (18+) was 1.74: CCRO, CAS/I ff. 234–49; CR 65 Bdl. 39.

43   Analysis of Easter lists points to an average turnover of *c*. 25 per cent in the householder population in any given year.

44   Source for Table 4: CCRO, CAS/I ff. 234–49.

45   Cf. Crossley Evans, pp. 102–3, 105, 107–8, and fn 57.

46   Beresford (ed), p. 171.

47 Wrightson, *English Society*, pp. 171–3.
48 J. J. Scarisbrick, *The Reformation and the English People* (1984), pp. 39, 162–4 and ch. 2 *passim*. But see Christopher Hill, *Protestantism and Revolution* (1958), p. 48.
49 The expansion of lay preaching has been explained in the same way: Sheils, pp. 174–5.
50 Crossley Evans, p. 105.
51 George Herbert, *A Priest to the Temple; of the Countrey Parson, his Character and Rule of Holy Life* (Everyman edn 1927), p. 269.
52 For example, CCRO, QSF/50 f. 48; /53 ff. 8–9, 10–11. Cf. Max Beloff, *Public Order and Popular Disturbances 1660–1714* (1963), p. 130.
53 Johnson, p. 45, cf. p. 88. There were 504 freemen in 1567, and 937 in 1641: see N. Alldridge, 'The mechanics of decline: population, migration and economy in early modern Chester', in Michael Reed (ed.), *English Towns in Decline* (Centre for Urban History, University of Leicester, Working Paper No. 1, 1986), Table 7 and sources given there.
54 Groombridge, pp. 69, 147. Johnson, pp. 36–48. The drift towards oligarchic control in towns was of course a general feature of this period: see Clark and Slack, *English Towns*, pp. 135–6.
55 Churchwardens' duties were laid down by canon law and regularly reaffirmed by bishops: see W. H. Frere (ed.), *Visitation Articles and Injunctions of the Period of the Reformation 1536–1575*, 3 vols., Alcuin Club Collections xiv–xvi (1910), *passim*. But those of swornmen and sidesmen – as separate offices – and the responsibilities of vestry commissions depended rather on local usage. For good Chester examples, see CDRO, P 20/13/1 (9 May 1644); P 63/7/1/ ff. 38r–40v, 84rv.
56 PRO, E 179, 244/29, unfolioed.
57 CDRO, P 29/7/1 f. 42.
58 CDRO, EDC 5 (1639) File 9.
59 CDRO, P 29/7/1 f. 42; P 20/13/1 (13 July 1632).
60 For example, CDRO, P 63/7/1/ f. 5r; P 20/13/1 (1 and 13 July 1632). Cf. Groombridge, p. 147.
61 CDRO, P 1/11 (19 January 1637); P 20/13/1 (4 April 1630); P 65/8/1 f. 66r.
62 For example, Bell and Newby, 'Community, communion . . .', p. 285. For a more open view, see Peter Burke, *Sociology and History* (1980), pp. 44–8.
63 CDRO, P 63/7/1 f. 64v.
64 CCRO, QSF/61 f. 120.
65 CCRO, QSF/35 f. 67.
66 For example, F. J. Furnivall (ed.), *Child-marriages, Divorces and Ratifications etc in the Diocese of Chester, AD 1561–6, etc*, Early

English Text Society, **108** (1867), p. 139.

67   For example, J. P. Earwaker, *The History of the Church and Parish of St Mary on the Hill, Chester* (1898), pp. 39–42.

68   CDRO, EDC 5 (1639) File 9.

69   *A Cheshire Sheaf* (3rd series), **12** (1915), pp. 14–15.

70   J. P. Earwaker, 'The Four Randle Holmes of Chester', *Journal of the Chester Archaeological Society* (n.s.), **4** (1890–1), pp. 113–35. BL Harleian MS, 2125 f. 23–58. *A Cheshire Sheaf* (3rd series), **23** (1926), p. 69. R. M. Lumiansky and D. Mills, *The Chester Mystery Cycle* (1983), pp. xvii–xx, xxiii.

71   The sample consisted of sixty-nine wills of Chester testators leaving charitable bequests, probated between 1551 and 1660: CDRO, WS, WI, WC and Enrolled Wills.

72   CDRO, WS 62/, Thomas Dewsbury, will (1613); WS, Thomas Benson, will (1614); WS, Christopher Barnard, will (1648).

73   T. Heywood (ed.), *The Diary of Rev. Henry Newcome (1661–1663)*, Chetham Society (o.s.), **18** (Manchester 1849), p. 89. Cf. Thomas, p. 240.

74   G. Ormerod, *The History of the County Palatine and City of Chester* (3 vols.) (2nd edn 1882), vol. 1 pp. 246–8.

75   Chester Public Library, MS F. 94.3 f. 23r.

76   John Ley, *A Pattern of Piety* (1640), pp. 1–4, 83, 104, 181–3.

77   See N. Z. Davis, pp. 65–6.

78   Ormerod, vol. 1, p. 194. Cf. Crossley Evans, p. 101. For the historical background to the arrangement of these churches, see *A Cheshire Sheaf* (3rd series), **13** (1916), p. 89.

79   CDRO, Enrolled wills, vol. 2, f. 244 (1603).

80   See *DNB* for both men.

81   CDRO, P 53/7/1 f. 5v.

82   *Victoria County History of Cheshire* (3 vols.), vol. 3 (1980), pp. 188–9.

83   Groombridge, pp. 52, 55, cf. 50.

84   *A Cheshire Sheaf* (1st series), **3** (1883), pp. 204–5; (3rd series), **13** (1916), pp. 86–7. CDRO, EDD 10/7/11; cf. Enrolled wills, vol. 2, f. 304 (1607). F. R. Raines, *The Journal of Nicholas Assheton of Downham*, Chetham Society (o.s.), **14** (1848), p. 37. Morris, pp. 170, 200. Daniel King, p. 21. Groombridge, p. 70. Simpson, pp. 34–5. D. Jones, *The Church in Chester 1300–1540*, Chetham Society (3rd series), **7** (1957), p. 113, fn 1 quoting BL Harleian MS 2150 f. 290. CDRO, P 63/7/1 ff. 38r–40v.

85   See *DNB* under James Ussher and Christopher Goodman.

86   R. H. Tawney, *Religion and the Rise of Capitalism* (Penguin edn 1977), pp. 158–9.

5 Common Prayer? Popular observance of the Anglican liturgy in Restoration Wiltshire[1]

Donald A. Spaeth

On 1 October 1673, John Mayo and twelve other inhabitants of the parish of Somerford Magna in Wiltshire appeared before the consistory court of the Bishop of Salisbury. They had been presented by their rector, Nathaniel Aske, for their neglect of divine service and, more importantly, for their failure to receive communion on the previous two occasions that it had been administered in the parish church. According to Aske, Mayo and his neighbours were nonconformists, and if his presentments were all we knew about the case we would probably believe him. Yet the rector told only one side of the story. The villagers responded by submitting a lengthy list of charges against their minister. They claimed that they longed to take communion but felt unable to receive it from Aske due to his numerous offences, and they petitioned the bishop to replace him with 'some other honest minister to administer the sacrament' to them.[2]

The petition of the inhabitants of Somerford Magna gives us a glimpse of a phenomenon about which we still know very little, namely the daily worship of Anglican villagers.[3] With a few notable exceptions, historians of early modern England have generally ignored the Church of England in their search for popular religious beliefs.[4] They have looked instead to heterodoxy, namely to religious dissent of all sorts – Puritanism, sectarianism, and nonconformity – and to magical and superstitious beliefs. The neglect of Anglican worship has been partly the result of inadequate sources. The problem is that conforming Protestant worship leaves very few records, because Protestantism lacks the rich ritual tradition of Catholicism. In theory, Protestant piety is private and in a largely illiterate society such as seventeenth-century England it therefore went unrecorded. Margaret Spufford summarized the problem well in *Contrasting Communities* when she noted regretfully that 'Orthodoxy, like happiness, has no history', although 'we can catch an echo of its existence from time to time'.[5] Heterodoxy, unlike orthodoxy, was prosecuted and thus created abundant records.

At the same time, historians have been unimpressed by Anglicanism (especially eighteenth-century Anglicanism). As Patrick Collinson has recently written, they have not been 'easily convinced that the Prayer Book and the Homilies can have defined and sustained the truly popular religion of early modern England'.[6] They have found dissent and magical beliefs more attractive subjects of inquiry. By differing from the Established Church, dissenters showed both that they had thought about their beliefs and that they were willing to suffer for them. We tend to admire martyrs for their courage in adversity. The very word 'nonconformist' sounds more attractive to our liberty-loving ears than the word 'conformist'. Yet, except during the Interregnum, Anglicans were not usually forced to suffer for their beliefs.

Modern observers are also intrigued by magical beliefs for their apparent irrationality. In recent years a number of historians influenced by Keith Thomas and Jean Delumeau have argued that most laypeople were indifferent to official, institutional religion.[7] According to this interpretation, most villagers either did not attend church or attended more out of obedience to the law than piety, and they generally misbehaved both inside and outside church. The exceptions were probably the more substantial parishioners. Popular religion has thus been described as 'folk-lorized Christianity', which in practice has seemed more magical than Christian.[8] One recent commentator has argued that we should not confuse attachment to official ritual and practice with ideological conformity to the Church.[9] Historians have found ample support for popular indifference to Christianity from jaded clerics such as the rector of Pewsey, who reported in 1668 that 'so many there are addicted to debaucherie & loosenes, if not inclin'd to Aitheisme that the publike service of God is too much neglected'.[10]

In this article I will argue that many villagers were conforming Anglicans in the *positive* sense of the word and that the Prayer Book played an important part in defining their religious beliefs and sense of proper worship. I will focus on the aspects of worship raised in the conflict between the rector and villagers of Somerford Magna, namely popular participation in communion and divine service. How often did villagers receive communion and attend church services, and did they observe the Anglican liturgy while they were there? If they conformed, did they do so out of obedience to the law or as an expression of their religious beliefs? And what implications did their behaviour and beliefs have for their sense of membership in the parish as a religious community?

My primary focus will be on the county of Wiltshire and elsewhere in Salisbury diocese after the Restoration. In the century after the Restoration, at least one-third of Wiltshire parishes experienced some conflict between minister and congregation, ranging from a single presentment of a neglectful cleric to long drawn-out battles which involved a series of presentments and counter-presentments, petitions, letters, and suits at law in both ecclesiastical and secular courts.[11] In the most serious incidents villagers might go on communion or tithe strikes or threaten to dissent from the church if they did not get a minister who would behave himself. Disputes arose over many issues, including clerical complaints that villagers did not conform to the Church or had defamed them and lay complaints that their minister had neglected his duties or performed them improperly. The evidence from such episodes will be supplemented by the regular presentments made by churchwardens to bishop, dean, or archdeacon. Although the quality of these presentments gradually deteriorated throughout the last half of the seventeenth century, churchwardens continued to present not only dissenters, but also worshipping Anglicans.[12]

Somerford Magna was a small parish which lay in the 'cheese country' of north-west Wiltshire, a region of pastoral farming, of cloth-making, and, it has recently been argued, of cultural and religious independence. We might therefore expect nonconformity to have been strong in the parish.[13] Indeed, according to the rector, dissent was a problem of major proportions. On two occasions in 1672 and 1673 he presented a total of seventeen members of his congregation for such offences as failing to attend divine service, coming to church late, some so late that they heard only the sermon, and, most seriously of all, failing to receive communion at Easter and on Whitsunday. In a letter written in July 1672, Revd Nathaniel Aske blamed the absence of his parishioners on the King's Declaration of Indulgence of that year. 'This late declaration of indulgence', he said, 'hath made the

church empty. . . . I warn comunions & none appears, & often
tymes read prayers to the walls.' Even Aske had to admit that his
recalcitrant parishioners were odd nonconformists, however,
for they made no attempt to respond to the rector's charges. In
'A Paradoxe to speake it a Drunken Swearing Puritan', he
commented.[14]

The explanation for Aske's paradox was that most of the
parishioners he had presented were not dissenters. True, there
were nonconformists living in the parish, accounting for eight of
sixty adults according to the Compton Census of 1676, although
there is no evidence that a conventicle ever met in the parish.[15]
Three of those whom Aske presented probably were dissenters,
for they made no attempt to respond to the rector's charges. In
September 1673, however, thirteen others petitioned the bishop
for assistance against their minister. In their petition and separate
articles of information 'which wee Alledge & cann prove against
Mr Nathanaell Aske', the villagers charged the minister with
numerous offences, including failing to baptize or bury on several
occasions, refusing to allow corpses to be brought into the church
unless he was paid to give a sermon, and using the churchyard as a
pasture for his cattle and pigs. They also claimed that both he and
the members of his family had themselves not received communion for two years.[16]

His worst offence, however, was his contentiousness. He 'hath
demeaned himself very troublesome & vexatious amongst his
parishioners by severall suits comenced against them, and citeing
of thirteen of them unto your Lordship's Courte, and by
indeavouring to procure & abett one Neighbour . . . to sue an
other'. On the day before they had drawn up their petition, Aske
had used his sermon to threaten them with further persecution:
'vizt that he had made a beginning with us, And those that were left
out should drinke of the same cupp for hee was resolved to fill the
courts with presentments against us'. It was on account of Aske's
numerous offences, and especially on account of his contentiousness, that the petitioners had stayed away from church and failed
to take communion. They and others of the parish felt that they
could not 'with a good conscience receave the Sacrament from his
hands' although, they said, 'we long to receave' it.[17]

In sum, the villagers whom Aske had presented claimed that
they were not dissenters at all; they were conforming Anglicans
who would do their duty if only they had a minister who would

behave. Do we believe them? After all, they could have been dissenters who were harassing their hapless minister in the hopes of replacing him with someone more theologically to their liking. In this fashion dissenters in the nearby village of Holt tried unsuccessfully to expel their curate by prosecuting him in the consistory court so that they could install a nonconformist preacher in his place.[18] Certainly, it is difficult to see some of their charges as more than harassment. It seems unlikely, for example, that they were seriously concerned that Aske's beasts did 'undecently tread downe & Roote upp the Graves there' since we know that in a number of other Wiltshire parishes villagers themselves used the churchyard as a pasture, workplace, storage yard, and playing field.[19] And how can Aske's litigiousness explain the petitioners' neglect of divine service and communion if their main example was his prosecution of them for that very neglect?

Aske's presentments were not the only evidence that he was a troublemaker, however. Although the rector piously told the bishop that he hoped that in his 'presentments there shall not be one drop of revenge, No such vinegar or gall in our ink',[20] he appears to have been an argumentative man who was only too happy to use the courts. In 1670, two years after his induction into the rectory, he sued his predecessor's widow and daughter for compensation for the poor state in which he allegedly had found the parsonage. Robert Butcher, of the neighbouring parish of Dauntsey, was so angered by Aske's suit against the late rector's family that he confronted him and charged him with simony, adultery, and drunkenness. Aske responded by prosecuting Butcher in the bishop's consistory court for attacking the clergy. Four years later, he took another man to court for vilifying him. John Atkins had made the mistake of calling Aske a rogue after the rector had charged him at assizes, ironically with bringing vexatious suits.[21] These secular cases upset the petitioners, just as they had angered Butcher, as can be seen from the wording of a testimonial in their support given by the incumbents of five neighbouring parishes. Although the petitioners would have preferred to have a new rector, the ministers reported, they would take communion from Aske 'if he shall lay by his Contention and inconvenient Disputes of Secular Affaires'.[22]

We can almost see the choleric rector shouting threats at his congregation: 'If the first court will not doe it, I will have you in the second: and if the second will not due it the third shall.'[23] Nor was this an idle threat. The bishop's official treated the petitioners gently when they appeared before him in October 1673. He dismissed the charges against them and cancelled their fees, at the same time warning them to take communion that Christmas.[24] Aske was outraged by what he termed 'my lords unparalelled patience and meekness'. '[A]las I fear that is not the way to deal with such rough dispositions as theirs are', he wrote; 'if that would availe they had all been my staunch friends ere this day'.[25] Five days after his previous action had been quashed, he once again asked the bishop's registrar to cite his congregation.[26]

Whether in reaction to Aske's new action against them or out of obedience to the bishop's admonition, it appears that most of the petitioners bowed to pressure and took communion at Christmas. By the end of December 1673, the rector had certified the submission of two of his opponents. But he refused to acknowledge the submission of the rest, leaving them little alternative but to write to the bishop's registrar themselves certifying that they had received Christmas communion from Aske.[27] Not surprisingly, their communion did not end conflict with the rector. One of the original petitioners, an 80-year-old widow whom Aske called 'a main fomenter of Phanaticisme in the Parish', continued to refuse to take communion from the minister and rarely went to church except to attend christenings and funerals. Aske complained that another petitioner sometimes laughed and whispered to his neighbours in church, while a third refused to pay his church rates. In 1674 he prosecuted two other opponents in the consistory court for failing to pay their tithes. In the long run, his parishioners found a new way to avoid receiving the sacrament from the rector's hands. On Whitsunday 1674 John Mayo, who was serving as churchwarden, failed to provide enough wine for communion to take place properly.[28] Aske's presentment of this incident in November 1674 is the last surviving evidence of conflict in the parish. Perhaps the appointment of a new curate in September had appeased villagers. Little more than a year later, early in 1676, Aske died and a new rector came to Somerford Magna.[29]

So behind Nathaniel Aske's presentments of apparent nonconformists there lay a bitter and prolonged struggle over religious worship in Somerford Magna. By failing to attend church or to receive communion, the parishioners expressed support for the Established Church and the sacrament of communion, not dissent or indifference. John Mayo and his neighbours refused to take communion from their rector because they thought he was unfit to administer the sacrament, for two reasons. The first can be traced directly to the Book of Common Prayer. The rubric to the communion service instructed the minister not to allow 'those betwixt whom he perceiveth malice and hatred to reign' to partake of the sacrament 'until he know them to be reconciled', and parishioners were warned that it could be dangerous to their souls to receive without first reconciling themselves with their neighbours.[30] Both villagers and clerics took this admonition seriously. Thus the vicar of Compton Chamberlayne forbade two of his parishioners who were embroiled in a lawsuit to receive communion and threatened them with suspension if they tried. A clerical prohibition of this sort might not be necessary, for some villagers disbarred themselves from communion. For example, after Robert Mortimer of Calne was involved in a fight which led to a suit at law he 'could not with a safe & quiet conscience come to the Holy Communion'. Only when the suit had been ended by each party signing releases did Mortimer feel that he could safely receive the sacrament again.[31]

To have allowed quarrelling parishioners to receive communion would have violated the spiritual function of the rite, both for communal and individual reasons. In addition to reminding villagers of how much they owed their Saviour, participation in communion symbolized their membership in the Church and their oneness with all other members, and this unity was clearly disturbed by disagreements between participants. Furthermore, anyone who was quarrelling with his neighbours was clearly not behaving with sufficient charity, despite repeated reminders in the liturgy.

If lawsuits with other laymen prohibited communion, how much more a legal dispute with the minister who was administering the sacrament must have done so. How was it possible to receive the body and blood of Christ from a man who had taken one to court? And if being out of charity with one's neighbours prevented one from receiving communion, how much more it must have seemed that it should prevent anyone from administering the sacrament. In addition to their concern about the safety of receiving communion from a man with whom they were in dispute there must have been some concern about the efficacy of receiving from an unworthy minister, despite the assurances contained in the 26th

Article of Religion that the benefits of the sacrament were not diminished if it was administered by 'evil men'.

To these theological explanations we must add the natural emotional reaction, which would make it unpleasant to receive the holy sacrament from a man whose behaviour made him objectionable. Villagers elsewhere in the Salisbury diocese sometimes refused to receive communion from ministers whose scandalous behaviour seemed to desecrate the sacrament. The inhabitants of Charlton, a chapelry near Somerford Magna, were scandalized by the behaviour of their vicar, who was a drunkard and sometimes fell 'acrying and belching as though he would vomitt and the like at the Administracon of the Sacrament therby making himself rediculous'. Not surprisingly, such antics gave 'a very greate offence and discouragement to the congregation in soe much that . . . divers . . . cannot frequent the said church in time of divine service and participate of the sacraments with any comfort'.[32] Lay neglect of communion can be traced back to conflict between the minister and his congregation in several parishes. In the chapelry of Knook, for example, few inhabitants received communion in 1667 'by reason of some difference betwixt' them and the curate. This dispute finally impelled villagers to lock the curate out of the church during Easter 1668, so that he was unable to administer the sacrament.[33]

In sum, villagers valued the sacrament of communion too much to risk taking it or to want to take it from a minister who they thought was unfit to administer it. Unfortunately for them, the official of the Bishop of Salisbury, however sympathetic he might be to their plight, could not countenance the unilateral decision of laypeople to stop taking communion from ministers they did not like. To do so would have been to relinquish control over worship to the laity and to provide a handy instrument to nonconformists. The Somerford Magna petitioners simply had to be forced to participate.[34]

The episodes in Somerford Magna and other villages suggested that villagers were conforming Anglicans whose religious beliefs were based on the Prayer Book. They might also lead us to believe that most Anglicans conformed to church requirements and took communion regularly, at least when they were on good terms with their minister. This conclusion appears to be confirmed by what scattered evidence we have on communion from Goodnestone in

Kent and the Nottinghamshire parish of Clayworth in the 1670s and from Southwark in the 1630s, where around 90 per cent of qualified adults received the sacrament.[35] Yet this interpretation does not hold true for Wiltshire parishes, where villagers rarely received communion and fell far short of official expectations, minimal as these were.

Observers since the seventeenth century have seen the frequency of communion as an important index of religiosity. As is well known, the Canons of 1604 required parishioners to receive communion at least three times a year, including once at Easter. Some ecclesiastics encouraged their clergy to administer it more often than thrice yearly to ensure that villagers had sufficient opportunity to receive, with the additional benefit that they could receive more often if they desired. Thus in 1662 Bishop Henchman of Salisbury charged his clergy to administer communion once a month, and George Herbert, author of the *Country Parson*, also advised monthly communion, although he thought five or six times a year was sufficient.[36] Despite these recommendations, churchwardens in country parishes usually purchased bread and wine, and therefore communion was administered, only three or four times a year, at the great feasts of the religious calendar – Christmas, Easter, Whitsunday, and sometimes Palm Sunday or Michaelmas.[37]

The laity rarely received the sacrament more than once a year, and over half received it even less often. In the parish of Pewsey, for example, only eighty-four people attended communion on Christmas Day 1709 or Easter 1710, although the parish had a population of around 400 adults.[38] Although no lists survive for other communions in that year, it seems unlikely that more than another eighty persons received at Whitsuntide and Michaelmas, assuming that the sacrament also was administered on those feast days. At most, then, about 40 per cent of adults took communion in Pewsey during the year 1709–10, and little more than 10 per cent received at Easter, figures which compare badly with the 90 per cent figures for Clayworth, Cogenhoe, and Southwark. The Pewsey returns were not atypical, however. Forty years earlier, the rector of Pewsey had reported that only half of his congregation received communion during the year. In 1743 Donhead St Andrew had only forty-five regular and twenty-five irregular communicants, although the parish had 456 inhabitants in Anglican families. Churchwardens' presentments from other parishes confirm this dismal picture. In Wokingham in Berkshire, it was reported in 1669, 'those that doth come are very few in comparison of those which doth not come'.[39]

   Testimony recorded in the deposition books of the Bishop of Salisbury makes it clear that villagers often went years without receiving communion. For example, Joyce Wordly of Downton ingenuously admitted to the court that she had not received for three years because 'her employment . . . [had] not permitted her to do it'. Even those who received the sacrament every year were unlikely to participate three times as stipulated by the Canons of 1604. A Downton brasier testified that 'for many years past he hath constantly received the sacrament . . . every Xtmas'.[40] Testimony on communion must be treated with care, since it came in response to questions asked by the defendent's proctor in an attempt to discredit the other side's witnesses. Yet witnesses freely admitted behaviour which fell short of canonical requirements, suggesting that whereas proctors knew the canon law, ordinary villagers did not. Lay depositions are also confirmed by other evidence, such as the 1668 presentment of the churchwardens of Landford that no parishioners 'refuse to receive once a year but scarce any receive thrice'. Similarly, in Pewsey more people participated at Christmas 1709 than at Easter 1710, and only eight received on both occasions.[41] This shows not only that villagers were unlikely to receive three times a year, but also that they made little special effort to receive at Easter, the one time at which everyone was supposed to communicate. Churchwardens' purchases of bread and wine for communion were only slightly, if at all, heavier at Easter than at other feasts.[42] Perhaps this was another reason why the inhabitants of Somerford Magna felt that their rector was being unreasonable in presenting them for absence from communion. After all, they had only missed two communions, at Easter and Whitsuntide.

   How do we explain this apparent neglect of communion by villagers? One possible explanation is that proper observance of communion fell off drastically after the 1689 Act of Toleration, which in practice may have licensed not only dissent but also absence from worship of any variety. The occasional churchwardens' presentment after 1690 of parishioners who failed to attend either church or chapel suggests that there was a general relaxation of religious observance after Toleration.[43] And it is worth noting that the rate of communion in Clayworth declined markedly from its peak of 90 per cent in 1677 to only 50 per cent in the 1690s.[44] Yet this does not explain the low rate of communion in Pewsey and Wokingham in the 1660s. Alternatively, perhaps the explanation is nonconformity. Certainly, Wokingham was a hotbed of dissent, with one Baptist and two Presbyterian meetings in 1669.[45] However, there is no evidence of active dissent in Pewsey after the Restoration, although its minister during the Interregnum had been a leading Presbyterian.[46] Nonconformity also does not explain the failure of forty-six inhabitants of Fugglestone St Peter – whom wardens described as 'Churchmen, but negligent' – to take communion in 1683.[47]

The episodes at Somerford Magna and elsewhere hint at another possible explanation. As we have seen, villagers sometimes refused to take communion from a minister who they thought was unfit to administer the sacrament. Perhaps they were also careful not to take it if they thought they were themselves not fit to receive. Thus the churchwardens of Imber parish presented in 1674 that some villagers had failed to take communion because they were waiting 'till they are better & fitter prepared'.[48] To understand the full implications of this statement, however, we must look outside Restoration Wiltshire. In 1692 the curate of Coddrington in Bedfordshire reported to the Bishop of Lincoln the unorthodox excuses that his parishioners gave for their failure to take communion. One man told the curate that communion 'did nothing but damn people; [because] it was impossible to receive it worthily & those that received it otherwise did damn themselves'. Another said 'that those were damned, that so much as laughed after they had received it'.[49] This belief was echoed in the presentment of the vicar of the Wiltshire parish of Winterbourne Monkton in 1783 that many were 'deterred from communicating under a notion that they thereby bind themselves to lead a better and more Christian life than they are otherwise obliged to do under a heavier and more severe punishment hereafter'.[50]

These statements all point to the same general interpretation. Villagers appear to have believed that the sacrament of communion represented a promise that the recipient had repented past offences and would henceforth commit no more. Violation of this promise might lead to eternal damnation. It was therefore safer to go without communion than to receive it and face the risk of being punished for failing to live a sufficiently virtuous life thereafter. The safest time to receive the sacrament was when one was old and thus unlikely to sin again.

In the clergy's eyes this lay belief was a 'misgrounded misapprehension'. It can, however, be traced directly to the wording of the communion service in the Prayer Book, just as could the reluctance of the inhabitants of Somerford Magna to receive from their troublesome minister.[51] On the Sunday or holy day which immediately preceded the administration of communion, the minister was supposed to announce the service and to warn the congregation to prepare themselves to receive the sacrament. He did so by reading an exhortation which instructed his hearers how to prepare themselves and described the dangers of receiving unworthily. Although the sacrament was spiritual food for those who received it worthily, it was 'so dangerous for them that will presume to receive it unworthily'. Those planning to participate were to examine their consciences, to bewail their sins, and to confess their sinfulness to God 'with full purpose of amendment of life'. Without repentance, the promise of amendment, and reconciliation with enemies, they were warned, 'the receiving of the holy Communion doth nothing else but increase your damnation'. The devil would enter their bodies and bring them 'to destruction both of body and soul'. This exhortation was not meant to deter people from taking communion, but only to make them think before they did so, as the term 'exhortation' itself indicates. The reformers who had designed the Anglican liturgy had wished to discredit the frequent repetition of the Mass and the superstitious uses to which it had been put, which they felt degraded the sacrament. Communion was to be taken seriously, after careful self-examination. Potential communicants were 'to consider the dignity of that holy mystery' and to search their consciences so that they 'may come holy and clean to such a heavenly feast', according to the communion service.

If too many in the congregation neglected their duty, however, the Prayer Book provided the cleric with a second, less frightening, exhortation. There was no excuse for not taking communion: 'If any man say, I am a grievous sinner, and therefore am afraid to come: wherefore do ye not repent and amend?' Yet although it asked absenters to consider 'how sore punishment hangeth over your heads', this alternate exhortation lacked the power and specificity of the first, with its mention of destruction by the devil.

Instead, it compared the failure to receive communion with the bad manners of someone who had been invited to dinner but refused to eat. Furthermore, evidence from the Oxfordshire parish of Caversham indicates that the second exhortation was likely to be read only when the minister was under pressure from his ordinary to increase popular observance. The curate reported in 1682 that 'In obedience to your Lordship's commands', he had given notice before Whitsun communion 'and to stir them up to their duty, I did read the second exhortation as is appointed in case of the people's negligence'. This tactic, combined with his decision to administer communion three times in the Easter season, had, he thought, increased the total number of communicants that year.[52]

Even if the minister read the gentler second exhortation the week before he administered the sacrament, the communion service itself probably cancelled its good work. Before the Confession, which came just before the congregation were to communicate, they were reminded of the dangers of receiving unworthily. When we receive communion unworthily, they were told, 'we eat and drink our own damnation', provoking God's wrath so that he will 'plague us with diverse diseases, and sundry kinds of death'. 'Judge therefore yourselves, brethren', the minister thundered, 'that ye be not judged of the Lord.'

This was a powerful threat. It is not surprising that such a fire-and-brimstone warning frightened its hearers. What is interesting is the way in which villagers in Coddrington and Winterbourne Monkton echoed the words and tone of the Prayer Book. When villagers said that communion bound them to live a better life 'under a heavier and more severe punishment' they repeated the communion service's threat of increased damnation for those who received without 'full purpose of amendment of life'. From the wording of the Prayer Book, it appeared that men had the power to damn themselves. Some of the punishments described in the communion service would be suffered in this world; unworthy reception provoked God to plague men with diseases and even death. Yet punishment might come in the next world as well. Anyone who received unworthily ate and drank his own damnation, bringing 'destruction both of body and soul'. Unworthy reception did 'nothing else but increase . . . damnation', a phrase reminiscent of the medieval Catholic concepts of Purgatory and of the Book of Life in which good works and sins were recorded and then balanced at death.

Any Protestant theologian would have rejected this lay interpretation of the liturgy, of course. The language of the communion
service in the Prayer Book was meant to be figurative only.
Unworthy reception 'damned' offenders only in the sense that it
increased their punishment on earth and revealed more clearly the
human sins which had already condemned them, through no fault
of their own, to damnation. Yet we can forgive villagers for taking
these words, which they heard before every administration of
commmunion, at face value.

Villagers seem to have believed, however, that their free will
worked in only one direction. Although they thought they could
damn themselves by unworthy communion, they do not appear to
have believed they could further their own salvation by their
actions, for example by receiving the sacrament. Men had
sufficient free will to refuse salvation, but only God had the power
to save them. A Salisbury woman testified to the strength of lay
anxieties when she confessed on her death-bed her fear that she
had 'damne[d] her body & soule' by perjuring herself.[53] In sum,
villagers found it difficult to accept the full implications of the
doctrine of predestination. Unknowingly, they adopted a position
similar to the Arminian doctrine of resistible grace.[54]

So far I have focused on individuals' concerns that their own
failings might make them unfit to receive communion. Yet
communion was also a social matter. Just as a minister who
degraded the bread and wine by performing the service improperly
or by taking his congregation to court might make the sacrament
worthless or even dangerous, so also if a sinner communicated it
was a matter of concern for the entire congregation. This was the
reason the vicar of Ramsbury asked the Dean of Salisbury to
explain why the husband in an incestuous marriage had been
absolved and was to be readmitted to communion. He wrote that
since the sinner still lived in incest, parishioners would 'be much
offended if they saw [him] be admitted to the sacrament before he
be reformed'. If they came to receive at the same time as he did,
the vicar reported, 'they will depart and not comunicate with
him and indeed some have expressed no lesse'.[55]

It would be rash to argue that these anxieties were felt by all
laypeople and provide a complete explanation for the behaviour of
those who failed to take communion regularly. Villagers might feel
unfit to receive the sacrament for other reasons, too, for example
because they did not know their catechism or were too poor to

afford 'cloathes fit for them to apear in, at the Worship of God'. In Pewsey, the leading inhabitants were three times as likely to receive communion in 1709–10 as were their impoverished neighbours. Villagers might also be prevented from receiving by sickness, business, or, of course, indifference.[56] Nor do villagers' fears explain why the rate of reception was so much lower in Wiltshire parishes than it was in some other parishes in England for which evidence survives. Yet anxieties about the danger of receiving communion unworthily do provide at least a partial explanation for popular 'neglect' of the sacrament.[57] Lay attitudes to communion were clearly complex. Despite their infrequent reception, many villagers appear to have thought highly of the sacrament, regarding it with a mixture of fear and respect. They were reluctant to receive it if they felt that either they, the minister of fellow members of the congregation were unfit, because they thought it was holy. Such behaviour casts doubt on the reliability of using the frequency of lay reception of communion as an index of popular religiosity.

Unfortunately, too little is known about popular attitudes towards communion in other periods to be able to explain the origin of these lay anxieties about communion. It is possible that popular concern about fitness to receive dated back to the sixteenth century or earlier.[58] Alternatively, it may have been a new phenomenon, perhaps the legacy of the exclusion of numerous parishioners from the sacrament by the Presbyterian and Independent clerics who entered many Wiltshire pulpits during the Interregnum.

Although parishioners may have respected communion, the infrequency with which they received the sacrament, and indeed with which the Church offered it, meant that it played little part in their normal religious life. The most common form of public worship was attendance at divine service, which might be performed up to two hundred times each year in every parish church in Britain.[59] The Canons of 1604 directed all parishioners to celebrate the days on which it was administered, not least by 'hearing the word of God' in church and by abstaining from ordinary labour. However, although the Church expected everyone to attend every performance of divine service, little attempt was made to enforce this. Even the most stringent anti-recusant legislation required only one attendance per week and churchwardens' presentments suggest laypeople generally satisfied, but did not exceed, this minimum requirement.[60]

Most villagers went to divine service once a week and abstained from labour on Sundays when possible, although there were naturally some who stayed away, preferring the alehouse or the churchyard to the church.[61] But they were unlikely to attend more than once on Sunday or to take much notice of all but the most important holy days. The churchwardens of Market Lavington reported in 1686, for example, that 'Parishioners for bear their ordinary labour and come tolerably well to Church on Sundays but upon Holydayes . . . the most of our parish follow their bodily imployments & but few come to church'.[62] The exceptions were the four great holy days on which communion was normally administered – Christmas, Easter, Whitsunday, and usually Michaelmas – two of which fell on Sunday. Lay failure to observe most holy days is best documented in Pewsey where a leading parishioner told the rector 'that there were but fower holy dayes to be observed throughout the year'. The rector's own thresher reprimanded him 'for not permitting him to work in [the rector's] barne as other daily labourers did'. The minister no doubt told his worker that labouring on a holy day violated the laws of the Church, for the thresher rebelliously told him, 'Let the Bishop & Church order what they please, I will worke upon all weeke dayes as well as other filke [folk]'.[63]

The importance of Sunday service can also be seen from the fact that the most frequent complaint made by churchwardens against their clergyman was 'for not letting us have prayer twice every Lords day', usually because he was a pluralist or served a parish with chapelries and was incapable of being in more than one place at the same time.[64] Yet despite such complaints villagers were unlikely to attend church more than once each Sunday. As the rector of Lydiard Millicent explained to the Bishop of Salisbury in 1749, they wanted two services so that they could attend the one which fitted best into their work schedule. Since the winter days were short, people spent their afternoons taking care of the cattle, 'so that he had a full congregation in the morning but in the Afternoon few or rather none at all'. In the summer, when the days were longer, parishioners had more time in the afternoon, so that he had 'twice the number of people to what I had in the morning'.[65]

Clearly, some 'ordinary labour' did continue on Sundays. The

rector of Lydiard Millicent was shocked by the practical considerations which determined his congregation's attendance patterns,
and he apologized to the bishop that 'such severe general
reflections (with a great deal of labor of mind) are suggested'. Yet
the Anglican liturgy did not forbid all Sunday labour. Although
the 1662 Prayer Book and Canons made no exceptions, earlier
church documents were more forgiving. Queen Elizabeth I's
Injunctions of 1559 echoed those of Edward VI twelve years
earlier in advising ministers to teach their parishioners 'that they
may with a safe and quiet conscience, in the time of harvest,
labour upon the holy and festival days, and save that thing which
God has sent'.[66] Without saying so explicitly, this Injunction
sanctioned essential labour of all sorts. The 1676 Act for the Better
Observation of the Lord's Day also exempted 'Works of Necessity'
from its general ban of ordinary labour on Sundays.[67] Whether in
harvest time or out, animals must be fed and cows milked,
especially in a dairying parish like Lydiard Millicent. Popular
observance of divine service shows that there was a delicate
balance between liturgical requirements and practicalities. A
compromise was possible on the fifty-two Sundays a year,
according to which villagers forebore all but essential labour. No
such compromise was possible on the other thirty-plus holy
days each year, which simply took too large a chunk out of the
work year.

It is no coincidence that the only holy days which villagers did
recognize were those on which communion was likely to be
administered. Popular observance of these days makes it clear that
the explanation for lay failure to take communion is not absence
from church. On the contrary, villagers might attend church for
years without receiving the sacrament. William Edom of Downton, his neighbours reported, 'seldom misses to go to his parish
church on Sundayes & holydayes', but only received the sacrament
once a year. When a fight broke out over the mayor's seat in
Devizes church in 1707, three witnesses reported that they had
never taken communion, although the eldest was 40 years old.[68]

So far, I have looked at the extent to which people *attended* divine
service. But how did they behave in church and what did they
think of the service? Unfortunately, the evidence on these
questions is not as plentiful or as clear-cut as it is for communion
and church attendance. Our general picture of popular worship,

based on Puritan and clerical complaints, is that much of the congregation did not pay attention and either fell asleep or behaved in a disorderly manner.[69] That such misbehaviour occasionally occurred is made clear by a presentment from Allington in 1689 in which the curate complained about an 'offencive pew . . . which overtops all the rest of the seats . . . serving onely for the more secure sleeping of those that sitt in it'.[70] To what extent is this an accurate portrayal of the role of the laity?

Divine service was long and left little room for lay participation or spontaneity. In the morning three services were usually read back to back: morning service itself, the litany, and the ante-communion service, which included a sermon. This was a lengthy service, which included substantial repetition. The Lord's Prayer may have been said as many as five times, two different creeds were used, and there were four readings from the Bible. Evening prayer was shorter, for the litany and sermon were usually omitted. The role of the laity in these services was rigidly predetermined and ritualistic. The congregation participated by reciting prayers along with the officiant, by giving the responses in the Prayer Book – especially important in the litany and the communion service – and by bowing, kneeling, or standing at specified times. It has been estimated that morning prayer, including communion but excluding notices, banns, and the sermon, gave the celebrant 3500 words to say, leaving the congregation with only 700.[71] Thus it would be no surprise if bored congregations all over Wiltshire failed to participate in divine service.

In some parishes laypeople seriously disrupted worship. In Hilperton, for example, parishioners apparently disturbed service regularly by talking in church and playing games in the churchyard, and on one occasion they rioted in the church. But such cases were unusual. Even the rector of Pewsey, who complained at length about the 'Aitheisme' of his congregation, had to admit that 'the misbehaviour or disorder is not such as to cause disturbance'. It was more common for parishioners to resort to church, 'abiding quietly in good order', as those of Codford St Mary did, according to a 1674 presentment. Where trouble broke out it often reflected tensions between clergy and laity rather than normal behaviour. Hilperton, for example, was the scene of thirty years of bitter lay–clerical conflict.[72]

These examples of lay inattention and disruption are also

balanced by other evidence that people paid attention to the service. Great Bedwin's wardens, for example, complained in 1692 that their elderly vicar's voice was 'soe much decayed, that few . . . of the congregacon can hear what hee reads or sayes'.[73] Literate villagers clearly followed along in their Bible when the minister read the Lessons, Epistle, and Gospel, for West Grimstead's wardens presented in 1668 that the church windows did not 'let in sufficient light for the Congregation to make use of their Bibles'. Several parishes charged their minister with failing to read sections of divine service. The most detailed of these presentments, from West Harnham, reported that their minister omitted the beginning of morning prayer and all of the ante-communion service except for a sermon and the Epistle and Gospel, which he read in place of the biblical Lessons prescribed for the day. These details show that some villagers knew the liturgy very well. Furthermore, since the omissions would have substantially shortened the service, villagers clearly were not so bored by worship that they wished for it to finish quickly.[74]

The laity generally preferred low-church elements of the service, such as the sermon, to high-church elements, such as ritual gestures. They expected regular sermons and complained when they did not get them, as in Laverstock whose wardens presented that they had only one sermon every three weeks.[75] With the exception of chapelries and parishes served by pluralists, most villagers got the regular sermons they desired, for over 90 per cent of incumbents had a licence to preach.[76] Wardens were thus able to present, as did those of Chicklade in 1662, that they did not need a copy of the Homilies because their parish was 'seldom destitute of a preaching minister'.[77] Laymen wanted not just a sermon but a good sermon, and they had their own opinion of what that meant. The parishioners of Downton, for example, reported in 1662 that their curate 'preached to the great content[ment] of many well affected people'. On the other hand, the inhabitants of West Harnham found their minister 'insufishent for preaching'. They complained 'that his sermons are only for sport for the rude people of Sarum the hole week following', so that they sometimes went into nearby Salisbury to hear better sermons, as Puritans had done earlier in the century.[78]

Parishioners appear to have been less committed to performing the ritual gestures prescribed by the liturgy, although the evidence on this question is mixed. All persons were to kneel during

General Confession and Absolution, the litany, prayers, and collects, as well as when they received communion; they were to stand during the reading of the Creed and the Gospel; and they were to show reverence for Jesus by bowing each time his name was read during the service. The parishioners of Somerford Magna apparently wanted to perform these gestures, for they complained that Nathaniel Aske did 'not att all speake out when he reades the comon prayer soe that wee know not in what posture to demeane ourselves either to stand or to kneele'. In other parishes such as Pewsey, however, few knelt when prayers were read, not everyone stood at the Creed and Gospel, and no-one made 'due reverence at the name of Jesus'. Even when parishioners did make the required gestures, they apparently did so without much enthusiasm. The wardens of Cricklade St Mary reported in 1668, for example, that although no-one refused to show reverence when Christ's name was read, they could 'not make an exact presentment' of those who did not 'because those who through forgetfulnesse as we suppose omit it sometimes with all reverence doe it other times', wording which suggests that popular observance was by no means complete and that the wardens did not wish to name offenders.[79]

In sum, villagers living in Wiltshire after the Restoration took communion relatively infrequently, some of them because they feared the consequences of reception if they or the celebrant was unfit; they usually attended church once a week on Sunday; they abstained from non-essential labour on Sundays but refused to do so on holy days; they listened attentively to the service and valued the sermon but were ambivalent about performing the ritual gestures which the liturgy prescribed.

They conformed and yet did not conform. This statement illustrates the difficulties involved in trying to decide whether villagers displayed religious commitment to Anglicanism. Depending on which evidence we choose, we may agree with the clergy that the laity were irreligious and ignorant, reflecting the sad state of the Church of England. Alternatively, we may decide that villagers were actually quite pious. Rather than asking how 'religious' villagers were, it therefore seems better to ask how they defined their religious beliefs, how religion fitted into their lives, and what social implications their patterns of worship had.

To start with, what implications did their failure to attend divine service more than once a week have for the position of the church as the centre of the community, both religious and secular? It appears that the classic image of the parish gathered to pray together each week was in practice rarely fulfilled, except perhaps on great feast days. The reception of communion by only a portion of the congregation present in church might have impaired the social function of communion as a communal celebration, rather as if half of the apostles had chosen to fast at the Last Supper. Yet lay patterns of worship brought into question, not the community of the parish, but the control of the Established Church and its clergy over that community. The unwillingness of villagers to receive communion along with known sinners shows that they still saw the sacrament as a social rite. The church building continued to be used as both a religious and secular community centre. The churchyard was still a parish meeting place, workplace, and, most important, playing field. Even nonconformity, which presented the greatest challenge to the unity of the parish in this period, does not appear to have split the community, for nonconformists continued to attend christenings and funerals in the parish church and even occasionally appropriated the church or churchyard for their own ceremonies.[80]

It is tempting to look for doctrinal beliefs in villagers' behaviour and statements. Villagers showed some affinity with Puritan views, ignoring most holy days, displaying little enthusiasm for bowing at the name of Jesus, and even 'gadding about' to hear sermons in other parishes. These similarities between village Anglicanism in Restoration Wiltshire and Puritanism in pre-revolutionary England are important because they may suggest that Puritan rule during the Interregnum had a lasting impact on parish worship. They may also help to explain the initial popularity of Puritanism to English men and women. Perhaps some parishioners were attracted to Puritanism because the low-church style of Puritan worship resembled their own worship far more than did high-church Anglicanism under Laud. Only when Puritans came to power after the Civil Wars and the full implications of their moral discipline became clear did villagers abandon Puritanism, either turning to more radical sects or returning to orthodox Anglican worship.

Yet if there were similarities with Puritanism they were mostly superficial ones. Whereas the Puritan attack on Anglican rituals grew out of a dislike of forms of worship which were not sanctioned by Scripture, village worship reflected both the simplicity and economic interests of parishioners. Villagers failed to respect holy days, not because they were unscriptural, but because they could not afford to observe them. Furthermore, as we have seen, they apparently rejected the doctrine of predestination, preferring to believe that they had free will even if it was only the power to damn themselves.

Although village Anglicans may have been confused about doctrine, the Prayer Book mattered to them. They worshipped as they had learned to worship, not only from family and neighbours, but also from their frequent hearing of the liturgy as it was read to them in church, week after week, year after year. The influence of the liturgy on their beliefs can be seen as one of the successes of its translation into the vernacular during the Reformation. It was not a complete success, of course, for they did not understand everything read to them. Like Menocchio, the sixteenth-century Italian miller of Carlo Ginzburg's *The Cheese and the Worms*, they reinterpreted what they heard, sometimes changing its meaning almost beyond recognition or taking it to extremes.[81] The frequent repetition of the Anglican liturgy created a strong sense of religious tradition, so that the replacement of the Book of Common Prayer by the Directory for Public Worship in 1645 must have come as quite a shock to villagers. No wonder that many continued to support the Prayer Book and welcomed its return in 1660.[82]

The most significant conclusion we can draw is that many villagers were independent-minded in their religious views. By their 'occasional conformity' they demonstrated that they were not simply passive conformists, sitting in church because they were obliged to. They thought about what they heard, and if they did not always understand it this was not their fault. These independent villagers could make life very uncomfortable for ministers like the rector of Somerford Magna. Their activity suggests that Restoration Anglicanism had a vibrancy which has not previously been suspected.

Acknowledgement

The author and publishers would like to thank Cambridge University Press for their permission to use this chapter, which will also be published in *Parsons and Parishioners in Restoration Wiltshire*, Cambridge University Press, as part of their series Studies in Early Modern British History.

Notes and references

1   Earlier versions of this article were presented at seminars at the University of Exeter and Cambridge University. I am grateful for comments I received on these occasions, and for suggestions from Sue Wright, Jonathan Barry, and David Bond. Unless otherwise stated, all manuscript sources are from the Wiltshire Record Office. The references use the following system of abbreviations for records of the Bishop of Salisbury: BABI=Act Books, Instance (vol.); BCP= Churchwardens' Presentments (year); BCit=Citations (bundle); BMCP=Miscellaneous Court Papers (bundle); BSD=Deposition Books (vol.). Also, DSCP=Dean of Salisbury, Churchwardens' Presentments (year).

2   BCit 17 (20 Oct. 1672, 10 June 1673, 18 July 1673); BMCP 39 (15 Sept. 1673 and n.d.).

3   Throughout this article, I use the word 'Anglicanism' to describe the religion of members of the Church of England, as opposed to nonconformity and recusancy.

4   Exceptions include Norman Sykes, *Church and State in England in the Eighteenth Century* (1934); John Morrill, 'The Church in England, 1642–9', in John Morrill (ed.), *Reactions to the English Civil War* (1982), pp. 89–114; F. C. Mather, 'Georgian churchmanship reconsidered: some variations in Anglican public worship 1714– 1830', *Journal of Ecclesiastical History*, **36** (April 1985), pp. 255–83; Arthur Warne, *Church and Society in Eighteenth-Century Devon* (1969); and Eamon Duffy, 'The Godly and the Multitude in Stuart England', *Seventeenth Century*, **1** (Jan. 1986), pp. 31–55.

5   Margaret Spufford, *Contrasting Communities: English Villagers in the Sixteenth and Seventeenth Centuries* (1974), p. 319.

6   Patrick Collinson, *The Religion of Protestants: The Church in English Society 1559–1625* (1982), p. 192.

7   Keith Thomas, *Religion and the Decline of Magic* (1971); Jean Delumeau, *Catholicism Between Luther and Voltaire* (1977), esp. pp. 161–74; Keith Wrightson, *English Society, 1580–1680* (1982), ch. 7; Barry Reay, 'Popular religion', in Barry Reay (ed.), *Popular Culture in Seventeenth-Century England* (1985), pp. 91–128.

8   For an exception, see R. W. Scribner, 'Ritual and popular religion in Catholic Germany at the time of the Reformation', *Journal of Ecclesiastical History*, **35** (Jan. 1984), pp. 47–77.

9   Reay, p. 94.

10   BCP, 1668, Cricklade and Marlborough deaneries, f. 4c.

11   This figure does not include tithe cases, which affected at least half of Wiltshire parishes in this period. BABI 55–63 (1661–92) and Exchequer Bill Books, Public Record Office, IND 16829–37 (1660– 1714).

12 I am currently preparing a book for publication using these sources, *Parsons and Parishioners in Restoration Wiltshire*.

13 David E. Underdown, *Revel, Riot, and Rebellion: Popular Politics and Culture in England, 1603–1660* (1985). For evidence of the high correlation between pastoral farming, cloth-making, and nonconformity in late seventeenth-century Wiltshire, see Donald A. Spaeth, 'Parsons and parishioners: lay-clerical conflict and popular piety in Wiltshire villages, 1660–1740', (unpublished Ph.D. thesis, Brown University, 1985), ch. 7.

14 BCit 17 (20 Oct. 1672, 10 June 1673, 18 July 1673).

15 Based on examination of conventicle returns (1669), licenses for meeting houses and preachers (1672), and certificates of dissenters' places of worship after Toleration. G. Lyon Turner (ed.), *Original Records of Early Nonconformity* (1911), vol. 1, pp. 106–27; *Calendar of State Papers, Domestic Series*, 1671–2, 1672; and Quarter Sessions, Certificates of Dissenters' Places of Worship, 1695–1745. The Compton Census figures for Somerford Magna are taken from Anne Whiteman (ed.), *The Compton Census of 1676: A Critical Edition* (British Academy Records of Social and Economic History, n.s. 10, 1986), p. 129.

16 BMCP 39 (15 Sept. 1673 and n.d.).

17 BMCP 39 (15 Sept. 1673 and n.d.).

18 BSD 58, ff. 26v–8v, 62–3 (1663/4–1666). See Spaeth, ch. 6, for other examples of nonconformist harassment of clerics.

19 See, for example, Dean of Salisbury, Visitation Book, 1670–3, f. 10c; Spaeth, pp. 132–7.

20 BCit 17 (6 Oct. 1673).

21 BABI 58, ff. 7, 23v; BABI 59, f. 37v; BSD 61, ff. 260v–255v, 84v–7, 88–9.

22 BMCP 39 (n.d.).

23 BMCP 39 (n.d.).

24 BCit 17 (10 June 1673).

25 BCit 17 (6 Oct. 1673). Despite the rector's rage, gentle treatment of non-communicants appears to have been common. See J. A. Vage, 'Ecclesiastical discipline in the early seventeenth century: some findings and some problems from the archdeaconry of Cornwall', *Journal for the Society of Archivists*, **7** (Oct. 1982), pp. 93–6, table 2. I am obliged to Anne Duffin for bringing this article to my attention.

26 BCit 17 (6 Oct. 1673, 29 Nov. 1673).

27 BCit 17 (30 Nov. 1673, 30 Dec. 1673, 11 Jan. 1673/4).

28 BCit 17 (6 Oct. 1673, 29 Oct. 1673); BCP, 1674, Malmesbury deanery; BABI 59, f. 37v.

29 Bishop of Salisbury, Subscription Books, 3 (1665/6–1680), 11 Sept. 1674; Bishops' Register, D1/2/23, f. 4v (5 April 1676).

30 *Book of Common Prayer* (1662).

31   BCP, 1674, Amesbury and Chalke deaneries (Compton Chamber-layne); Dean of Salisbury, Visitation Papers, Letters, 3 Oct. 1669 (Calne). For evidence of a similar connection between the resolution of legal disputes and the ability to take communion, see David Warren Sabean, *Power in the Blood: Popular Culture and Village Discourse in early modern Germany* (1984), pp. 37–60, esp. 47–51.

32   BSD 62, ff. 2v–3 (*c.* 1668).

33   DSCP, 1668, f. 11; 1669, f. 41.

34   Thus Bishop Henchman asked in 1662 whether any refused to receive communion from the minister, 'taking exception against him'. 'Articles to be Enquired of in the Diocese of Salisbury . . . 1662', House of Commons, *Parliamentary Papers*, 1867–8, vol. 38, pp. 610–13, title 6, query 5.

35   Based on figures given in Peter Laslett, *The World We Have Lost*, 2nd edn (New York, 1971), p. 74; Peter Laslett and John Harrison, 'Clayworth and Cogenhoe', in H. E. Bell and R. L. Ollard, (eds), *Historical Essays, 1600–1750, Presented to David Ogg* (1963), pp. 162–71; and Jeremy Boulton, 'The limits of formal religion: the administration of holy communion in late Elizabethan and early Stuart England', *London Journal*, **19** (Winter 1984), pp. 145–6. The figures for Clayworth and Cogenhoe were peaks and should be compared with 50 per cent communions in Cogenhoe in 1612 and in Clayworth in the 1690s.

36   'Articles . . . 1662', title 10, query 10; George Herbert, 'A Priest to the Temple, or the Country Parson his Character, &c' (1632), in F. E. Hutchinson (ed.), *Works* (1941), p. 259. For a more detailed discussion, see Boulton, p. 138.

37   See, for example, Grittleton, Churchwardens' Accounts, 1677–1799 (WRO 1629/17). Churchwardens' accounts rarely make it clear whether communion was given just on Easter Day or also on Palm Sunday or Good Friday.

38   Pewsey, General Entry Book, 1608–1855 (WRO 493/49). The adult population figure is taken from BCP, 1668, Cricklade and Marl-borough deaneries, f. 5d.

39   BCP, 1668, Cricklade & Marlborough deaneries, f. 5b (Pewsey); Donhead St Andrew, Tithe Survey, 1742 (WRO 1732/15); DSCP, 1669, f. 36 (Wokingham).

40   BSD 61, ff. 61, 77.

41   BCP, 1668, Chalke and Amesbury deaneries, f. 3; WRO 493/49.

42   Based on the examination of several sets of churchwardens' accounts, including those for Grittleton, 1672–83 (WRO 1620/17), Calstone Wellington, 1716–30 (807/18), and Alton Barnes, 1677–84 (496/1).

43   See, for example, Chicklade, BCP, 1716, Amesbury and Chalk deaneries.

44   Laslett and Harrison, pp. 162–71.

45   Turner, p. 125.

46   Based on the sources cited in note 15; BCP, 1668, Cricklade & Marlborough deaneries, f. 4c; and Whiteman, p. 127. Pewsey's minister from 1646 to 1662 was Humphrey Chambers. A. G. Matthews, *Calamy Revised*, (1934), p. 107.

47   BCP, 1683, Wilton and Wylye deaneries.

48   BCP, 1674, Avebury and Potterne deaneries.

49   Lambeth Palace Library, MS 633/9.

50   Mary Ransome (ed.), *Wiltshire Returns to the Bishop's Visitation Queries of 1783* (Wiltshire Record Society 27, 1971), p. 238.

51   The quotations in this and subsequent paragraphs are taken from the communion service in the *Book of Common Prayer*, (1662).

52   Mary Clapinson, (ed.), *Bishop Fell and Nonconformity: Visitation Documents from the Oxford Diocese, 1682–83*, (Oxfordshire Record Society 52, 1980), pp. 7–8. I am grateful to Sue Wright for bringing this to my attention.

53   BABI 57, ff. 141–141v (1681).

54   The extent to which the Calvinist doctrine of predestination was accepted by the Church of England under Elizabeth and James I is currently the subject of a debate. See Peter White, 'The Rise of Arminianism Reconsidered', *Past and Present*, **101** (Nov. 1983), pp. 33–54; P. G. Lake, 'Calvinism and the English Church 1570–1635', *Past and Present*, **114** (Feb. 1987), pp. 32–76.

55   DSCP, 1670.

56   For examples of other excuses, see Alton Pancras, DSCP, 1676; Winterbourne Bassett, BCit 41 (clothes unfit for divine service); Pewsey, WRO 493/49. For Pewsey, the leading parishioners are defined as those who were in the top quartile of ratepayers in 1710 or served as churchwardens or overseers for the poor in 1700–10, the poor as those on a list of alms recipients in 1705.

57   For confirmatory evidence, see Mather, p. 273, esp. n. 89.

58   Stephen A. Ozment argues that popular anxiety about freedom from sin was one of the causes of the Reformation. *The Reformation in the Cities: The Appeal of Protestantism to Sixteenth-Century Germany and Switzerland* (1975).

59   The Book of Common Prayer of 1662 listed thirty feast and holy days and three solemn days on which service would be read twice, plus sixteen eves of holy days on which service might also be read. Another nine holy days fell on Sundays.

60   Namely the Act of Uniformity, *Statutes of the Realm*, 1 Elizabeth c. 2.

61   Prosecutions of such offenders were numerous. For examples, see Calne, DSCP, 1676 and 1685 (tippling); Collingbourne Kingston, BCP, 1708, Cricklade and Marlborough deaneries (youths playing games).

62   BCP, 1686, Avebury and Potterne deaneries, f. 20.

63 BCP, 1668, Cricklade and Marlborough deaneries, ff. 4c–4d.

64 South Marston, DSCP, 1671, f. 12.

65 Bishop of Salisbury, Faculties, Various Petitions, 1747. For a similar report from Oxfordshire, see Clapinson, pp. 8–9.

66 Edward Cardwell, *Documentary Annals of the Reformed Church of England . . . from the year 1546 to the year 1716*, 2 vols. (1844), vol. 1, pp. 15–16, 24.

67 *Statutes of the Realm*, 27 Charles II c. 7.

68 BSD 61, f. 77; BSD, Bundle 1 (1708).

69 Wrightson, p. 213.

70 BCP, 1689, Amesbury and Chalke deaneries.

71 J. Gordon Davies, 'The 1662 Book of Common Prayer: its virtues and vices', *Studia Liturgica*, **1** (Sept. 1962), p. 173, cited in Horton Davies, *Worship and Theology in England*, vol. II, *From Andrewes to Baxter, 1603–1690* (Princeton, 1975), p. 388.

72 BCit 43 (n.d.) (Hilperton); BCP, 1668, Cricklade and Marlborough deaneries, ff. 5b, 5d (Pewsey); BCP, 1674, Wilton and Wylye deaneries, f. 27 (Codford).

73 DSCP, 1692, f. 31.

74 BCP, 1668, Chalke and Amesbury deaneries (West Grimstead); DSCP, 1668, f. 16 (West Harnham).

75 BCP, 1689, Chalke and Amesbury deaneries.

76 Bishop of Salisbury, Diocese Books, 1680 and 1683.

77 BCP, 1662, Amesbury and Chalke deaneries, f. 22.

78 BCP, Wilton and Wylye deaneries, ff. 39b, 41b (Downton); DSCP, 1668, f. 16 (West Harnham).

79 BMCP 39 (n.d.) (Somerford); BCP, 1668, Cricklade and Marlborough deaneries, ff. 5b (Pewsey), 4 (Cricklade).

80 Spaeth, ch. 6.

81 Carlo Ginzburg, *The Cheese and the Worms*, trans. John Tedeschi and Anne Tedeschi (1980), *passim*.

82 Morrill, pp. 104–14.

6 The parish in civic life: Bristol and its churches 1640–1750

Jonathan Barry

Little historical attention has been paid to the significance of the parish in English towns after 1640 until the decades when rapid urban growth demanded a restructuring of the whole parochial system. But the period between the collapse of the Laudian Church and the growth of industrial cities saw a major challenge to the assumptions and structures which had made the parish church the centre of religious experience and loyalty for most English people before 1640. The emergence of nonconformity and subsequently of Toleration, which effectively allowed non-attendance at church, struck at the foundations of parochial life.[1] The aim of this essay is to examine the impact of this change on the role of the parish in the life of one city and its individual citizens. How far did the aspirations towards religious unity, which the parish had represented, continue to be an important consideration in urban life, and was the parish now seen as a help or a hindrance in establishing such unity?

No single town can be regarded as an ideal case-study in trying to answer such a question. The medieval inheritance of parishes varied from town to town, as did the presence and power of cathedrals, the strength and character of nonconformity, and the rate of urban growth. The best argument for studying Bristol is that it was a city where both the parish structure and noncon-formity were strong, and which experienced considerable growth after 1640, without the spectacular expansion of some of the new towns.

How viable was the parish structure in Bristol during this period? The answer must be ambiguous. Bristol had eighteen parishes to cater for a population rising from 15,000 or so in 1640 to just over 20,000 in 1700 and 40,000 by 1750. Had the population been spread evenly across these parishes then the numbers, though growing large, would not have been unmanageable. But there was a clustering of small parishes around the city centre. Repeated plans to rationalize these arrangements only bore fruit when two were absorbed into larger parishes in the later eighteenth century.[2] Several formerly rural parishes outside the city began to become populous and some of the suburban parishes within the city also grew far too large for effective parochial organization. During the eighteenth century a number of the churches were extended or rebuilt, but these were often inner city churches, not those most in need.[3] By the 1750s the parishioners of St Michael's wished to rebuild their church, which could hold only 550 people from a population of 2000. Although 200 dissenters would not attend, and another 500 were considered to have a good excuse to miss the Sunday service, that left 750 souls uncatered for, who were liable to use the argument that the church was full to 'stay at home or wander to other parishes'.[4] Another anomaly was created by building over the Castle site after 1655, as the area remained extra-parochial. Thereafter its inhabitants, who claimed the right to attend any parish church, became notorious for non-attendance or nonconformity.[5]

Most Bristolians throughout our period lived close to a parish church, but the ties between neighbourhood and church were weakening. There seems to be a correlation between unusually large, suburban parishes and strong nonconformity in the eighteenth century, particularly in St James and Ss Philip and Jacob, although nonconformity was also strong in several artisan parishes nearer the city centre and south of the river.[6] Social composition may be a more important variable than parish size alone, as the city centre remained the area of greatest wealth, and parts of the suburbs were relatively poor.[7] It may be significant that the expanding but fashionable suburb of St Augustine's seems to have become *less* prone to nonconformity over time. St Augustine's, however, also contained the cathedral and the civic chapel of St Mark's, so it was hardly typical.[8] It contrasts sharply with St James, where most of the nonconformist meeting-places were built, and where dissenting chapels may have seemed to offer the most convenient local place of worship.

Mention of the cathedral and civic chapel should remind us that the parish system did not exist in a vacuum. The most prestigious civic occasions were celebrated in these two buildings, facing each other on College Green. The Dean and Chapter and the city council, known as the corporation, appointed ministers to most of the parish livings, and between them they exerted great influence over the city's religious life.[9] Several factors, however, served to limit this influence and allow the parishes and parishioners a certain autonomy. The first was the ongoing rivalry between the corporation and the cathedral, expressed in disputes over jurisdiction and civic ceremony.[10] This served to weaken further the already precarious position of the episcopacy within the city. Created in 1542 using a former monastic church, the see was poorly endowed. The bishop held a divided responsibility over both Dorset and a small deanery comprising Bristol and its immediate hinterland. The bishopric was unpopular and most incumbents spent little time in Bristol, while many of the prebends were largely non-resident. Although there were periods, such as the 1680s and early eighteenth century, when the cathedral sought to be a force in Bristol's religious life, they were the exception.[11]

The corporation were undoubtedly the greater force. By the early seventeenth century they were actively involved in providing lectureships and overseeing the religious life of the town, and they continued to support two weekly lectureships throughout our period, while claiming a right to veto other schemes of a similar kind.[12] As the JPs for the city the mayor and aldermen were key figures in the response to nonconformity, and even after 1688 they remained arbiters of religious controversy. In 1700, for example, when the ex-Quaker George Keith sought a public debate with his former Friends, the mayor was asked to chair the occasion.[13] Religion was so integral to civic life that the corporation were bound to take an interest. The civic calendar involved an intricate round of visits to the parish churches, as well as the celebration of the major public holidays with processions to church and sermons. Parish churches had tables on the walls listing the names of parishioners who had been mayors, and special seats were reserved for visiting councillors.[14] Similar patronage might be given by the guilds, particularly the Society of Merchant Venturers who met annually at St Stephen's. Sermons given before the corporation, guilds or other societies were quite often published, and these were clearly important patrons for the parish clergy.[15]

However, such civic patronage was outweighed by the role of

parishioners in determining the character of parish life. The minister depended heavily on his relationship with the vestry and his parishioners. Although they did not choose him, they were the paymasters who controlled his income, as well as church expenditure in general. As in other towns, tithes had all but disappeared as a means of support for the clergy, and the property or other fixed income attached to livings was generally very small. To make a decent living the clergy needed fees from performing services, together with voluntary contributions from the congregations. In addition to regular collections they could usually rely on money for preaching gift sermons, to commemorate particular occasions, while some vestries arranged regular subscriptions for extra lectures or prayers.[16] Such dependence ensured that Bristol's clergy were active in their parishes, or at least arranged for regular deputies.[17] Although the clergy of the city appear to have received a reasonable stipend, they depended heavily on voluntary public support. Repeated efforts were made by supporters of the clergy to remedy this. Some plans involved the merging of small parishes to create more viable units; others contemplated compulsory rating of citizens to provide an urban tithe. Both the corporation and the cathedral supported such plans, but at different times, and none of the schemes succeeded. The parishioners appear to have resisted the idea, and could play off the city and the church against each other to stop such proposals.[18]

This put pressure on the clergy to court popularity with their parishioners, or at least with the vestry. Like parts of London, Bristol had developed well before 1640 a system of select vestries, in which fifteen to thirty parishioners, usually the wealthier men, appointed all the parish officials and chose their own successors.[19] Disputes make clear the power vestrymen had to influence the lives of the minister, though only in one such case do we know that some of the ordinary inhabitants objected to the lack of general parish democracy. This case, in the parish of St Mary Redcliffe in 1725, uncovered several potential areas of conflict. Although the 1725 dispute was not overtly concerned with religion or politics, it becomes clear that in the past the vestry had been split between Whigs and Tories, especially around 1710–14, and that earlier nonconformists had been active in the vestry and made the minister's life very difficult. In 1725, however, the main issue appears to have been rivalry to become a vestryman caused by the power of the Redcliffe vestry, which was a major property-owner, in addition to controlling the grandest parish church in the country.[20]

As this example suggests, parish control brought power, both religious and secular. Vestries controlled the running of the churches. They also had major functions in local government, if not quite the same concentration of powers that might be found in a rural parish. The city was also divided into twelve wards, each under an alderman, and many issues were resolved through the wards and ward presentments. Before 1696 the most important task left to the parishes was poor relief, although even here they were subject to the aldermen as JPs, who intervened to distribute money away from the richer to the poverty-stricken parishes.[21] In 1696 a Corporation of the Poor was established which removed the care of the poor on the rates from the parishes. This was resisted strongly well into the eighteenth century, as we shall see.[22] But even when this function was removed, the parishes retained a considerable poor relief function through the funds which they controlled. The tables of charities which hung in parish churches were constantly requiring additional entries recording private bequests, while the new method of gift by subscription was taken up to support charity schools as well as church maintenance.[23]

The parishes, moreover, were important cultural and ideological centres in urban life. Despite their close contiguity in a crowded city, they strove to retain their separate identities through special saints' days and through perambulations on rogation day. Most parishes held the latter every two or three years, taking the children round to check the boundaries, with cakes and ale to refresh the participants.[24] Civic ritual depended heavily on the parishes and reinforced their significance. Parishioners were expected to ring their bells and decorate their towers on public holidays. As we have seen, the corporation, guilds and societies, even if they had their own headquarters, still used the parish churches for public gatherings. Although subordinate to the history of the city as a whole, the separate histories and traditions of the parishes were an important ingredient in the understanding of the town's heritage, just as the churches were the most notable buildings within the city, at least until the new classical building of the eighteenth century. Even then, the churches were soon rebuilt or renewed to retain their impressiveness. Visitors to the city were quick to comment on the splendour of the churches (though they found the cathedral disappointing) and the excellent order in which they were maintained.[25]

Despite these indications that the parishes played an important part in Bristol life, it is difficult to document their importance to the individual citizen. Until the mid eighteenth century we have few personal documents, such as diaries or autobiographies, to show how people felt about the parish. Indirect evidence, however, suggests that by 1640 the parishes already had two main problems to face in their attempt to provide an ordered setting for the religious experience of the community: pietism and indifference. The rationale behind the parish was the belief that religion was indivisible from the life of the community. The individual's religious growth depended on the support of household, neighbourhood and government, which in turn depended on religious uniformity. This could best be ensured through a parish church and its minister, offering a regular framework, both in space and time, to meet the religious needs of the average parishioner. The ideological tensions associated with the Reformation, and the socio-economic pressures which had increased the secular role of the parish, had encouraged an emphasis on the parish to the neglect of alternative religious institutions. In some respects this development seemed particularly necessary in towns, where the danger that society might fragment, in the face of social inequality, anonymity and indiscipline, brought a particular emphasis on institutions which might reinforce communal solidarity and order. But in other respects the complexity and variety of town life militated against a parochial monopoly of religious experience. Some people would wish to enjoy a broader religious diet than one parish could provide, while others would evade parish life altogether.

The initial problem does not seem to have been absenteeism, although it is plausible to suggest that the poor were never assiduous attenders, and that churchwardens never really hoped to enforce their attendance. The able-bodied adult poor, however, were a minority in a town where most householders were freemen. Meanwhile almshouses and charities helped the aged and the orphaned, but made this conditional on religious worship.[26] In 1642–3 two Anglican ministers, discussing the collapse of church authority at the onset of Civil War, were worried not by non-attendance, but by the character of the relationship between the parish clergy and their parishioners. Like many later commentators they emphasized the crucial role of the minister. He had to set a good example and hold his flock together. But this was not easy, largely because of the attitude of the congregation. The laity were ever-eager to criticize their clergy, and lacking in true respect for the church's observances. They talked through the sermons or played with their children. Their participation in church was perfunctory, except when the minister's message was new and controversial. The parish clergy were, they claimed, under pressure to play up to this 'itch' for novelty by using their sermons to question authority, in Church and state. If they did not do so, their flock would leave them for other parish ministers, or to attend 'strangers', that is itinerant clergymen or even lay preachers.[27]

When these complaints were being expressed Bristol was experiencing for the first time a serious nonconformist challenge to Anglicanism. There is very little sign of separatism within the city before 1640, although we know of 'godly' groups collecting to hear lectures and discuss sermons, and one such group was gradually moving towards independency.[28] It is not possible here to describe all the complex changes in nonconformity in the next two decades, but a number of points are of relevance to our parish theme. In the first place it is clear, as Collinson has emphasized, that 'the godly' were seeking less to supplant than to supplement the parochial system.[29] Provided they found sympathetic ministers, the emerging Baptist and Congregational churches, as well as Presbyterians of course, were generally prepared to exploit the parish system. The Baptists still took the sacrament from ordained parish ministers, while also having their own preacher, who was happy to hold a corporation post as a city lecturer.[30]

There were certainly signs of greater hostility to an Established Church. In the years before 1640 Laudian innovations had made many suspicious of the liturgy and the notion of the church as a sacred space. Meeting in private houses or refusing to celebrate holidays became a symbol that the godly would not accept such a demarcation of 'the sacred'. This tradition continued to have some appeal within the sects, and particularly among those who broke off to form the earliest Quaker movement.[31] But most of the godly did not wish to break so firmly with established forms of worship. There was also strong public hostility to those who challenged the Church. The separatists before 1640 had been attacked for meeting in 'a church with a chimney' and for not celebrating holidays, and the Quakers attracted deep hostility after 1654.[32] The Presbyterians before 1660, and the Anglicans thereafter, could reinforce their general arguments for a national Church with specific appeals to the notion of civic unity. They portrayed sectarianism as a breaking of unity and brotherhood within the city, and associated it whenever possible with the baneful influence of outsiders. The fault lay with itinerant preachers, who were either self-seeking mountebanks or, even worse, emissaries of Rome and the Devil, come to sow discord among Protestants.[33]

Although such criticisms were levelled at various sects, it was the Quakers who seemed the ultimate and most dangerous expression of this tendency, which helps to explain the hysterical reaction they provoked. The clamour for the punishment of James Naylor, after his blasphemous ride into Bristol on a donkey, had a local as well as a national dimension. To outraged Bristolians, Naylor, whose ride parodied the conventions of civic ceremony as well as of Palm Sunday, had to be punished to vindicate Bristol's honour.[34] Whether Naylor acted deliberately or not, however, his gesture was only one of many symbolic protests by which the Quakers threw down a public challenge to the city of Bristol to decide between salvation and destruction. They combined the frequent disruption of church services and the rejection of civic ceremony and public holidays, with extravagant 'warnings' to the city to repent, such as processing in sackcloth and ashes to the High Cross. The Quakers also attracted massive numbers of citizens to public meetings in the open spaces of the city or nearby fields, employing revivalists techniques to stir the hearts of all classes.[35] After the Naylor affair, however, the Quakers began to adopt the quietist tradition of the later sect. Many of their permanent converts came from the pre-existing churches, including a fair number of well-established merchants and traders.[36]

In the first two decades of nonconformity I believe we can already discern the characteristic features of the dissenting churches and their relationship to the parish, which can be traced, with obvious modifications, in the subsequent century. Despite the prominence of a separatist, evangelical wing of dissent, most of those attracted to nonconformity were 'pietists', who wished to supplement the kind of low-key religiosity which the established parish round could offer with a more strenuous form of religion, and with a more vital union of 'the godly'. An obvious parallel can be drawn with the pre-Reformation guilds, but in the political circumstances after 1660 such pietism was often forced outside the Established Church. Because separate churches became established, and history has been written from such denominational perspectives, especially those of the ministers, it has been assumed that such divisions were intended and inevitable, and that they shaped the religious experience of the laity. This may be a mistaken view.

For one thing, as John Triffitt shows in his essay, nonconformist churches, like parishes, contained members with varying levels of commitment. An inner core, rather like a vestry, tended to run affairs, while there was a broader membership in communion but not so active. Many of these were women, who appear to predominate in several sects and may have found a greater opportunity for involvement than in the Church of England, though usually still subordinate to men. But beyond this membership there was the broader range of 'hearers', who attended more or less regularly but lacked the full commitment. It seems likely that many of these remained Anglicans, nominally at least, and occasionally conformed. We know that the Presbyterians, in particular, practised occasional conformity, and also participated in parish affairs, getting elected on to vestries and the like.[37]

To many Anglicans this was a hypocritical attempt to retain the advantages of Anglican membership, because nonconformists were exluded from offices of all kinds. Perhaps it was, but it was also an expression of ecumenism, and a protest by these Protestant dissenters against being ejected from the national church and their particular parish against their will. From the viewpoint of the layman, moreover, the difference between the various churches may not have seemed great. No great doctrinal divides distinguished the churches, except the Quakers, until the arrival of Unitarianism, which itself split all the churches into various factions. The Calvinist/Arminian divide is notoriously hard to translate into denominational terms, and most groups established some working compromise. For the laity such doctrinal complexities probably mattered little. Most churches offered the layman a similar mixture of regular preaching, a fairly simple form of service, and infrequent communions, perhaps every one or two months.[38] The difference between the churches was primarily one of style, and spiritual autobiographies suggest that the young frequently tried out various churches before settling on one which suited their mood.[39] These personal accounts tend to come from those who found a secure identity in one church; many others must have shared in the search with a less definite destination.

Competition for hearers, however, made all the churches very concerned with education and the maintainance of a core of members through the influence of family and patronage. This encouraged each church to become a separate community, reproducing in miniature the parochial model of unity. Baptists, Quakers and, to a lesser extent, Presbyterians offered their poorer members relief and education, while they all sought to control the morals of their congregation.[40]

Many parallels existed, therefore, both in conditions and varying levels of commitment, between parish and sect membership after 1660. In another way also the divergence between the two was lessening. Before 1640 the puritan form of pietism was to a considerable extent defined by dissatisfaction with the 'Popish' elements in the Church of England. But after 1660, as Protestantism divided on issues of worship and discipline, pietists began to emphasize inner spirituality as the essence of true godliness. Concern with morality, or good works, was combined with a strong mystical tendency. This trend in religiosity can be observed across a broad spectrum from the Quakers through Latitudinarianism to the High Church Anglicanism of William Law. Such pietism displayed less concern with external details of worship than with their proper use to further devotion.

Such priorities fostered an ecumenical attitude towards the varying practices of different churches. If we look at the religious activity of a pietist such as the accountant William Dyer and his friends in the mid eighteenth century, we find a frenzied search for pious activity with little discrimination between denominations. In an average week Dyer might attend services in his parish church of Redcliffe, other Anglican churches and the cathedral, as well as early morning Methodist gatherings and an evening gathering led by an independent preacher. One of the Dyer's best friends was the rector of St Werburgh's, Richard Symes, who was active among a group of Anglican clergymen who sought close ties with evangelically inclined dissenting ministers.[41] Underlying such activity was a very strong sense that the religious needed to unite against the dangers of unbelief and ungodliness, and that the real distinction in religion was between the children of God and those of the Devil, not between churches.[42]

Pietism of this kind did not directly challenge parochial forms of worship. These people were often devoted and active members of their parish, eager to participate in the sacrament. They did not challenge the authority of the minister, and some of the clergy sympathized with their search for religious unity and a more vital religion. But the restless search for extra religious experience was, at least implicitly, a challenge to the assumption that the parish and its minister could satisfy all legitimate religious needs. These issues came to a head with Methodism.

It must be stressed that the Methodist movement was not initially a denominational one, intended to establish a separate church. Rather its Anglican leaders, whose English mission started and flourished in Bristol, sought to appeal across church boundaries to the pious of every denomination. They were very careful not to take converts away from the existing churches. Meetings were always timed and envisaged as supplementary to ordinary church services, and their members urged to be exemplary in their performance of church functions. The Methodists sought to cultivate ties with influential lay and clerical members of every group, Quakers, Baptists, Congregationalists, Presbyterians, low and High Church, often with considerable success. In Bristol, at least, a working partnership gradually developed, helped by the fact that many young Methodist preachers became Anglican or nonconformist clergymen when they settled down after a period of itinerancy. Bristol was a centre of resistance to the establishment of a separate Methodist church in the 1790s.[43]

Naturally not all Anglicans viewed the Methodists as allies. The Wesleys and Whitefield record the hostility they met from many of the clergy and the Church hierarchy. As with the nonconformists a century before, they were hounded out of many parish churches by those who viewed their activities as dangerous. They were portrayed as breakers of unity, subverting the ties of family and neighbourhood in pursuit of a godly perfection which, it was often suggested, must be a cover for faction, treachery or immorality. Methodism was brought by outsiders, itinerant tricksters or subversives, who were associated with Jacobitism, popery or the Devil. They represented a return to enthusiam, threatening to overturn the order and harmony of city life. Like the Quakers before, therefore, they were legitimate targets for mob hostility, and for harassment by church and civic authorities.[44]

The danger that they posed to parochial order, however, arose less from their appeal to the pious than from their evangelical efforts to reach the indifferent, seen most vividly in the revivalist mass meetings they held, complete with scenes of spiritual frenzy. During the late 1730s and early 1740s the Methodist leaders record in their journals frequent gatherings of many thousands in the poorer parts of the city and the countryside nearby. Combined with theatrical entrances to the city, accompanied by supporters, these ensured that a very public challenge was issued to Bristol to seek repentance. In common with earlier dissenters they embraced the role of prophets in the city, while repudiating civic holidays and ceremony except in times of fasting.[45] Like the development of itinerant preaching, the intention of all these forms of publicity was to ensure that their message reached all classes of society, in particular the poor. The content of that message, moreover, was of a kind which could tap the dramatic imagery of popular religiosity. Whether Calvinist or Arminian, the evangelical preached a message of sudden conversion, of the struggle of God and Devil for the soul, which clearly struck deep chords in the psychology of the crowds.

This was a kind of preaching which had not been heard in the parishes for many years. Historians have rightly stressed how such religiosity had become discredited by its association with Civil War radicalism. But at a deeper level one can question, as Dean Tucker did at the time, whether the once-and-for-all message of evangelical conversion could ever be the standard fodder of parochial religion.[46] The latter was bound to emphasize steady practice of Christian virtues over intense changes of heart, and to emphasize the unity of the whole congregation over the deep division between the saved and the unregenerate. If popular indifference could only be overcome by such measures, then possibly the remedy was worse than the disease.

Even the Methodists had to face up to this dilemma, once the initial period of enthusiasm was over. After a massive early response, Methodist membership settled by the 1740s to a level of between 500 and 1000, at which it remained until late in the century. Most of these members were probably active before in other churches, and often remained so. Although not drawn from the elite of Bristol, most were from the trading, artisan and respectable working classes, again with a high female representation. Like other sects they came to stress the community of the godly, and their steady search for perfection. John Wesley also noted, and struggled against, a strong tendency towards mysticism and morality, characteristic of the introverted pietist, rather than the outgoing mood of the evangelical. This pietism shared many of the cultural presumptions of popular religiosity, in its biblical emphasis on God's providence and the struggle of good and evil spirits, but it was increasingly contained within the boundaries of respectable civic piety.[47]

In the opening section I sought to emphasize the continued, if limited, importance of the parish in civic life, while stressing that other institutions played a vital role in providing the religious dimension considered so necessary to urban life. In the second section I examined how various forms of extra-parochial activity, notably dissent, satisfied kinds of religious aspiration that the parish could not meet. In one sense they threatened the parochial monopoly, but the challenge was often unintentional and limited. Furthermore, the rival churches that emerged came to share many of the aspirations and characteristics of parochial life, as they settled into a routine This had a paradoxical effect. On the one hand the similarities, especially as experienced by the laity, encouraged weak denominational boundaries, and aspirations for unity among Protestants. On the other hand, *as* communities, both parishes and nonconformist churches aroused powerful feelings of loyalty. These became focused on their ministers, and on the political and social issues that were inseparable from religious divisions during this period. The rest of this essay will explore this final dimension.

An appropriate starting point is a book published in 1759 by Edward Goldney, a member of a leading Bristol Quaker family. He had been converted to Anglicanism, chiefly by the preaching of Bishop Secker and his 1737 visitation sermon on 'the unhappy divisions of the Church of England'. Goldney offered 'scriptural remedies for healing the divisions in the Church of England, particularly of those people called Methodists', and the main theme of the book was the 'dreadful reproach' that Christianity had been 'itself made the occasion for animosities and contentions'. As befits a former Quaker Goldney repudiated any suggestion of forcing uniformity against conscience, but he believed that the Anglican clergy and laity could recapture the people if they reformed themselves. The laity had to set a good example by moral behaviour, and by reverence at service time and in their treatment of the clergy. But the principal responsibility lay with the clergy. They had to be resident, evangelical and preach plain, simple doctrines to all classes, not 'showy, pompous sermons'. Divisions came because the careless and lukewarm clergy made a trade of the Church and neglected the spiritual message which was the necessary complement to its decency and order, important as such qualities were. The clergy also had to set an example of charity and morality for the laity to follow.[48]

Such trite sentiments hardly seem worth close analysis, yet I suspect that their very naivety catches precisely the general attitude of the time. Goldney's analysis bears a striking resemblance to that of the Anglican clergy in 1642–3, and to many later visitation sermons and other comments on religious division.[49] We have already seen how nonconformists were equally convinced that churches were judged by the lives of their adherents. The 'decency and order' of services was naturally a theme of particular appeal to the Church of England. From the late seventeenth century it is clear that Anglicans began to devote much effort and money into improving the standard of furnishings and services. Edward Colston was only the most lavish of many benefactors to this cause.[50] It is tempting to see the Church reaping the benefits of this in the apparent decline of dissent during the mid eighteenth century. Reports to the bishops in 1736, 1764–6 and 1784 suggest a confident Anglicanism, despite the evident problems in adjusting to population growth discussed above.[51]

The key, however, was seen to lie in the hands of the clergy. Recent historical work has emphasized how the Reformation, far from degrading the role of the priesthood as once thought, led to a great emphasis on the professional training and position of the minister, above all as a preacher.[52] We have already seen how dependent, financially and organizationally, the minister was on his laity. But this does not mean that the minister did not wield considerable authority. Several visitors to Bristol noted the respect paid to the clergy, in their distinctive clerical dress, and one visitor in 1735 even accused them of tyrannizing the citizens, a point which Chatterton later echoed.[53] The chief instrument of any such tyranny must have been the sermon. The visitor in 1735 claimed Bristolians were as fond of sermons 'as Presbyterians'.[59] The rich diet already available was continuously expanded by new bequests and subscriptions, and the printing of sermons was the mainstay of local publishing. The dissenting churches were equally concerned to raise funds to maintain a preaching ministry. One of the reasons why both Anglicanism and nonconformity were so strong in towns was that towns attracted ambitious clergymen, and offered teaching, medical or other positions to help congregations hold a well-educated ministry. Only the Quakers rejected outright the notion of a professional preaching ministry, and even they developed an unofficial preaching elite. References to the panic felt by ordinary Quakers at first testifying in public (an activity only imaginable when sustained by the Holy Spirit), suggest why most laypeople took for granted the need for an intelligentsia to interpret the Word and to speak to them and for them.[55]

The relationship between the minister and the parish, however, was problematic. Parishioners often had inordinate intellectual, moral or social expectations of the ministers. Visitation sermons alternate between urging the clergy to live up to such standards and pleading with the laity to tolerate human failings in their pastors. Moral lapses or an insufficiently genteel life-style by the clergy would expose the Church to contempt.[56] So sensitive was the matter that the Anglicans established in 1692 a Society of the Clergy and Sons of the Clergy to ensure that aged clerics and their relations did not fall into poverty, and that their children could find respectable callings.[57] But if the minister had to be an educated gentleman, would he be an effective communicator with all his flock? This problem came to the fore when a liberally educated clergy began to question Trinitarian doctrines.[58] Too sophisticated a theology, then as now, might arouse popular hostility, but how could a minister satisfy a congregation running the social gamut from merchants and professionals aware of new ideas, through to the humblest poor? The evangelically inclined Dr Stonhouse, who combined a city lectureship with a country living, distinguished very clearly between the simple rural audience and the sophisticated urban audience. He was all too aware that the latter expected intellectual entertainment as well as spiritual nourishment. His solution, possibly copied by many good ministers, was to emphasize the pastoral role of the minister as a visitor of the sick, in order to reach the poor at a time and in a form where they would be receptive. In this respect the minister himself might welcome a series of alternative settings to the regular Sunday sermon, each of which would provide an occasion to preach a particular kind of doctrine to a particular kind of audience. Sermons on holidays, at society meetings or at assizes offered one kind of opportunity, but others were offered by the Lent lectures sponsored by Colston, by work with charity schools or hospitals or by visiting prisons or almshouses.[59]

Both the Anglican minister and his parishioners faced a dilemma when nonconformists refused to attend their services. Many believed that the nonconformists were being led astray by unscrupulous preachers or particular factions, and that the honest majority would be won back to the Church by experience of a good parochial ministry.[60] The notion of tolerating permanent divisions within a Christian community was very slow to develop. But some saw the answer in enforcement of uniformity, others in efforts to broaden the Church and persuade the moderate dissenters to return. Those emphasizing the need for uniformity could play on the deep sense of loyalty to the parish and its minister, viewing the nonconformists as schismatics.[61] Those stressing the need for comprehension could emphasize that the purpose of the parish was to articulate neighbourhood harmony, and that persecution could only destroy such sentiments. They stressed the common front among Protestant fellow-citizens against the alien threat of popery.[62] Both sides, in other words, deployed the language of community and unity, but to opposite ends.

As this deadlock developed, political parties emerged, which we label for convenience Whig and Tory. Although other issues were involved, these owed their main foundation to this disagreement about the best means to restore a united Church. The Tories sought to portray the Whigs as the party of dissenters, but, as Whigs insisted, they were a mainly Anglican party, though obviously attracting Presbyterian and other sectarian support.[63] Both sides were engaged in a bitter struggle in the decades up to and around 1700 for control of the parishes, as well as the other institutions of the town. This struggle could divide vestries and set ministers against vestries, as well as setting parishes against the corporation. After 1700 the parishes increasingly became strong-holds of Tory power, while the corporation was increasingly Whig, leaving the ministers an uneasy mixture of both parties according to the influence of patrons or congregation.[64]

Commenting on this position Arthur Bedford, Whig vicar of Temple church, claimed that, despite the Tory assertion that they were the 'church party', in fact both groups were 'state parties', neither fully representing the interest of the Church.[65] There seems to have been a rising sense in the eighteenth century that the party battle, once intended to defend the parish, now involved the exploitation of the parish, and the Church generally, for political ends. Such exploitation was almost inevitable. Not only were religious issues central to politics, but the parish, or the nonconformist church, formed a natural ideological and organizational centre in a city still possessing only a limited number of meeting-places and kinds of organization. Party campaigns exploited the use of church bells; ministers contributed with their sermons and by leading their parishioners to vote. The parishes formed a manageable basis on which parties could organize. Although the Tories established a city-wide Steadfast Society to co-ordinate their campaigns in the 1730s, this was merely an umbrella organization over a series of parish or 'independent societies', which retained considerable autonomy.[66] The Tories undoubtedly used their stronger presence in the parishes to counteract the Whig control over the corporation and hence, through the aldermen, over the wards. In addition to the ideological significance of holding positions of prestige, both sides also exploited the patronage which went with them, in particular over the poorer classes, who relied on charity or being granted an alehouse license.[67]

The position of the parish in Bristol became a controversial issue because the competing sides in this struggle for power sought to weaken or strengthen its position as best suited them. During the Interregnum a degree of parish autonomy suited the Congregationalists and Baptists, as well as closet Anglicans, and they united in opposition to the plans of the Presbyterian corporation to streamline the size and finance of the parishes under corporate control.[68] After 1660 both the corporation and the parishes were divided between tolerant and persecuting Anglicans, while Presbyterians and other sectarians still sought to participate in parish life. Not to do so would have been to risk greater persecution, and to relinquish a say in the secular affairs of the parish, such as poor relief, for which they were all paying rates.

The same confused position continued through the 1690s, but around 1700 various efforts were made to resolve the struggle by rendering the parish less central. The most important of these was the establishment of the Corporation of the Poor, removing responsibility from the vestries to a city-wide body with guardians elected by all rate-payers, regardless of denomination. The prime mover behind the scheme was the radical Whig John Cary, who probably hoped to set up a third, democratic force in city government independent of both parishes and the oligarchic corporation. In the event the corporation welcomed this chance to centralize power, while the parishes resisted. An act was passed, however, and the scheme began, although it was subject to bitter Tory criticisms as it developed. Exploiting the Tory parliaments of 1710–14 supporters of the parishes mounted a campaign against the Corporation of the Poor, in favour of parish responsibility, but they also tried to turn the organization into one dominated by Anglicans and supportive of the parishes, by making the church-wardens of each parish *ex officio* guardians for the year. When they got a sympathetic parliament, the Whigs attempted to reverse this, but only succeeded partially. Thereafter the Corporation of the Poor became an increasingly effective champion of the parishes in their attempts to resist further centralization in such matters as lighting and the watch.[69]

The Corporation of the Poor was intended not merely to administer poor relief but to discipline the poor through the threat and experience of work, to educate their children until apprentice-ship, and to care for the sick poor. All of these were functions which the parishes had performed in a haphazard fashion before 1696, and which the charities they administered continued to perform. But there were also several other experiments in organizing such activities, through voluntary societies. In 1699 a Society for the Reformation of Manners was established, which lasted until 1705, meeting regularly to discuss how city and parish officials and private citizens could best ensure that the laws on such moral issues as drunkenness, swearing and Sabbath observance were put into execution. After a successful start, however, support tailed off.[70] Arthur Bedford, an SPCK correspondent, encouraged the society to concentrate on the education of children as a way to promote better manners. Parishes were urged to mount subscrip-tions to pay teachers to take on the poor, and richer parishes to donate funds to poorer ones. This led to clashes with the Corporation of the Poor.[71] A few years after the society and its schemes lapsed, the emphasis on education was revived by a wave of charity school foundations, based again on subscriptions but encouraged by donations from the Tory philanthropist Edward Colston. Between 1708 and 1722 a variety of schools were started, mostly in the poorer, peripheral parishes, although more were planned than finally emerged. The impetus then slackened, although a few more did emerge in later decades.[72] Finally, in 1737, an infirmary was established, again by subscription, to care for patients, particularly the acutely ill and accident cases, who were ineligible for the Corporation of the Poor but could not afford private treatment. By the early 1760s this provided 132 hospital beds, as well as out-relief by infirmary apothecaries and nurses.[73]

The most significant common feature of these various schemes was that they relied on membership subscriptions rather than public funding. Each sought to attract subscribers from every religious and political persuasion, and all subscribers had a share in managing the activities. Thus they hoped to avoid the controversies inevitable when public funds or organizations were exploited for sectarian ends. More than that, some participants believed that these new forms of philanthropy would bring together the divided religious groups in a common Christian effort to help the poor, advance morality and provide an uncontentious religious education. The individual citizen would perform his religious duty and aid the community through this voluntary association, now that public bodies like the parish were divisive.[74]

In practice these hopes were often dashed. It was extremely hard to get members of different denominations to work together. Those within each church who welcomed such ecumenism came under pressure from others who feared the effects, especially in periods when political tensions ran high. These tensions helped to destroy the Society for the Reformation of Manners, and caused problems for the Infirmary, though mostly after 1750.[75] The charity school movement was always closely associated with the parishes and their ministers, and this, together with Colston's extreme Toryism, made it difficult for non-Anglican subscribers to believe that the schools would not function chiefly to win the poor to Anglicanism. in 1722 the Presbyterians retaliated by establishing their own charity school. Although they declared their school open to the children of all the poor of St James, Presbyterian children had priority.[76] The Quakers had never been prepared to give up the schooling and poor relief of their own members based on the workhouse they established in 1697.[77] The heavily religious element in primary education, and the bringing of schoolchildren to the services of the sponsoring church, made non-denominational education very unlikely. It was also an integral part of the image of any church as a community to offer such care for their poor members.

More practical considerations also favoured the churches over voluntary organizations. It was hard to maintain the funding and bureaucratic support for societies after initial enthusiasm, whereas churches had an established array of officials to deal with administrative matters. Bequests were much more readily left to churches, which donors believed would survive, than to societies with no officials who could act as trustees.[78] Subscription-raising events tended to require annual meetings, with sermons, processions and dinners, to maintain their popularity and civic notice. As we have seen, parishes formed a natural focus for such occasions. The infirmary, for example, held an annual service at St James' church, with a sermon by an Anglican minister. How the active Quaker committee members felt about this is not clear. They also tolerated an unofficial arrangement whereby an Anglican clergyman acted as chaplain, but they drew the line when it was proposed that this post should be funded by the subscriptions, causing a prolonged crisis in the early 1770s.[79] While religion was still an indispensable ingredient of public action in the town, the Church of England was bound to have an advantage which its adherents were tempted to exploit and its rivals to resent.

No simple formula can capture the position of the parish in urban life in the century after the Civil Wars, least of all one which contrasts Anglican parish loyalty with nonconformist separatism. There were still many pressures, both practical and ideological, encouraging an emphasis on the unity of the religious with the secular community. Both the city and the parish held a dual role, and some kind of church establishment to express this unity seemed desirable to most. But religious pluralism, and the political divisions this engendered, increasingly meant that the parish minister and parish administration became the focus of conflict, which seemed to threaten civic unity. This encouraged initiatives to bypass the parish in various areas of town life. These often expressed the conviction that true religion could only promote unity, not division. The chief threat to the parish in this period came not from religious indifference or social change, nor from the open opposition of sectarians or secularizers to this relic of religious uniformity. Rather they came from gradual adjustments in religious aspiration, as the parish ceased, once again, to be a credible single focus for communal religious solidarity, and a pluralistic system, reminiscent perhaps of the late Middle Ages, emerged.

Notes and references

1   The best introductions to this theme are G. V. Bennett, *The Tory Crisis in Church and State* (1975) and P. J. Corfield, *The Impact of Towns 1700–1800* (1982), pp. 138ff. But see also M. D. Watts, *The Dissenters* (1978); A. D. Gilbert, *Religion and Society in Industrial England* (1976); F. C. Mather, 'Georgian churchmanship reconsidered', *Journal of Ecclesiastical History*, **36** (1985); and Sykes, *Church and State*.

2   Estimates of parish population can be found in: A. Whiteman (ed.), *The Compton Census of 1676*, (British Academy Records of Social and Economic History, N.S. vol. 1, 1986), pp. 546–51; P. Clark (ed.), *The Transformation of English Provincial Towns* (1984), p. 153 (based on 1696 tax census); E. Ralph (ed.), 'Bishop Secker's Diocese Book' in *A Bristol Miscellany* (Bristol Record Society, vol. 37, 1985), pp. 21–69. For the two small parishes see W. Barrett, *The History and Antiquities of the City of Bristol* (1789), pp. 478–9, 506.

3   See C. W. Chalklin, 'Financing of church building in provincial towns of eighteenth-century England' in Clark, *Transformation*, pp. 284–310.

4   Bristol Central Library, Bristol Collection (hereafter BCL) 7952 f. 73.

5   Whiteman, p. 551; Ralph, p. 36; M. Caston, *Independency in Bristol* (1860), pp. 39–79.

6   Whiteman, p. 551; BAO EP/V/3 presentments, especially for 1670, 1674–85; Ralph, pp. 21–69; Barrett, p. 404.

7   J. Barry, 'The cultural life of Bristol, 1640–1775' (unpublished D.Phil thesis, University of Oxford, 1985), pp. 146–9; E. Baigent, 'Bristol society in the later eighteenth century' (unpublished D.Phil thesis, University of Oxford, 1985).

8   Whiteman, p. 551; Ralph, pp. 34–5; R. H. Quilici, 'Turmoil in a city and an empire: Bristol factions 1700–75' (unpublished Ph.D thesis, University of New Hampshire, 1976), pp. 38ff.

9   Barrett, pp. 128–9, 280; J. Latimer, *Annals of Bristol in the Seventeenth Century* (1900), p. 97.

10 Latimer, pp. 29–31, 84, 378–9, 389; Bodleian MSS Gough Somerset 2, f. 60; BAO Common Council Proceedings, Nov. 1739; *Felix Farley's Bristol Journal* (hereafter *FFBJ*), 10 Nov. 1759.

11 *HMC Fourth Report*, pp. 141–4; BL MSS Additional 5811.ff. 69, 97; T. Newton, *Works* (2 vols., 1782), vol. 1. pp. 96–7, 111.

12 Latimer, pp. 14, 23, 48, 66, 284, 425, 448; T. Thompson, *A Friendly Farewell* (1616), dedication and pp. 57–9; J. Chetwynd, *A Memorial for Magistrates* (1682), dedication.

13 G. Keith, *A Narrative of the Proceedings* (1700), pp. 27–30; B. Coole, *Honesty the Truest Policy* (1700), p. 97.

14 E. Fawcett and E. Ralph (eds), 'Mugleworth's Diary', *Transactions of Bristol and Gloucestershire Archaeological Society* (hereafter TBGAS), **61** (1939), pp. 246–70; Barry, pp. 309, 334–5.

15 Barry, pp. 77–9.

16 Ralph, *passim*; Barrett, pp. 130, 467–8, 478, 480, 486, 496, 501, 510, 525, 546, 560, 579, 589; *A Letter from the Vestry of St Mary Redcliffe* (1725), p. 6.

17 J. Gaskarth, *Sermon . . . at Primary Visitation* (1685), p. 24; BAO Temple Ka 4, f. 25; *Letters of the Reverend Job Orton and Sir John Stonhouse to the Reverend John Stedman* (2 vols, 1800), vol. 2, p. 41.

18 Latimer, pp. 75, 208, 221, 237, 273–4, 287, 378–9; Barrett, pp. 83, 130; BAO 04417 (1) under 30 Nov. 1656; BAO Temple E4, letters 1707–12; *An Apology for the Clergy of the City of Bristol* (1712); *Reasons offer'd to the Inhabitants of Bristol against a Tax* (1712); *A Letter from a Freeman of Bristol . . . in relation to the Clergy's Petition* (1712); Bodleian GA Glos B4a no. 858.

19 Quilici, pp. 43ff.; S. and B. Webb, *English Local Government Volume One: Parish and County* (1906), pp. 175, 182–3. For disputes in Temple parish see BAO EP/V/3 1705 and Temple Fa 1(1), 4–7, 9.

20 *A Letter from the Vestry*; J. Gibb, *An Account of the Minister's Conduct* (1725), pp. 4–5, 12–13; *A Letter to the Reverend Mr Gibb* (1725). Another minister in conflict with his parish was Thomas Godwyn: see his *Phanatical Tenderness* (1684), pp. 11–12 and *passim*.

21 The clearest introduction is in E. E. Butcher (ed.), *Bristol Corporation of the Poor* (Bristol Record Society, vol. 3, 1932).

22 See references in n. 69.

23 These comments are based on the churchwardens' accounts in BAO; Barrett, *passim*; T. J. Manchee (ed.), *Bristol Charities* (2 vols, 1831). See also nn. 71–2 below.

24 Barry, pp. 141–3, 309, 334–5; Fawcett and Ralph. For saints' days see, e.g., churchwardens' accounts kept by St Mary Redcliffe; *FFBJ* 10 May 1755, 6 June 1761, 30 May 1767, 2 June 1770. For perambulations: BAO 37541 end-pages; BCL 6494 f. 113; Bodleian MSS Gough Somerset 2, ff. 173–4; *Bristol Journal* 27 May 1775.

25 BL MSS Additional 5811, ff. 56, 91 and 15776, f. 92; *FFBJ* 12 Oct. 1754, 24 Jan. 1761; D. Defoe, *A Tour through . . . Great Britain* (2 vols, 1778 edn), vol. 2, pp. 246–7.

26 The 1675 presentment for Christchurch parish in BAO EP/V/3, after listing non-communicants and non-attenders by street, as well as

others who came to church but not communion or missed Easter communion, referred to some 'other very inconsiderable people which we thought fit purposely to omit by reason of their poverty'. For freemen see Barry, p. 316.

27 R. Towgood, *Disloyalty of Language Questioned and Censured* (1643), pp. 19–21, 43–5; R. Standfast, *Clero-Laicum Condimentum* (1644), *passim*, but especially p. 24.

28 Thompson, pp. 66–7; *HMC 4th*, pp. 141–4; R. Hayden (ed.), *Records of a Church of Christ in Bristol 1640–83* (Bristol Record Society, vol. 27, 1974), introduction and pp. 83–97; M. Stieg, *Laud's Laboratory* (Lewisburg, 1982), pp. 283–91; J. G. Fuller, *The Rise and Progress of Dissent in Bristol* (1840); Caston; J. Murch, *History of the Presbyterian and General Baptist Churches in the West of England* (1835).

29 P. Collinson, *The Religion of Protestants* (1982).

30 Hayden, pp. 99–103, 115–16; R. Purnell *et al.*, *The Church of Christ in Bristol* (1657), pp. 42–3, 63; R. Farmer, *Satan Inthroned in his Chair of Pestilence* (1657), pp. 45–7. A classic Bristol statement of ecumenism among the godly is R. Purnell, *Good Tydings for Sinners, Great Joy for Saints* (1652).

31 Hayden, pp. 85–6; Purnell *et al.*, pp. 3, 11; Farmer, pp. 47–8; *Rabshekah's Outrage Reproved* (1658).

32 Hayden, p. 86; Farmer, pp. 55–9; J. Besse, *A Collection of the Sufferings of the . . . Quakers* (2 vols, 1753), vol. 1, pp. 39–42.

33 S. Kem, *Standfast: A Sermon* (1647), pp. 11–15; R. Farmer, *The Great Mysteries of Godliness and Ungodliness* (1655), dedication and pp. 77–9; B. Blaugdone, *An Account of the Travels, Sufferings and Persecutions* (1691), pp. 5, 28; R. Towgood, *The Almighty his Gracious Token of Love* (1676), dedication and pp. 13–19; R. Standfast, *A Sermon . . . at the Assizes* (1676), *passim*, especially pp. 26–30; E. Phileroy, *A Satyrical Vision* (1684).

34 Farmer, *Satan*, p. 43; W. Grigge, *The Quaker's Jesus* (1658).

35 Besse, vol. 1, pp. 41–2; G. Bishop, *A Book of Warnings* (1661); T. Speed, *Reason versus Rage* (1691), p. 28; R. S. Mortimer (ed.), *Minutes of the Men's Meeting . . . 1687–1704* (Bristol Record Society, vol. 30, 1977), p. 83; R. Bury, *A Collection of Several Messages and Warnings* (1701); Bury, *A Collection of Sundry Messages* (1728).

36 C. Marshall, *Journal* (1844); Mortimer, *Minutes 1687–1704*; Mortimer, *Minutes of the Men's Meeting 1667–87* (Bristol Record Society, vol. 26, 1971).

37 Hayden, pp. 144, 220 gives two lists of Baptist members, 100 and 166 respectively. Watts, pp. 495, 503, 506 discusses the 1715 figures for different Bristol churches. Later Baptist numbers can be found in the Western Assocation MSS at Angus Library, Regents Park College, Oxford (ref. 18c 13e for 1736–44). Presbyterians were urged not to

split from the church, e.g. in E. Hancock, *The Pastor's Last Legacy and Counsel* (1663). In 1684 the Rye House plotter James Holloway claimed 'I am not a dissenter from the Church of England nor joyned with them altogether' (*Free and Voluntary Confession* (1684), p. 13). The limited membership of the large Lewin's Mead Presbyterian congregation can be traced in BAO 6687 (1) and (4). Their early eighteenth-century minister, Michael Pope, actually left £50 for a sermon at St James' parish church (Barrett, p. 397). Ralph, p. 47 includes Dean Tucker's comment in 1766 on the dissenters in his parish, St Stephen's, that they were not 'of the rigid sort, many occasionally come to church'.

38   Ralph shows monthly or quarterly communions the norm, and BAO 6687 (1) suggests the same for Presbyterians.

39   *Some Particulars relating to the Life and Death of Rebecca Scudamore* (1790), pp. 23–4; *The Life of Mary Dudley* (1825), pp. 2–23. On 12 May 1745 John Ryland, trainee Baptist minister, noted a great number of spectators who came to see new Baptist members received in (Angus Library 6e 27 (6)).

40   Manchee, vol. 1, pp. 202ff., 275ff. summarizes the Presbyterian and Baptist charities, for which see also BAO 6687 (3) and BD/A2/1 and M1/2. BAO also holds the Quaker poor records. For a typical moral exhortation see: *Some Admonition and Tender Advice to . . . Friends in Bristol* (1706).

41   J. Barry, 'Piety and the patient', in R. Porter (ed.), *Patients and Practitioners* (1985); A. B. Sackett, *James Rouquet and his part in early Methodism* (Wesley Historical Society Publications, no. 8, 1972); L. E. Elliott-Binns, *The Early Evangelicals* (1953), pp. 332–7. The pietist atmosphere can be captured in three diaries of the period: John Ryland's in Angus Library 6e 27; William Dyer's in BCL 20095–6; and the Rev. Bowen's in BCL 6492.

42   *Letters of Orton and Stonhouse*, vol. 2, p. 31.

43   For Bristol Methodism see: J. W. Raimo, 'Spiritual harvest: the Anglo-American revival in Boston, Massachusetts and Bristol, England 1739–42' (unpublished Ph.D thesis, University of Wisconsin, 1974); J. Kent (ed.), 'Wesleyan Membership in Bristol in 1783' in *An Ecclesiastical Miscellany* (Bristol and Gloucestershire Archaeological Society, Records Section, vol. 12, 1976); A. C. H. Seymour, *The Life and Times of Selina Countess of Huntingdon* (2 vols, 1844), vol. 2, pp. 352ff; E. Welch (ed.), *Two Calvinist Methodist Chapels* (London Record Society, vol. II, 1975), pp. 29, 35. The best general account of Methodism's link to other churches is J. Walsh, 'Origins of the evangelical revival' in G. V. Bennett and J. D. Walsh (eds), *Essays in Modern Church History* (1966), but see also D. Hempton, *Methodism and Politics in British Society 1750–1850* (1984).

44   Raimo, pp. 197–9; *London Magazine* (July 1739), pp. 340–3; W.

Dowers, *Errors in Part Discovered* (1746) pp. 8–9, 15, 26, 30; T. Jackson (ed.), *Journals of Reverend Charles Wesley* (2 vols, 1849), vol. 1, pp. 244, 248; J. Telford (ed.), *Letters of John Wesley* (8 vols, 1931), vol. 1, p. 291. Ralph, p. 46 includes the following comment by the vicar of Sts Philip and Jacob in 1784: 'Families about 2,600, of which 400 church, 50 Presbiterians, 65 Anabaptists, 10 Papists increasing, 14 Quakers, 60 Independents. The rest of no religion. Of the above greatest part Methodists, numbers increasing. All, male and female, pretend to be preachers.'

45 Raimo, pp. 141–77 explores the links of Methodist with earlier Bristol enthusiasm, while pp. 209–32 discuss this brief phase in 1739–42.

46 J. Tucker, *A Complete Account of the Conduct of that Eminent Enthusiast Mr Whitefield* (1739), especially p. 36; Tucker, *An Apology for the Present Church of England* (1772), pp. 4, 11, 44. For popular religiosity see M. MacDonald, 'Religion, social change and psychological heaing', *Studies in Church History*, **20** (1983), but see also E. Duffy, 'The godly and the multitude in Stuart England', *The Seventeenth Century*, **1** (1986).

47 Kent; *Letters of John Wesley*, vol. 5, p. 341. Quakers contrasted their pietism with Wesley's evangelism: *Life of Mary Dudley*, pp. 13–18; J. Helton, *Reasons for Quitting the Methodist Society* (1778).

48 E. Goldney, *Epistles to Deists* (1759), especially pp. 160ff. and sections dated Whit Tuesday and entitled 'Scriptural Remedies'.

49 See above n. 27 and below n. 56.

50 The mass of information in churchwardens' accounts and vestry books in BAO is usefully summarized in A. Harvey, 'Church Furniture and Decorations', *TBGAS*, **32** (1909), pp. 140–64. Bodleian MSS Gough Somerset 8 includes mid eighteenth-century sketches of several church interiors. For Colston's gifts see E. G. Clarke, *The Life of Edward Colston* (1895). A typical statement stressing Anglican decency and order is S. Seyer, *A Serious Address to Members of the Church of England* (1772).

51 Ralph. See above nn. 2–8.

52 Collinson, *Religion*; R. O'Day, *The English Clergy* (1979).

53 D. S. Taylor and B. Hoover (eds), *The Complete Works of Thomas Chatterton* (2 vols, 1971), vol. 1, pp. 365, 404, 413, 421–2, 546–51; L. Dickins and M. Stanton (eds), *An Eighteenth-Century Correspondence* (1910), p. 21.

54 Dickins and Stanton, p. 21.

55 Marshall, pp. 11–12; *Life of Mary Dudley*, pp. 23–5.

56 Gaskarth; G. Smalridge, *The Charge . . . at his Primary Visitation* (1716); J. Harcourt, *The Duty of not Giving Offence* (1735); E. Collins, *The Saints Backsliding* (n.d.); and see n. 27.

57 Barry, pp. 172–3; *An Exact and True Account of All the Moneys [of] the Society of the Clergy* (1724).

58 E. Harwood, *A New Introduction to the Study and Knowledge of the New Testament* (2 vols, 1767), vol. 1, p. xviii.

59 *Letters of Orton and Stonhouse*, vol. 2, pp. 15–25, 51–2, 76, 89, 92. J. Stonhouse, *Every Man's Assistant and Sick Man's Friend* (3rd edn, 1794). For the Lent sermons established by Colston see B. Bayly, *Fourteen Sermons* (2 vols, 1721), vol. 1; J. Tucker, *Seventeen Sermons* (1776), sermons 9 to 14. Tucker's infirmary sermon of 1746 caused such a stir locally that he too was attacked in the streets.

60 For example, Gaskarth.

61 Standfast, *Assizes Sermon*, pp. 26–30; R. Kingston, *Vivat Rex* (1683), pp. 7–8, 42–3; *Bristol's Second Address* (1681); *The Report from the Committee of the Commons . . . to Consider the Petition of Richard Thompson* (1680); *The Vizor Pluck't Off from Richard Thompson* (1680), p. 3. Godwyn, pp. 14–16, 35 noted those ministers who would not support persecution and called them 'timorous and half-sized men keen to be thought moderate' by neglect of duty to their superiors and 'obsequious deference to inferiors', for example by waiving the ceremonies of baptism and churching and joining the attack on Thompson. Judge Jeffreys in 1685 noted the 'differences' among the clergy, who, he claimed, 'ought to preach peace and unity to others' J. Evans, *Chronological Outline of Bristol* (1824), pp. 236–9. Hayden, p. 145 only identifies four Anglican ministers active in persecution.

62 Besse, vol. 1, pp. 45–6 quotes Bishop and Speed telling the magistrates that Quakers were 'of the city and in the city, inhabitants and interwoven are we therein and with the people thereof, as a man's flesh in his body and his spirit in his flesh'. See also Speed, p. 24; T. Cary, *A Sermon . . . at the Monthly Fast* (1691), pp. 12–14; B. Bayly, *The True Notion of Moderation* (1711).

63 BAO Temple Ka 4, ff. 77, 93, 246. For examples of religious interpretations of parties see: BCL 9992, f. 199; *HMC Thirty-Sixth Report*, vol. 7, pp. 404–5; Speed, pp. 1–2, 13–14, 20; *A Letter to an MP from a Gentleman of Bristol* (1715); BCL 11156 handbill 'A Letter to a Friend'; *The Bristol Contest* (1754), pp. 48–52.

64 The evidence of pollbooks on clerical voting is confirmed by the remarks on political allegiance in Ralph.

65 BAO Temple Ka 4, f. 93.

66 BAO Temple Ka 4, ff. 66, 72, 77–8, 84, 93; Angus Library FPC D21 sermons of Andrew Gifford, a Baptist, especially 30 Jan. 1701, 1 Jan. 1705, 10 Apr. 1719; BCL 11156 (1739 election) and 10944–74 (1754 election) and 5433, f. 29 (1768 election); *Bristol Contest*; Philalethes, *A Stroke at Pulpit Time-Serving* (1763), p. 8; L. Colley, *In Defiance of*

Oligarchy (1982), pp. 139–40, 166–7; N. Rogers, 'The urban opposition to Whig oligarchy 1720–60', in M. C. and J. Jacob (eds), *Origins of Anglo-American Radicalism* (1984), pp. 137–9, 142–4. E. D. Bebb, *Nonconformity in Social and Economic Life 1660–1800* (1935), pp. 52, 83 quotes the Evans MSS of 1715 on the voting power of dissent in Bristol (over 700 of *c.* 4000 voters) including the dubious claim that 'the strength of all the dissenters in Bristol may justly be reckoned much more than that of all the low church party there'.

67 Barry, pp. 334–5. For the growing Presbyterian influence in the corporation see Quilici, pp. 215–7, 222–3, 233–58.

68 Latimer, p. 227.

69 Butcher (ed.); H. Waterman, *A Sermon . . . before the Court of Guardians of the Poor* (1699) pp. 23–4; J. Cary, *An Account of the Proceedings of the Corporation of the Poor of Bristol* (1700); *Some Considerations offered to the Citizens of Bristol* (1711); *The Bristol Watch-Bill* (1756), pp. 5, 11; J. Johnson, *Transactions of the Corporation of the Poor* (1826); Colley, pp. 134–5.

70 BCL 10162. See also D. W. R. Bahlman, *The Moral Revolution of 1688* (Yale, 1968); W. Speck and T. Curtis, 'Societies for the Reformation of Manners', *Literature and History*, **3** (1976).

71 BCL 10162, 13 Aug. 1700, 27 August 1700 and on, e.g. 12 Dec. 1700.

72 Barry, pp. 33–5; D. G. Cooke, *The Story of Temple Colston School* (1947); *Some Considerations offered*, pp. 5–6. See also M. G. Jones, *The Charity School Movement* (1938).

73 G. Munro Smith, *A History of Bristol Royal Infirmary* (1917). For background see J. Woodward, *To Do the Sick No Harm* (1974).

74 For example, *The State of the Ladies Charity School* (1756) claimed 'nobler and better motives than sect or party' (p. 4). But the school, masterminded by Tucker, had morning and evening prayers, taught the girls the Church catechism, and took all the pupils to church on Sunday, unless their parents were dissenters (*FFBJ*, 1 Feb. 1755).

75 BAO Temple Ka 4, ff. 102–3. *Bristol Journal*, 10 Dec. 1774, advertises a volume urging Anglican solidarity against dissenters, who, it claims, planned to subvert the Church through supposedly charitable subscriptions and collections.

76 The records of the Presbyterian school are in BAO 6688 (1–2). Typically Anglican rules for the other schools can be seen in BAO 28049 (25) or *The Rules of Pile Street School* (1764).

77 Mortimer, *Minutes 1687–1704*, pp. 112ff; BAO SF/A9/1.

78 See Barrett and Manchee volumes, *passim*; *An Account of the Hospitals, Almshouses and Public Schools in Bristol* (1775). The other great repository of charitable trusts was that other perpetual, but political, body, the corporation.

79 Smith, *Infirmary*, pp. 34–5.

7 Believing and belonging. Church behaviour in Plymouth and Dartmouth 1710–30

John M. Trifitt

On 6 November 1720 Pentecost Barker was received as a communicant member of the Batter Street Presbyterian meeting at Plymouth, a group with a select inner circle of perhaps a hundred communicant members.[1] At the same time Barker had committed himself to a demanding spiritual regime – two lengthy sermons on Sunday and one on Wednesday, a monthly period of self-examination in preparation for the communion, besides a routine of personal devotions and reading. He also began to keep a spiritual journal, the surviving fragment of which gives us a glimpse into the business of belonging to a church in Plymouth in the early eighteenth century.[2]

Barker had lived a very debauched life until his 'Reformation'. With his friends at the White Ale House, he had drunk himself deeply into debt and endangered his marriage.[3] In 1720, however, his 'mind was strangely awakened' and he determined on a new start.[4] It was hardly surprising that he should turn to the Batter Street meeting, for his father was a committed Presbyterian, as his grandfather had been, and his sister had married a dissenting minister. He was encouraged by Peter Baron, the new minister whom he was eventually to consider 'my dearest friend' and who encouraged him to read spiritual books and to begin his journal.[5] Barker's membership of the congregation sprang from a tangle of intentions – a determined attempt to overcome his drinking problem 'which perfectly rises a Devil in Me' and a spiritual experience which was no doubt genuine.[6] The fact that the Presbyterian meeting was his chosen medium reflected, in addition, an attempt to reintegrate himself with family and friends, bidding for the forgiveness of his father, from whom he had been forced to borrow heavily.[7]

There was more to it than this. Barker's father-in-law was mayor of Plymouth in 1717 and Pentecost had some modest political ambition. In 1717 he became a constable for his ward and in 1718 a freeman voter.[8] In November 1720, ten days after his first communion, he wrote to Sir John Rogers, MP for the town and special friend of the Presbyterians, reminding him of his father-in-law's political services and asking to be considered for a government job.[9] As a result he became a purser at the Royal Naval dock, and thus obtained the chance to rescue his finances. Besides its personal assocations, therefore, Barker's reformation was closely linked to his entry into public life – together they constituted a package of new choices. In turn, belonging to the Presbyterian meeting associated Barker with a tight group of Rogers' supporters, many of them occupying government jobs.[10] He became a regular visitor to the Rogers' country house at Blatchford and borrowed money from his political friends.[11]

Barker was a Presbyterian because he had experienced an authentic spiritual awakening. But it was also because he was husband, brother and son, companion of the local minister, beset with personal problems, anxious to protect his new salary, continually in debt and prompted by an informed political interest. Belonging to the meeting meshed very closely with the many concerns of his everyday domestic, business and public life.

Barker was by no means unusual in his experience. In the memoirs of another Plymouth dissenter, John Fox, we find a number of people like him, although Fox's own disillusionment with the Church casts them all in a cynical light. One was John Huxham, an able if vain physician who came from a dissenting background and trained at Leyden, arriving in Plymouth with the recommendation of a Presbyterian minister. It was, wrote Fox, 'sufficient to put him under the protection of the Dissenters, who were immediately his friends'.[12] Huxham accordingly set up practice among the dissenters – at least, until his Anglican rival began to show signs of insanity. Then he 'began to be taken notice of by the Church party as well as Dissenters upon which he began to show his gratitude to the latter by declaring that he never thought himself in the least obliged to them'.[13] If Huxham's Presbyterianism had become as much a vehicle for his career as a spiritual home, Mark Batt, a young lawyer, attended the meeting purely for family reasons. His father had intended him for the ministry but a spell in the minister's household 'had a quite contrary effect on him . . . and gave him such dismal ideas of living

and conversing with such sort of people that he was soon
determined never to engage in that way of life'. He therefore
attended an inn of court where he became a deist. 'However he
had address sufficient to conceal his sentiments especially from his
father and conformed very cheerfully when he was at home . . .
going to meeting and conversing with dissenters'.[14]

Nor was this muddle of attitudes peculiar to dissent. Benjamin
Smithurst was the town's most successful bookseller. When he
came to Plymouth, Fox tells us, he was a thorough-going Anglican,

full of zeal for the clergy and their establishment. . . . He was [a] very strict
observer of all the ceremonies of the Church, gave very dilligent
attendance to the sacrament whenever it was administered and always
manifested great seriousness in his public devotions. He kept Sunday and
holy-days very strictly and was unquestionably a man of true piety.[15]

Then Smithurst fell in with a local deist and shifted his ground. 'He
was a great despiser at last of priests and bigotry as any man.' He
continued, however, his religious observance.

He seemed to forget all his notions when he was at Church. I have often
heard him rail at and expose the Athanasian Creed out of it and laugh at
many practices as mere superstitions, but when he was in he would
reverence that creed, and comply with what he would break jest on the
next day.[16]

Fox thought the explanation lay in his upbringing – 'so great was
the prejudice which his parents had instilled into him from
infancy'. Perhaps it owed something also to Smithurst's business
sense, bookseller as he was to a town with two SPCK schools.

Many, like Barker, had a variety of reasons for being in the pew,
whether it was concern with kin, trade or politics or a truly
spiritual experience. The impact on the character of church
congregations was inevitable, giving those at the centre a tight and
many-sided sense of belonging, but introducing on the fringe those
with a variety of casual interests. Such a pattern is indeed
suggested by the evidence of attendance and membership. When
in 1715 figures were returned for John Evans's census, 500
'hearers' were recorded at Batter Street.[17] In contrast, the
baptismal register reflects a group of three to four hundred, while a
list of communicants, beginning with Pentecost Barker and kept
up-to-date for a number of years, reveals that only one in three of

this inner group ever took on full membership.[18] We might assume that the Evans figure is mere optimism. But the gulf between census and baptismal register is suggestive, for it is characteristic of other congregations in the south west for which both totals can be discovered.[19]

I suggest that this pattern represents different levels of commitment within the meeting. There were no doubt those townsmen who went along from time to time, for whatever reason, but stopped short of real commitment. They were 'hearers', precisely as the Evans census terms them. Perhaps they drifted from denomination to denomination or went to the parish church as often as they attended a meeting. Perhaps they sometimes stayed at home. A smaller number had identified sufficiently with the meeting to have their children baptized by the Presbyterian minister. Only a fraction engaged themselves completely. If this interpretation is accurate, a meeting like Batter Street would have been a broadly based organization with a dense and complex structure, its wide outer circle centred around a distinct inner set and a committed core.

The more serious members were probably bound together by ties of kinship and business, although substantial evidence is hard to collect. Certainly Barker was related to the Martyns, the Winchelseas, the Cocks and perhaps other families within the congregation. Sometimes he did business on their behalf.[20] It may be that, in John Huxham, they shared a Leyden-trained physician with other well-to-do dissenters. When a man like Barker attended church, he expected to find a supportive and familiar circle, enriching his world with a series of social contacts.

The innermost core was more than a circle of friends and relations. Some committed members were no doubt spiritual athletes who, like Barker, had experienced a spiritual awakening. Perhaps they were also people with the time to devote to a rigorous spiritual schedule, for the devout spent time each day in prayer, reading and writing, and heard three long sermons a week. Two of the sermons, indeed, were delivered on Sunday, which at Plymouth was post day and therefore a day for business.[21] These were, however, also the people with money. The core of the meeting represented the rich of the congregation – men like Amos Doidge, a successful merchant; Elias Lang, a prosperous sailmaker; and Mordecai Cockey, a wealthy brazier. There was almost certainly an inner court of leading men, trustees who governed the affairs of the meeting. Although we do not have any trust deeds for the Batter Street meeting, those we have for Presbyterian meetings in Bridgwater, Dartmouth and Tiverton contain almost exclusively merchants, sergemakers, fullers, mercers, grocers and skilled artisans – a baker, a saddler, a couple of tallow chandlers.[22] All these occupations suggest more than average personal income. The closer we penetrate to the heart of the meeting, the richer are the individuals we encounter.

At the very heart of the Presbyterian meeting was the minister. Barker was devoted to Peter Baron, and admired most of the ministers he knew, noting that Nathaniel Harding, minister of the Plymouth Independents, 'always drops some good expressions'.[23] John Fox was less complementary. According to his memoirs, Harding 'had always the art of keeping great authority over his hearers', conversing 'with none but such as were bigots to him, and over whose faith and conversation he had got the ascendant'. Meanwhile John Enty, Baron's senior colleague at Batter Street,

set out in the world full in the belief of his divine commission and always expected the full respect to be paid to it which he tho't was due to it. . . . He had a great ascendant over the most considerable part of his hearers.[24]

Whether we believe Barker or Fox, we are left in no doubt that the committed members, enclosed in a solid framework of common loyalty and shared life, were further bound together by the authority and charisma of the capable minister.

Within the casual sphere of the Sunday congregation at Batter Street was thus a dense inner circle, centred about a rich, organized and articulate leadership and focused on the minister. This was a pattern broadly shared by other denominations in Plymouth. Monthly minute books suggest that the local Quakers revolved around a core of rich merchant families, especially the Ceanes, Colliers and Hingstons. They met so frequently at Henry Ceane's home that it was eventually registered as a meeting house. They had no minister, but the monthly meeting exercised such authority over the members – whether in collecting cash for their poor brethren, ordering them to sell their houses to meet their debts or instructing them to moderate their 'conversation' – that the unity of the meeting was greater rather than less.[25] At nearby Kingsbridge, the status of the monthly meeting was such that it was used as a court for the settlement of disputes, whether the quarrel was about unruly mastiffs or imported tobacco.[26] These meetings revolved around their central, moneyed core, just as Barker's meeting in Batter Street. Nor were the parish churches fundamentally dissimilar. A vestry book survives from Charles Church, the more outlying of the town's two Anglican parishes. Of course, it tells us nothing about attendance at services. But it does reveal that the vestry was run in the 1720s by a wealthy little group – perhaps half a dozen rich men who were senior wardens and provided over half the signatures at the vestry meetings.[27] As we shall see, the leading men from Charles Church worked together in other enterprises too and it would not be surprising to find that this vestry and its congregation exhibited all the close communal feeling of a dissenting meeting during this period.

Churches like Batter Street balanced a casual outer sphere with tight and increasingly committed inner circles. Drawing on the diverse intentions pooled by their adherents, they fulfilled, moreover, an impressive range of functions. For the indifferent they offered weekly ritual and a focus for local affairs; for the committed they bred an environment of strong loyalty and common interest. As institutions, they combined broad appeal with a dense communal struture. In this lies their importance for urban society, for such structures were bound to acquire social weight beyond their formal capacity. Indeed, the churches were without rival in towns of this period, when occupational guilds were in decline but had yet to be replaced by clubs and associations. In towns such as Plymouth, where the churches were by far the most impressive organizations outside the corporation itself, this was to create serious problems for local society and especially for local government.

We have begun gingerly to step outside the familiar ground of early eighteenth-century church studies, for the impact of the churches upon local society in this period – not only for religious and cultural life, but also for order and politics – has not been appreciated. The problem is methodological – the narrow perception we inherit from ecclesiastical sources. We might say that the character of an institution derives from the interplay of structure and performance. The structure is built out of offices, ideas and ceremonies: the performance is staged by a public caught up in the pressures of everyday life. The structure may be complex and subject to variations – but it will be essentially ordered and purposive. It will also govern the written record that the institution may generate, and will therefore very readily dominate our historical perspective. But the performance may be fluid and confusing. It will have to be decoded from hints in the institutional records – or culled from some other source altogether. Church structure is formal, hierachic, professional, given to ritual, fixed or slowly changing, devoted to a few objectives defined by the institution itself. Performance, however, may be extempore, unpredictable, open, amateur, given to theatre, endlessly various, invaded constantly by the values of society at large. Membership of a church, writes Demerath,

need not connote a commitment to religion. It may make a status claim to serve as a vehicle for mobility. . . . It may be prerequisite for credit or a job. . . . Or it may simply represent a penchant for formal associations.[28]

Only when we understand the complexity of this performance by examining the churches from outside their own range of sources and outside their own preoccupations do we guage their importance in the everyday life of eighteenth-century society.

Distracted by the formal structure of the churches, or by their theology, we easily overlook the many mundane reasons which took people to church and filled their Sunday experience with secular meanings. Those writing on the early eighteenth-century churches in the tradition of Dean Sykes have focused on the modest, pastoral approach of Anglicans in the face of a hostile intellectual climate and the challenge of dissent. Although Sykes recognized that reasons for church-going were not straightforward, he did not pursue the idea.[29] Nor has it been taken up by those who have followed his method. Working very largely from sermons, clerical diaries, episcopal correspondence or visitation records, these historians have been concerned only in passing with the local congregations, dismissing the laity because it appeared to be apathetic and uninformed.[30] Other historians, using the peculiar richness of dissenting sources, have constructed socio-economic interpretations of denominational membership in this period.[31] Drawing this work together, Watts has given us a portrait of eighteenth-century dissent which encompasses theology, worship and discipline, and also notices social patterns within the membership.[32] Although this approach comes much closer to the reality of local church life, the concern of such historians has remained almost exclusively the religious practice, and not the wider concerns of the laity. Inheriting the work of these twin traditions, it is therefore hardly surprising that historians of early eighteenth-century society are tempted to overlook the huge social and political significance of weekly, institutional religious behaviour.

Recently these strands of denominational research have blended with sociological theory to suggest the broader social and communal significance of the churches. Writers such as Hurwich and Gilbert have set the churches in a global context, as vehicles of social aspiration as well as centres of worship and belief.[33] Although their concern has remained largely with the interior dynamics of the churches, they draw out the secular associations of church membership and so point towards interactions between social and religious arenas. Following this lead, we can ask wider questions about the importance of the churches within local society and begin to unveil the dynamic role they played in local life.

The case of Pentecost Barker and his Plymouth contemporaries suggests that the churches did indeed play a very forceful role in the early eighteenth-century town. More striking evidence of problems created by a successful church is found at Dartmouth, Plymouth's Devon neighbour. It is important because it reveals how a parish church might attract bitter quarrels within local society and sharpen them into political conflict. Equally, it uncovers crucial ambiguities in the institutional structure of the parish, which redoubled its divisive character.

Dartmouth was served by three Anglican churches. High on the hill, overlooking the town, stood the parish church of St Clement's, while at the town centre stood its chapel of ease, St Saviour's. On a promontory at the harbour mouth stood St Petrox's, a second chapel of ease, in the parish of Stoke Fleming.[34] In 1701 Michael Peach was elected master of the Latin school by the town council and at about the same time was chosen curate of St Clements. In 1709 he also became minister of St Petrox's, chosen by the parishioners and confirmed by the distant rector of Stoke Fleming.[35] A year later the bishop appointed William Pritchard as vicar of St Clement's, the corporation (which held the advowson) being apparently unable to agree on the appointment.[36] Peach had been the only active clergyman in the town during the old vicar's last illness and might have hoped to secure the position himself. Within months, curate and vicar were at loggerheads – quarrelling over fees, subscriptions, the frequency of the Eucharist and of preaching.[37] Pritchard, who concentrated his work at St

Saviour's (whenever he was in Dartmouth, having another cure elsewhere), summarily dismissed Peach as curate. The bishop, when asked to adjudicate between them, counselled Peach to be content with his poisition at St Petrox's.[38] By 1710, the town was therefore divided into two Anglican districts – St Clement's and St Saviour's on the one hand, St Petrox's on the other. A smouldering sense of rivalry continued between the two clergymen. In 1714 Peach published a long account of the struggle that had ensued. It is an extraordinary document, written by an articulate and difficult man whose experience can hardly have been typical.[39] But it unmasks much about the town parish in this period which otherwise could only have been painstakingly reconstructed.

It shows, first of all, that this was far from a simple case of professional competition. For, despite the manner of his appointment, Pritchard was championed from the start by an aggressive and dominant clique within the town council.[40] Led by the town clerk Thomas Newman, and his ally Joseph Bully, this knot of councillors used their command of the corporate machinery to spur on the vicar and to hound the curate. They made official complaints to the bishop about his conduct, prosecuted him at the county sessions over the keeping of the parish registers, and charged him in the town court with assault and abuse.[41] They had Bully elected churchwarden of St Petrox's, along with the parish clerk Joseph Martin, a notorious local adventurer. Absenting themselves from services, the new wardens allowed the chapel to fall into disrepair, forbad the sexton to toll the bell, refused to open the doors on Christmas Day and presented articles against Peach at the triennial visitation. When the time came again to elect wardens, they arrived early, locked minister and people out, and re-elected themselves. The curate caught cold from the broken windows and found cobwebs in the chalice.[42] He was charged with being drunk and with reading the marriage service instead of the funeral. He discovered a rumour that he kept his servant as a 'concubine'.[43]

Peach put up a stubborn defence until Bully and Newman finally lost their majority in the council and their campaign ground to a halt. But why had his ordeal taken on such proportions? Bully and Newman – at least, as they appear in Peach's account – treated the church as a meeting-place for the people of the parish, and the work of the vestry as an element in town administration. They used, in other words, a civic rhetoric which addressed the parish primarily as a unit of obligation and control within the structure of local government.[44] Town notices were to be called and poor rates read out after the service. Baptism and marriage, being a means of acquiring a settlement, were rites of entry both to Church and parish and the clergyman had to observe his duty to help keep vagrants out. Employing this myth, Bully and Newman assumed righteous magisterial indignation when worshippers migrated from other parishes or vestry officers favoured the dissenters; or when Peach suppressed council proclamations, married couples without settlement and baptized their children, or kept the parish registers at his lodgings.[45]

But there was more to it than this. Increasingly people had begun to drift out of the town to worship in Peach's congregation. Anxious to impose a high Tory regime upon the borough, Bully and Newman feared his moderate reputation, recognizing that he could quickly become a focus for opposition. The corporation had direct control over St Saviour's, the chapel of ease at the centre of the town, where it put in the town serjeant each year as warden and probably ran the accounts.[46] But there was no such tradition of control at St Petrox's. The magistrates became determined to annex this parish too, turning the corporate machinery into a 'petite Inquisition' in order to close Peach down, resorting to the rhetoric of parochial obligation to justify their behaviour.[47] In this lies the significance of the case. St Petrox's had apparently come to represent a serious menace in the eyes of town government.

Peach knew that St Petrox's could not be run along the lines of a formal administrative unit, for success in an outlying parish depended on the support of the laity. Like any contemporary, of course, he made formal appeal to the local elite as a measure of self-protection. One disputed churchwarden, he argued, was the properly selected deputy of Josias Southcote, patron of the living. His decision to expel Joseph Martin as parish clerk had been, after all, supported by the 'Principal Inhabitants of St Petrox,' who 'being throughly convinc'd how ill he has us'd me, and how unfit he is for a Parish clerk . . . Certify'd under their Hands, in so many Words'. Such patrician figures were also said to have backed his line on council notices and given him a general certificate of character.[48] But this was little more than a hollow pretence, for the wealthy of the parish were as divided among themselves as any social group. Visit St Petrox's today and you will find the aisles paved with the memorials of Holdsworth and Newman families.

This rich cousinhood represented the most successful overseas businesses of the period and boasted several local magistrates. It must have been a formidable presence within the parish. Yet Peach received scant backing from this quarter, the heart as it was of local whiggery.[49]

In reality, Peach's behaviour was governed not so much by the elite as by the mass of parishioners who had chosen him as their minister, who occupied his pews and who sent their children to his school. He introduced a bi-monthly Eucharist on the 'Pious desire of a Person of the Town. . . . He assur'd me, that I should not want a sufficient Number of Communicants, and I thank God, I have all along had very good Encouragement'.[50] Unlike Pritchard, he depended on the subscriptions of the townspeople for his income. Unlike Pritchard, he visited the sick – rich or poor. Unlike Pritchard, he preached regularly, twice on Sundays. And unlike Pritchard, he saw his pews fill to overflowing as people were drawn from all over the town.[51]

More than this, Peach was able to win the affection of his people. The councillors disrupted poor relief in St Petrox's and blamed the minister, tried to prevent him teaching, diverted his subscriptions and blackened his reputation by gossip – all calculated to erode his points of contact with the parishioners. Peach, however, was able to raise a special collection to restore the church after its two years of neglect. The parents continued to send their children to school and signed a certificate of good conduct in the master's favour.[52] The Sunday congregation remained unmoved. When Peach dismissed his treacherous parish clerk he replaced him by a man the magistrates called a 'vagrant'. But when one Sunday Peach was away and Martin assumed the clerk's pew again, the congregation met him with stony silence and finally laughed him out of his stall.[53]

As we have seen, however, the motives of church-goers are rarely straightforward. No doubt Peach profited from the willingness of some individuals to seek out religious provision to their taste, attracted by the manner of the preaching and the regularity of the sacraments – ecumenists who easily crossed parish and denominational boundaries in search of religious satisfaction. There were undoubedly others whose motives were not so transparent. Peach proposed three major reasons for his success. Some came along to 'indulge' him in his sufferings, some on account of the regular preaching. Others, he admitted, simply deserted

St Savour's when Bully and Newman introduced pew rents, although he added significantly that 'if there was no Preaching [at St Petrox's], in all probability, several of them would run to the Meeting'.[54]

Bully and Newman muttered that Peach's congregation were papists, an illiterate mob which attended the Eucharist for a drop of wine, adding that 'the farr greater part besides go there not out of any Zeale to Religion but for the sake of a Walk the Church being situate on the sea-side'. They also warned ominously that 'the leaders and better sort of them confess they do Not go there out of Devotion, but purely to Create and keep up a faction'.[55] Although Peach repudiated the charge there was probably some truth in it, for Bully and Newman were cynical operators, pushing a controversial, radical programme. They must have had many enemies, not least because their own attitudes towards the Church were so ambiguous. As Peach remarked,

the Story is pretty notorious, that Mr *Mayor* [Bully], in the time of his *Whiggism*, rode out of Town, and receiv'd the Sacrament at a Country-Church; and after the Holy Solemnity was over, spent the remaining part of the Day over a Bowl of Punch, for Joy that himself and his Friends (some of 'em *rigid Dissenters* . . .) were thus Qualify'd to act against the *Church-Interest*.[56]

Bully's newfound Tory zeal for the Established Church cannot have carried much conviction. Many must have known that Thomas Newman – who attended church 'extreme seldom' – held nightly court at the Hole-in-the-Wall, where he regaled the tailors and cobblers with political argument and persuaded them to serve a turn for him on the town jury.[57] His campaign for control of St Petrox's smacked equally of opportunism, particularly when he locked Samuel Whalley, the archdeacon's surrogate, out of St Saviour's, saying that 'he car'd not a Fig for Mr Whally, nor for the Archdeacon himself'.[58] It would not have been surprising if some townspeople, with equal cycnicism, had been willing to use the beleaguered minister of St Petrox's as a champion, and his church as a platform for their challenge to the ruling clique. Indeed, when Peach comes to list his supporters, the magistrates he names were precisely those – Nathaniel Terry and Thomas Floud – who led a moderate caucus within the council, eventually to ally with the Whigs and topple the Bully–Newman regime.[59] His ordeal was just one element in a struggle for mastery among the political factions of the town.

The congregation of St Petrox's grew and grew, in part from authentic piety – as the people of Dartmouth encouraged Peach to preach and to celebrate more often – and in part because the church was becoming a centre of opposition to the governing regime. No doubt, as the drift along the shoreline grew, particularly among the wealthy and influential, some went along with an eye to prospects in trade or employment. As it gathered momentum, St Petrox's was acquiring a profile very like that of the Plymouth churches, assembling a broad casual fringe around an articulate clergyman, careful to meet the demands of his congregation, but looking in particular to a central group of the committed and the wealthy.

In so doing, this church became the most important vehicle for sectional conflict within Dartmouth society. Town government inevitably suffered. Sunday by Sunday the mayor and councillors processed to their ceremonial pew in St Saviour's, but the congregation around them dwindled away. Meanwhile, St Petrox's, with its wealthy friends, its wide public and its complement of vestry officers, lay at the southernmost tip of Dartmouth, where the authority of the corporation was at its weakest. In these streets, complained Bully and Newman, Peach was now 'Mayor, Justice and every Thing'.[60] The magistrates' ruthless, increasingly disreputable and finally vain struggle against the curate must have cost them dearly in public esteem. For a campaign mounted against minister and schoolmaster could not be conducted in secret. As Bully and Newman canvassed unsuccessfully from house to house to close Peach's school or to divert his subscriptions, and as the town clerk was shouted down in the town court from the public gallery, the authority of the ruling junta ebbed away.[61] St Petrox's was becoming a key issue in the local party struggle of this time. More than this, the structure of town government was itself being shaken by the affair.

Michael Peach was an angular and difficult man; Joseph Bully was a notorious local trickster and Thomas Newman arguably a crooked attorney. However it was not unusual for church affairs to take on an extraordinary local political importance. In Plymouth both the dissenters and the men from the outlying Charles Church found themselves excluded from high town office. Accordingly they joined together, at first in a Corporation for the Poor and in two SPCK schools, but soon in joint political activity also.[62] By the 1720s this ecumenical and philanthropic connection had become a formidable presence in local politics, a platform from which the excluded were able to score resounding victories against the council, particularly over the vexed issue of the franchise. Most notably, in 1728, an open alliance among freemen from dissenting meetings and those from Charles Church outvoted a majority in the council and saw Sir John Rogers' son elected as mayor.[63] This type of political pattern recurred in town after town. In Taunton a caucus of dissenting sergemakers, clubbing together in charitable work and in a local canal project, engaged in long and bitter feuding with the town council. In Tiverton, where factional conflict led to the collapse of the corporation, vestry elections became the focus for local rivalry. In Tavistock control of the vestry machinery was the central issue of local politics for twenty-five years after 1710.[64] Everywhere in these parliamentary boroughs the dissenting churches were treated as a distinct political entity, a recognizable force in local affairs. Everywhere the relationship between council and vestries experienced strain and conflict. In all of these towns confrontation between church-based groups, and suspicion between local government and the churches, could not but become a very public spectacle.

It is no exaggeration to say that these were the dominant features of the political landscape in many ordinary market towns and ports, both in the early years of the eighteenth century and in other periods too.[65] Before we can understand either the churches or the course of political events, we have to grasp this close correspondence between them, and understand why such a correspondence should have occurred. Combining formal structure and ritual with broad casual membership and a tight sense of commitment within an inner circle, the churches were a redoubtable social force, an ideal vehicle for political action, attracting to themselves all manner of local conflict. On the other hand, the structure of local government was fundamentally weak, lacking both formal cohesion and basic resources. The relationship between corporation and parish was both crucial and peculiarly ill-defined. Central questions, for example on matters of poor relief, were decided in the vestry while the parish church was the setting for much of the corporate ritual calendar. Town councils had no direct say in these affairs, even if they often chose the incumbent and serviced elements of his pay.[66] If the corporation took control of a parish at the town centre, its influence over others remained a matter of contention. These problems were compounded where dissenters were prominent in the community. While Baptists and Quakers had their own mechanisms for relief of the poor and discipline of members, Presbyterian and Independent congregations looked to the civic institutions for these services and expected to hold office within them.[67] Although in practice they often did, their position was always questionable. These issues took on particular potency in a town like Plymouth, where councillors, including those who were dissenters, served an apprenticeship in vestry office, and where the council had the gift of a living.[68] The course of Plymouth politics was decisively changed when, in 1711, the mayor was removed for breaking open the town chest and making off with the seal. This desperate course of action arose from his determination to win for his candidate an election to the living of Charles Church.[69]

More fundamentally, local administration was overstretched and under-resourced. It depended entirely on broad public co-operation if its many offices were to be filled satisfactorily and its numerous duties performed.[70] The trick of achieving such consensual, voluntary self-government could be impossible to perform when a significant sector of the public was divided between churches which were broadly recruited, highly organized and influential. It was all too easy for local disputes to gravitate towards the churches as a vehicle for collective conflict, while local government fell into the hands of a religious (or, at least, church-based) faction. Religious division became a sharp, organized, long-term political struggle. Ultimately it might threaten the whole business of local administration.

Within many early eighteenth-century towns such as these, the churches were the only institutions to pose such a threat to order. If the churches were therefore a focus of division within society, they were themselves moulded by the heavy burden they were expected to bear. The clergy could not, for example, avoid becoming embroiled in local politics. Every year there was a sermon to be preached on the choosing of the mayor, while a proportion of clerical income often derived from funds serviced by the corporation. Canon Gilbert, of St Andrew's in Plymouth became embroiled in a long dispute with the corporation over payment of rent for tithes and other moneys. William Pritchard was compromised on his arrival at Dartmouth by his need to secure a lease of the tithes from the impropriators, the corporation. Peach blamed this for the vicar's unwillingness to oppose corporate policy.[71] Peach himself – who suffered the loss of his schoolmaster's salary from the corporation rather than compromise with his antagonists – followed the advice of the old vicar of Tounstall, claiming that he 'never espous's any Party at all'. But this proved no insulation from local politics, either for Peach or for his mentor, whom Joseph Bully had dubbed 'Cardinal-Primate, God Almighty's Dragon, and other wicked and opprobrious Names'.[72]

The political importance of the churches also meant that they were cynically invaded by individuals with political ambition. The episode at St Petrox's demonstrates how very vulnerable the machinery of the vestry could be, and how disruptive a political incursion. Joseph Martin would entertain the congregation during a poll by selecting psalms with an appropriate election flavour.[73] Worse still, after two years of legal conflict the parish stock was exhausted and a neighbourhood subscription necessary to get the chapel back into repair.[74] Meanwhile, as we have seen, at St Savour's in Dartmouth the vestry had been annexed completely by the corporation, the parish, as it was formally constituted, almost entirely separated from the worshipping group. Even within the congregation, however, political calculations were being made. Prestigious pews fetched large sums, and disagreements led to fighting during services.[75] Worse still, legislation against occasional conformity could make church attendance a farce. At Bridgwater, where dissenters were threatened with exclusion from council office after the Occasional Conformity Act, six promptly converted to Anglicanism. There ensued a weekly pantomime in which the new arrivals were scrutinized by Anglican agents during morning worship. Formal affidavits record that they failed to kneel in the right places and that James Bowles stooped 'in a sleepy posture from his comeing into the church unto the end of the sermon'. The converts in turn retorted that their behaviour was beyond reproach and that their failure to kneel was due to the gout.[76] It must have been a struggle to sustain public worship in an atmosphere such as this.

Paradoxically, the complexity of motive among those who attended churches proved also to be some protection against the ill winds of doctrinal controversy. Lay people had invested too heavily of their time, emotion and money in the churches to be easily swayed by disputed theology. What was to become the Salters' Hall controversy broke at Exeter in 1719, when two Exeter ministers were ejected for Arianism. The affair at once drew in all the Presbyterian and Independent ministers from Devon and Cornwall, together with a good many from Somerset. The issue at the heart of the affair – the right of the Exeter Assembly to lay down doctrinal standards for the clergy of the region – had been brewing for some time.[77] The Batter Street congregation at Plymouth found itself deeply embroiled, for its minister, John Enty, was one of the loudest orthodox voices in the Assembly, along with his Plymouth contemporary, Nathaniel Harding, and their friend from Tavistock, Jacob Sandercock. John Fox, moreover, was one of several heterodox pupils from Hallett's Academy whose examination was one cause of the stir. A member of Harding's meeting, he probably preached at Batter Street too. It was an episode which caused Fox to despise the 'the paultry spiritual wickednesses with whom it was my ill luck to be concern'd' and eventually to leave both ministry and Church.[78] Plymouth nonconformity cannot but have been rocked by the controversy. Yet it was at this very moment that Pentecost Barker's mind was 'strangely awakened' and his name entered as the first in a list of new communicant members at Batter Street. Over the next fifteen years the body of communicants apparently maintained its strength, or grew slightly, while the number of infant Presbyterians coming for baptism held its own. By the end of the 1720s, when Barker's surviving journal allows us to watch the Presbyterians at close hand, the Trinitarian question had apparently been forgotten. There is, indeed, no sign that the meeting suffered at all on account of the controversy. Nor do the Presbyterian registers of Tavistock or Taunton suggest any ill-effect in these congregations.[79] We underestimate the resilience of lay church practice if we assume that the theological heart-searching of the ministers in 1719 had much impact on dissenting strength. The same could probably be said of the Hoadly controversy within Anglicanism. There is in consequence no reason to suppose that the churches lost their potency as a source and expression of social and political division, at least until the rise of Methodism and probably not even then.[80] For even if the dissenting churches were eventually to lose their way, narrowing their appeal to a thin band of the socio-economic spectrum, it is unclear whether such small, tight congregations would have been any the less potent a political force than their growing, looser forerunners at the turn of the century. Membership of a church was too complex and too deep an activity to have been materially softened by difference over points of dogma, and too wide-ranging a business to be lightly written off.

The motives of those who sat in the pews were rarely uncluttered by everyday concerns, for church-going was closely meshed with the anxieties and values of society at large. The result for church practice was profound and the impact upon society hardly to be overestimated. It may be that the first decades of the eighteenth century were a moment of peculiar religious and political tension, as dissent procured a constituency in the wake of Toleration, as local government worked through a legacy of political tension from a century of conflict and civil war, and as many towns experienced a moment of prosperity. But at root the junction of believing and belonging is a reality to be confronted in every period.

Acknowledgement

I am very grateful to the other contributors for their encouragement and guidance in the preparation of this paper.

Notes and references

1   PRO RG4/4091 f. 18 Batter Street Presbyterian Meeting register; list of communicant members.
2   WDRO 581/14 ms. Journal of Pentecost Barker 1729–31.
3   Barker's Journal, entries for 15, 29 Jan. 1730 (on drink and on the death of an alehouse friend), 16 Aug. 1730 (a sermon on hardness of heart).
4   Barker's Journal, 2 Jan. 1731.
5   Barker's Journal, 1 June 1730 (his sister), 25 Sept. 1730 (his father and grandfather), 2 Jan. 1731 (Peter Baron).
6   Barker's Journal, 15 Jan. 1730.
7   Barker's Journal, 14 Nov. 1730 (asking his father's forgiveness, should he ever discover the journal).
8   WDRO W 52 Plymouth Corporation minute book, ff. 106, 113 minutes recording Barker's election as constable 17 June 1717 and as freeman 6 Oct. 1718.
9   WDRO Passy Papers (uncatalogued), Pentecost Barker to Sir John Rogers, 17 Nov. 1720. Barker's request was backed by letters from

his father and from his wife's family. Passy Papers, Gregory Barker to Rogers 21 Nov. 1720; Joanna Beere *et al.* to Rogers to 17 Nov. 1720.

10 Rogers' activity at Plymouth is examined in John M. Triffitt, 'Politics and the Urban Community. Parliamentary Boroughs in the South West of England 1710–1730' (unpublished D.Phil thesis, University of Oxford, 1985), pp. 210–18.

11 Barker's Journal, 29 Dec. 1729, 8, 20 Jan. 1730, etc. (visits to Rogers); 7 Sept. 1730 (an evening with the Governor of the Citadel) 'I cannot retire from the world. I am in many people's debt and this makes me sneak and cringe, in hopes that I may one time or other get into some Business whereof I may be inabled to discharge what I owe.'

12 J. B. Rowe (ed.), 'Eighth Report of the Committee on Devonshire Records', *Transactions of the Devonshire Association*, **xxix** (1897), p. 80. On Huxham, see G. S. Holmes, *Augustan England. Professions State and Society 1680–1730* (1982), p. 209.

13 Rowe, p. 81.

14 Rowe, pp. 82–5.

15 J. B. Rowe (ed.), 'Seventh Report of the Committee on Devonshire Records', *TDA*, **xxviii** (1896), pp. 171–2.

16 Rowe, p. 172. See also very similar influences among converts to catholicism in E. Duffy, ' "Poor Protestant Flies". Conversions to catholicism in early eighteenth-century England', *Studies in Church History*, **xv** (1978), pp. 289–304.

17 Dr Williams' Library ms. 706 E 22, f. 7 Evans list for Plymouth; PRO RG4/4901 Batter Street baptismal register, calculating an approximate figure by multiplying average annual total by thirty.

18 Dr Williams' Library ms. 706 E 22, f. 18.

19 For example, 2000 hearers (Evans) and 700 (register) for Paul Street Meeting, Taunton; 600 hearers (Evans) and 300–400 (register) for Abbey Chapel, Tavistock. Dr Williams' Library ms. E 22 ff. 28, 99 Evans lists for Tavistock and Taunton; PRO RG4/2030, 1567 registers for Abbey Chapel, Tavistock and Paul Street Meeting, Taunton.

20 Barker's Journal, 9 Jan. 1730, (trip to Launceston 'by wish of bro[ther] W[inchelsea]') 23 Feb. 1731 (death of Anne Martyn), 28 Mar. 1731 ('Bro[ther] Cock') 22 May 1731 (theft from 'My Bro[the]r Winchelseys'). It is informative to compare Bossy's comments on the importance to fraternities of 'greeting, meeting and eating', Bossy, pp. 57–60. Compare, too, W. J. Sheils, 'Oliver Heywood and his Congregation', *Studies in Church History*, **xxiii** (1986), pp. 261–77.

21 Barker's Journal, 7 Dec. 1729 'O that I could remove from Plymo[uth] into some Place where the Lord's day is not post day, for this is a sad Snare to Me.' Collinson's warning against assuming too severe a separation of the believers on the evidence of spiritual

autobiographies is, however, worth recalling here. P. Collinson, *Godly People. Essays on English Protestantism and Puritanism* (1983), pp. 527–62.

22   Tabulated in Triffitt, pp. 348–9.

23   Barker's Journal, 31 Aug. 1730 (on a visit to Harding).

24   Rowe 'Seventh Report', pp. 149, 166–7.

25   Swarthmore Settlement, Plymouth ms. E 11, Plymouth men's monthly meeting book 1669–1717, f. 188 entry for 5 Dec. 1710 and *passim*; ms. E 12, Plymouth men's monthly meeting book 1717–1772, *passim*. I am indebted to Mr W. Brown and Mrs J. Lawson for allowing me to consult these documents.

26   Swarthmore Settlement, ms. E 2, West Devon monthly meeting book 1708–1748, ff. 6, 74, entries for 6 Sept. 1708, 1 Nov. 1725.

27   WDRO 258/1/22, 32 Charles Church, churchwardens' accounts, vestry book.

28   N. J. Demerath III, *Social Class in American Protestantism* (New York, 1965), pp. 7–8, quoted in R. Currie, A. Gilbert and L. Horsley, *Churches and Churchgoers. Patterns of Church Growth in the British Isles since 1700* (1977), p. 19.

29   N. Sykes, *Church and State in England in the Eighteenth Century* (1934), p. 231. Sykes's analysis is most comprehensive in his *Church and State*. But see also, among others, *From Sheldon to Secker. Aspects of English Church History 1660–1768* (1959), *Edmund Gibson, Bishop of London 1689–1748* (1926), *William Wake, Archbishop of Canterbury 1657–1737* (2 vols, 1957).

30   For example, S. C. Carpenter, *Eighteenth Century Church and People* (1959), primarily concerned with theology; G. V. Bennett, *The Tory Crisis in Church and State* (1975), principally national politics; J. H. Pruett, *The Parish Clergy under the Later Stuarts. The Leicestershire Experience* (Illinois, 1978) and W. M. Jacob, 'Clergy and Society in Norfolk 1707–1806' (unpublished Ph.D. thesis, University of Exeter, 1982), little beyond the clergy.

31   Early attempts were E. R. Bebb, *Nonconformity in Social and Economic Life* (1935) and D. Coomer, *English Dissent under the Early Hanoverians* (1946); more comprehensive are recent books such as R. T. Jones, *Congregationalism in England 1662–1962* (1962), C. Bolam *et al.*, *The English Presbyterians. From Elizabethan Puritanism to Modern Unitarianism* (1968), R. T. Vann, *The Social Development of English Quakerism, 1655–1755* (Harvard, 1969).

32   M. R. Watts, *The Dissenters. From the Reformation to the French Revolution* (1978).

33   J. J. Hurwich, 'Dissent and Catholicism in English society. A study of Warwickshire 1660–1720', *Journal of British Studies*, **xvi** (1976), pp. 24–58; ' "A Fanatick Town": the political influence of dissenters in Coventry, 1660–1720', *Midlands History* iv (1977), pp. 15–47; A. D.

Gilbert, *Religion and Society in Industrial England. Church, Chapel and Social Change 1740–1914* (1976) (including a survey of events before 1740); Weber's seminal work in this field is most easily read in H. H. Garth and C. Wright Mills (eds.), *From Max Weber* (1946). Subsequent studies are accessible in R. Currie, *et al.*

34 DRO DD 63926 account of the vicarage of Tounstall, 24 Apr. 1727.

35 DRO SM 2003 Dartmouth Corporation constitution book, f. 41, election of Peach as schoolmaster, 15 Sept. 1701. I have used the term 'minister' because it was employed by the people of the town at this time.

36 The living was held by the corporation, but Pritchard was apparently collated by the bishop owing to lapse of time. It seems likely that the corporation was divided over the appointment. Seale family papers, at Slade House, 'Institutions to the Vicarage of Townstall, extracted from the Principal Registry of the Bishop of Exeter'. I am grateful to Sir John Seale for his permission to consult these papers.

37 M. Peach, *The Case of Mr Michael Peach or, a Faithful Relation of the Hardships He has lately met with at Dartmouth* (1714), part i, pp. 21–3.

38 Peach, part iv, pp. 6–7 (Peach's account of Pritchard's demands and the bishop's decision).

39 Peach's letters to Browne Willis reveal a sharp and hasty temper. Bodleian Library ms. Willis 48, ff. 171–84, Peach to Willis, March 1715 to Jan. 1716.

40 Dartmouth affairs in this period are discussed in Triffitt, pp. 252–4.

41 Peach, part i, (articles presented to the bishop and Peach's response); part iv, pp. 8–16 (prosecutions against Peach).

42 Peach, part ii, p. 9 (election of wardens), p. 12 (Christmas) and part iii 'Narrative of the Unpresidented [sic] Behaviour of Mr *Joseph Bully* and *Joseph Martin*, during their Two years Church-Wardenships for the Parish of St Petrox', *passim.*

43 Peach, part i, p. 35 (the funeral); also part ii, p. 20, 'I was so civil', reported Newman, 'as to invite him to my Feast, where he, like a Beast as he is, got so Drunk, that he would have fall'n in the Canal at the Door, had not Jo. Martin succour'd him.' DRO Diocesan ms. cc 47 concerning the case of Peach vs. [Joseph ?] Martyn for defamation.

44 The idea of the parish as 'unit of obligation' belongs to the Webbs, but reflects their interpretation of formal parish structure as they found it in the pamphlet and legal literature of the period. S. and B. Webb, *English Local Government from the Revolution to the Municipal Corporations Act. The Parish and the County* (1906), pp. 9–41.

45 Peach, part i, p. 3–8, (articles submitted to the bishop); part ii, pp. 3–4 (articles submitted at the triennial visitation).

46   Both surviving early eighteenth-century mayoral accounts include the entry 'To Thomas Carter to serve as Churchwarden 10s'. Carter was town serjeant and appears in parish papers as warden for many years. DRO DD 63771, 63825 Dartmouth mayoral accounts 1714, 1719; DRO 1579A/24/43 (10) settlement certificate, St Saviour's parish 27 June 1718; DRO diocesan principal registry 510, D2/186 St Saviour's parish petitions 1726, 1729.

47   Peach, part iv, p. 8.

48   Peach, part i, pp. 31–2 (parish clerk); part i, pp. 26, 42 (certificates); part iv, p. 23 (notices).

49   Triffitt, pp. 53–4, 252–3. Lines within Dartmouth council are difficult to trace, owing to the paucity of our documents. But Peach never hints at support from the Holdsworth connection besides signatures to general petitions in his favour. It seems beyond doubt that the Holdsworths were aligned with the 'Whiggish or Dissenting Party' which Peach self-consciously avoided. Peach, part i, p. 31.

50   Peach, part i, p. 22.

51   Peach, part i, pp. 23–4 (full church and preaching); part iv, p. 35 (visiting).

52   Peach, part i, p. 20; part iii, p. 12 (subscriptions); part i, p. 47–8 (school); part iv, p. 22 (poor relief). Jacob is certainly wrong in the Sykesian view that 'the general public in the eighteenth century . . . conceived of the clergyman's role only in terms of the performance of public worship'. W. M. Jacob, ' "A practice of very hurtful tendency" ', *Studies in Church History*, **xvi** (1979), pp. 315–16.

53   Peach, part ii, p. 4 (the new clerk); part iv, p. 21 (Martin's return).

54   Peach, part i, pp. 23–4.

55   Peach, part i, p. 5 (the sea-side, the faction); part iii, p. 11 (the wine).

56   Peach, part i, p. 11.

57   Peach, part iv, p. 12.

58   Peach, part i, p. 30.

59   Peach, part i, p. 48 (visit to Bully's accompanied by Floud and Terry). This moderate group is discussed in Triffitt, pp. 243–4.

60   Peach, part iv, p. 22.

61   Peach, part iv, pp. 16 (the courtroom). The vulnerability of town government to popular dissatisfaction is suggested in Triffitt, pp. 263–99.

62   WDRO W 733, Passy Papers (uncatalogued), list of Hospital officers 12 May 1713; 423/4/1 Charity School accounts 1714ff.; 3/1 Charity School minutes 1735ff.; SPCK, abstract letter books 4.3713, 3747; 5.3838, 3934/5; 6.4335/6, 4606; 7.5188; 8.5551 John Gilbert to the Society 15 Oct. 1713, Sir John Rogers to same 6 Nov. 1713, James Yonge to same 10 Jan. 1714, 19 Nov. 1715, 7 Apr. 1717, 23 Mar. 1718, Yonge and Gilbert to same 12 Mar. 1714, 19 Nov. 1715.

63 Triffitt, pp. 235–6.

64 Triffitt, pp. 231–3, 307–8, 318–19. M. Dunsford, *Historical Memoirs of the Town and Parish of Tiverton in the County of Devon* (1790), p. 445 n.

65 See, for example, P. A. Slack, 'Religious protest and urban authority; the case of Henry Sherfield, iconoclast, 1633', *Studies in Church History*, **ix** (1972), pp. 295–302; A. Fletcher, 'Factionalism in town and countryside; the significance of Puritanism and Arminianism', *Studies in Church History*, **xxvi** (1979), pp. 291–300, D. Fraser, *Urban Politics in Victorian England. The Structure of Politics in Victorian Cities* (1976), pp. 25–111.

66 Although badly flawed in its interpretation, the best account of parochial structure remains S. and B. Webb, *The Parish and the County*. For some corrective with respect to poor relief, see G. W. Oxley, *Poor Relief in England and Wales 1601–1834* (1974).

67 Watts, pp. 336–43.

68 Parish Officers at St Andrew's, Plymouth are identified in parish petitions DRO diocesan papers C12/11, principal registry 510, D2/112, petitions 1718–25.

69 WDRO W 52 ff. 63–4 Plymouth council minutes 30 Aug. to 14 Sept. 1711; WDRO 224/1 Statement of the case Roche vs. Berry, Queen's Bench, 1712, J. J. Beckerlegge (ed.), *James Yonge. Plymouth Memoirs* (1951), pp. 57–9.

70 This point of view is argued at length in Triffitt, pp. 139–58.

71 WDRO W 388–90 bond, judgement and release concerning Gilbert's dispute with Plymouth corporation, March to June 1716; Peach, part i, p. 17.

72 Peach, pp. 10–11 (party), p. 46 (school).

73 Peach, p. 32.

74 Peach, part iii, p. 12.

75 For example, DRO R4/1/Z Tiverton Pew Rental 1724ff., in which sums of £20 were paid for prize positions; DRO 1579A/22/16 and Diocesan PR A1760, papers concerning Totnes pew dispute 1706–8; E. Windeatt, 'An old lawsuit relative to the rights to seats in Totnes church', *TDA*, **xix** (1887), pp. 538–46; SomRO D/D/Cd 115 ff. 26–9 depositions relating to pew dispute at Bridgwater, 1721. This pattern is a stage in what Bossy has called the 'enclosure movement', the taking over of church space by individuals. Bossy, p. 33.

76 SomRO D/B/bw 1980 depositions of John Symes and James Bryant 28 June 1718, Henry Player and Richard Coles 2 July 1718, John Slape and John Weeck 28 [illegible] 1718.

77 A. Brockett, *Nonconformity in Exeter 1650–1875* (1962) pp. 74–95; R. Thomas, 'The Non-Subscription Controversy among dissenters in 1719', *Journal of Ecclesiastical History*, **iv** (1953), pp. 162–86; F. J. Powicke, 'Arianism and the Exeter Assembly', *Transactions of the*

    Congregationalist Historical Society, **vii** (1916), pp. 34–43; Bolam *et al.*, pp. 150–73.

78 Rowe, 'Seventh Report', 129–47.

79 See Table 1 and notes.

80 An ebbing of religious fervour as a divisive force in English society was supposed in early work on dissent, and in Sykes's disdain for the laity. It inevitably colours political accounts – for example those of W. A. Speck and G. S. Holmes in J. Cannon (ed.), *The Whig Ascendancy* (1981).

Table 7   *Baptisms 1717–40*

	Plymouth, Batter Street	Taunton, Paul Street	Tavistock, Abbey Chapel
1717	9	19	8
1718	2	37	14
1719	5	33	12
1720	7	29	10
1721	16	20	12
1722	13	23	17
1723	19	28	22
1724	10	36	11
1725	11	26	13
1726	13	27	13
1727	6	21	10
1728	3	20	13
1729	6	15	10
1730	8	24	13
1731	6	10	19
1732	3	24	5
1733	2	24	18
1734	8	18	6
1735	3	23	8
1736	8		24
1737	6		8
1738	11		15
1739	7		10
1740	8		14

Sources: PRO RG4/4091 (Plymouth); 1567 (Taunton); 2030 (Tavistock). The Plymouth register is headed 'Baptized by me Peter Baron' and may therefore include only a proportion of the total baptized at the meeting. Baron was assistant minister until 1720, when he became pastor, to be joined subsequently by other assistants.

8 Confirmation, catechism and communion: the role of the young in the post-Reformation Church

S. J. Wright

The reasons for belonging to a particular religious community, as several of the papers in this collection illustrate, could be many and varied. The householder was susceptible to a range of political and social pressures when deciding which church to frequent. With fewer public responsibilities, and hence less need to preserve their reputation, women and young people were freer to indulge their religious sentiments or to eschew all forms of worship. The former often played an important role in Catholic or dissenting churches. The young were frequently criticized for their failure to attend church. One has only to dip into the records of church visitations to find numerous complaints about young men and women who preferred the lure of the maypole, the alehouse and the gaming table, or who spent their Sundays 'going a nutting' or 'playing bandy ball', as Henry Newcome lamented that he had done.[1] But apart from such references to the 'ungodly' activities of the young all too little is known about the early years of the individual's spiritual career or about the extent to which one member of the family influenced another. It is impossible, even if the documentary evidence were available, to deal with all the tantalizing questions concerning the role of children in the church in one article. I intend, therefore, to focus on the stages which led up to the assumption of full church membership, namely catechism, confirmation and communion, although brief consideration will also be given to the question of church attendance and to the other responsibilities which faced the young parishioner.

In his autobiography, compiled shortly after the Restoration, Oliver Heywood mentioned that,

When I was about 14 yeares of age I was entertained into the society of some godly christians, we were aboue twenty young men and others who joyned together by the instigation of an ancient godly widow woman, and propounded necessary questions and held conference every fourtnight and prayed our course about.[2]

Heywood was encouraged to join the widow's classes by his parents and before then had often accompanied his mother when she attended lectures in the Bolton area. Richard Baxter's account of his spiritual career also emphasizes the importance of regular worship as a child and of being brought up in a godly household. Indeed the latter owed far more to the influence of his father than to the Established Church, for he spent his early years in a parish which was served by an octogenarian, who deputized whenever he could, and later by a stage player with forged orders and a common drunkard.[3] Men like Baxter and Heywood may, of course, be far from typical, yet their accounts prompt a number of questions about the provisions which were made to prepare the young for the assumption of full church membership.

As far as the Church authorities were concerned the best way of 'initiating' the individual was to hold regular catechism classes. During these classes children were taught the Lord's Prayer, the creed and the catechism. They were subsequently tested on their knowledge and only then were considered fit to receive communion. Collinson's description of the early seventeenth century as 'an age of catechizing' is particularly apt for this was a period when a large quantity of popular catechisms and commentaries were published and presumably read.[4] But the emphasis on training was by no means new. The Church made limited attempts to ensure that the laity could recite the basic articles of faith in the early sixteenth century and the state took over the initiative with the ruling in the 1549 Prayer Book that catechism classes should be held 'once in six weeks at the least . . . upon some Sunday or holy day half an hour before evensong'. In 1562 this was extended to demand training every holy day and second Sunday in the year and from then onwards Church and state alike made many attempts to check up on catechism, references to the former in royal injunctions and visitation queries strongly outweighing references to confirmation.[5]

Although contemporaries distinguished between children and youths, it was accepted that religious instruction should begin as early as possible and should be continued throughout the 'dangerous' years of adolescence.[6] Six was cited as an ideal starting point in many episcopal injunctions and from 1562 onwards anyone with 'children of eight years and upwards' or servants and apprentices over 14 who could not say the catechism was liable to a fine of 10s. unless the default was 'in the want of capacity of the youth'.[7] Meanwhile, although individual orders vary, 20 seems to have been recognized as a point beyond which it was virtually impossible to enforce attendance.[8]

To understand the preoccupation with formal training we need to remember that the weekly catechism classes were not only intended to prepare the individual for communion. They facilitated the dissemination of religious knowledge in an age of illiteracy. They helped to keep a check on religious conformity, for children and adults alike were subject to periodic tests.[9] At a more practical level, people also saw the classes as a means of enforcing order and instilling in the young and potentially unruly a sense of respect for their elders, factors which were obviously important to the parishioners of St Mary's in Leicester. As they noted in a complaint about the inadequacy of the vicar's stipend, they had to put up with 'unlearned ministers, vnable to instructe them as appurteignethe through the want whereof dyverse of the younger sort are become verrie vndewtifull, lewde and disordered'.[10]

In an age when the enforcement of all forms of church attendance was difficult, the attempts to ensure that children attended catechism classes met with qualified success and it is clear that the regulations were increasingly neglected. The laity complained of uneducated ministers and absenteeism. The clergy protested that even if classes were restricted to Lent, the usual season for religious instruction, their parishioners found numerous excuses for not attending. They ranged from the amusing case of the Essex man who refused to send his children for fear that they 'should be boxed about the ears' to fairly common complaints about the weather.[11] Sometimes it was the distance from the parish church or the need to help with the harvest. Sometimes, as Bishop Fell lamented, 'it is said that the Youth are backward and have no mind to come and parents and masters are negligent to send them'.[12] Servants were a particular problem. As the rector of Finmere in Oxfordshire pointed out,

I cannot complain of the neglect of parents in sending their children to me for this purpose: but no servants come as thinking themselves (I suppose) too old or too big for this Discipline: but these, as they are constantly shifting from Place to Place are likely to be always the most disorderly part of my Parish.[13]

While local sources often refer to catechism it is difficult to establish whether any other provisions were made to involve the young in parish life. Were special services held for children in the post-Reformation church? Did the authorities encourage them to join their parents at morning and evening prayer? Did the individual become more involved in his local religious community as he approached the 'years of discretion' or, remembering the complaint about servants in Finmere, should we assume that it was impossible to enforce regular attendance once the child had left home? Piecemeal evidence makes it clear that young people did go to church. We know, for instance, that Nehemiah Wallington, the son of a London turner, had been 'brought up in the ways of God from a child' and had learned to go to church 'not only on the Sabbath day but also on weekdays to the lectures', and that John Pawson's parents had 'obliged us constantly to go to church'.[14] But they came from devout Puritan households and, like so many diarists, were not necessarily typical. Official inquiries and complaints about disorder also hint at the presence of a younger element in the congregation. One of the questions raised in the Buckinghamshire Visitation of 1662 was whether you 'suffer no misbehaviour or disorder to be done by men, women or servants or children in your church?', and in reply to a similar demand in 1634 the authorities at Salisbury Cathedral desired redress 'for ye ordinarie trudginge vp and downe of youthes, and clamours of children to ye greate disturbance of ye preachers in their sermon'.[15] Unfortunately what such examples do not reveal is whether the children who attended divine service were in a miniority or whether they were more likely to frequent church at particular points of the year rather than on a regular basis. Nor, and perhaps even more interesting, do we know how many people actually witnessed the administration of the sacrament before assuming a participatory role. In one village in the Diocese of Durham, that of Allanton, it was reported that five or six hundred people took communion at Easter 'at which time the people in regard of there great number doe make such a confusion and noise and thronging that often times the young and old people are carried downe with there crowding'.[16] Here at least, if we can assume that the vicar was referring to children rather than adolescents, it seems that the individual may have been exposed to the sacrament before his first communion. But in London the vicar of St Pancras, Soper Lane, obviously felt that children should not be present for he allowed a 13-year-old to witness the sacrament, but noted that 'there is no assenting order of the church thereto since in this business witnesses ought to be participators in and of sufficient age to participate in the Holy Supper'.[17] Was he correct or should we assume that, as with attendance at divine service or catechism classes, practice varied considerably from one parish and one family to the next?

Another issue which it would be interesting to learn more about is whether child-attendance varied significantly over time. It would be rash to lay down a rigid chronological framework on the basis of circumstantial evidence alone. The factors which influenced the individual's early involvement with the church were, in any case, very diverse. However, several suggestions can be made. For instance, given the changes in the timing and organization of the service, it is quite likely that attendance at Mass was more common than at Holy Communion. Before the Reformation it is also possible to pinpoint several dates in the ecclesiastical calendar which were particularly associated with the young. Christmas and May Day are obvious examples. But there were other occasions too when frivolity and excess were accompanied by some form of religious service. In some parishes girls accompanied their mothers when they processed to church with a candle at Candlemas and All Souls was an occasion when boys had fun apeing the church elders by dressing up as the Bishop and his retinue and delivering special sermons.[18] On 'Frick Friday', just before Whitsun, the women and youths of St Thomas's in Salisbury gathered to dance and carry lights to the church and the 'virgins' at Leicester carried an image of Mary during the Whitsun processions. A little later in the year the wardens at Leicester gave 'poynts and ribbons' to the children who joined the Rogationtide perambulations.[19] In other communities parents took their offspring to the services which preceded church ales and the annual feasts of craft and parish guilds.[20]

Some of these activities faded out at the Reformation. Others did not vanish entirely despite attacks by the more puritanically minded.[21] However, they became increasingly secular in content and were far less likely to involve formal worship. Did anything replace them in the seventeenth and eighteenth centuries? Or should we assume that, with the exception of the catechism class, nothing was done to cater for the younger element? In the seventeenth century it has been suggested that the custom of preaching to children was fairly common, for a large number of sermons were published for young people, and special youth services were occasionally held. However, they were geared towards apprentices and older adolescents, those who were bound by law to attend church, rather than to the younger child, and they were held in centres like London where the variety of religious opportunities was far wider than in the average parish.[22] Deprived of some of the more colourful events in the ritual year and with less excuse to attend with their peers, the church must have seemed an increasingly dull place to children from 1600 onwards. Can we wonder that many preferred to spend Sundays loitering in the churchyard, as they appear to have done in a number of Wiltshire villages, or dancing to the tabor and pipe, a regular pursuit in Baxter's village of Eaton Constantine?[23]

If children did attend church in the seventeenth century it was more likely to be as part of the household than with their peers, a development which was facilitated by the increasing tendency for people to rent family pews rather than sitting in occupational groups or with members of the same sex. The Puritans were particularly anxious to promote family worship.[24] Indeed, as many contemporary works emphasize, it was one of the duties of the 'godly householder' to ensure that his family went to church regularly, that they joined together to pray and read the Bible and, whilst catechism was primarily a parochial activity, to see that his children and servants were adequately instructed.[25] Unfortunately, despite the efforts of the authorities and of individual writers, neglect of all forms of religious observance increased, albeit because of apathy, or, as Spaeth suggests, because of the shortcomings of the clergy. In consequence the young probably had less and less opportunity to familiarize themselves with the church. Yet there were several developments during the eighteenth century which helped, on a limited scale, to counter this tendency. One was the encouragement of lay participation in ritual and, in particular, the spread of psalm-singing after the Restoration. Congregational choirs, composed largely of adolescents, were founded in many parishes and, although often lax in attending the lengthy sermons which were so popular with the Puritans, children evidently enjoyed the opportunity to sing in church.[26] Another

development, and one with a greater impact, was the establishment of charity schools to teach reading and religious knowledge
to poor children. Originating in London under the auspices of the
newly founded Society for the Promotion of Christian Knowledge,
the schools gradually spread throughout the country.[27] They
cannot all have been as successful as that established in Box
where, 'most of the young men and maidens and little children of
the parish . . . were very desirous to be admitted'.[28] Yet the
movement drew many children to church who would not normally
have received much encouragement.

Although many cases could be cited which demonstrate how
provisions for the young changed over time, I do not intend to
pursue the subject here but wish to turn instead to the second stage
in the spiritual life-cycle, confirmation. In theory this was the
crucial point in the process, the spiritual 'rite of passage' when the
individual affirmed his baptismal vows and accepted a place in the
parish community with all the religious and secular obligations that
this entailed. The 1549 Prayer Book laid down that 'there shall
none be admitted to the Holy Communion, until such time as he
be confirmed'. It also made the local clergy responsible for
ensuring that those who were ready to receive the sacrament
attended the confirmation services which, in theory, were held
every three years during episcopal visitations.[29] The 1549 rulings
marked a change in attitude. After the Reformation confirmation
was no longer held to be a sacrament as it had been in the past and
the more extreme reformists demanded that it be abandoned
altogether. They claimed there was no scriptural authority for
confirmation and emphasized that the important thing was not the
service itself but the period of training which preceded it.[30] There
were, of course, various shades of opinion on the issue. Many
moderate Puritans objected to the fact that priests were not
allowed to confirm and that, in consequence, the episcopate found
it impossible to examine all candidates or to conduct regular and
ordered services. Yet they agreed that there was a need for a
formal initiation into the Christian community.[31] Meanwhile, on
the conservative side some wished to revive the sacramental
character of confirmation, whereas others recognized the practical
problems of holding regular services and ensuring attendance and
were prepared to compromise by allowing people to take
communion without obtaining the bishop's blessing.

Conflicting opinions meant that the degree to which the Prayer

Book rulings were enforced varied over time. During the 1550s and the Civil War the administration of confirmation was particularly irregular.[32] Complaints were also made of general neglect in the latter decades of the sixteenth century when the church hierarchy was dominated by a reforming element. In 1587 Robert Cawdry noted that 'the bishops themselves, for the most part, these 29 years had not observed it' and four years later Whitgift criticized his fellow bishops because they had 'generally begun to neglect to confirm children, at least to call for, and exact the use of both it and catechizing'.[33] During periods of 'retrenchment' and conservatism, however, attempts were made to tighten up the system. Visitation articles dating from the 1630s and 1660s illustrate an increased stress on the need for confirmation. Conservatism also marked the first half of the eighteenth century, although by then the emphasis had shifted and while a minority still insisted on the sacramental character of confirmation, other ecclesiastics were more concerned to regularize proceedings and impart an element of solemnity to the occasion. The Bishop of Oxford, Thomas Secker, sent out tracts to improve the standard of preparation and issued tickets to prevent people attending more than once. He also instructed churchwardens to ensure that there was sufficient space 'to prevent noise and confusion that so this holy rite may be performed in a most solemn and edifying manner'. Other active reformists included Gibson of London and White Kennet, Bishop of Peterborough between 1720 and 1728.[34]

What was going on at the parish level? Did the clergy ensure that suitable candidates were submitted for confirmation and, more important, was there a demand for the ceremony among the laity? Again opinion varied considerably. Some priests were diligent and made every effort to adhere to the Book of Common Prayer. Indeed one Oxfordshire vicar commented in 1748 that his predecessor had been so conscientious that 'I found a girl who was confirmed at five years old and several before they were ten'. However, numerous examples of neglect could also be cited.[35] Many people criticized the way confirmation services were organized. But despite this, contemporary descriptions suggest that they attracted crowds of candidates. In Toby Mathew's diary we learn how, after confirming over a thousand at Ripon in 1607 and a similar number at Malton 'I nearly melted away with the heat and did indeed earn the right to go to bed'.[36] Another bishop wrote in 1649 of 'the over eager and tumultuous affection with which confirmation was sought in Devon and Cornwall' and added that,

it cannot be spoken with what fervour and violence of desire that people were wont to sue for this sacred ceremony. . . . How have we been tired with the importunity of suitors, impatient of either denial or delay! How have we been oppressed with the throngs of the multitude, striving for the first admission![37]

In the eighteenth century too the evidence points to mass gatherings throughout the country, although White Kennet may have been slightly over-optimistic in claiming that 'there was never a better disposition in the people to conform to all the rites and duties of the church'.[38] In the diocese of Lincoln, for example, Wake confirmed nearly 13,000 people in 1709 and over 18,000 three years later, whilst the Bishop of Gloucester dealt with '8922 or thereabouts' in Halifax and Ripon in 1737.[39]

Such figures obviously need to be treated with a certain amount of caution. Sometimes the staggering numbers reflected the need to catch up on an earlier backlog. As Taylor observed in 1663, when confirmation began to be more carefully ministered after the initial upheaval of the Reformation, 'people ran to it in so great numbers that churches and churchyards could not hold them'.[40] In the 'small, unpeopled' diocese of Carlisle the lack of visitations between 1684 and 1702 meant that five and a half thousand people were confirmed by the new bishop at his first Visitation, and Archbishop Blackburn left his successor 'an arrear of 12 years neglect' so that he confirmed over 30,000 in his first year at York.[41]

Unfortunately it is impossible to establish how many were never confirmed or, even more important, to ascertain whether the individual candidate was motivated by genuine piety or by the persuasions of his parents or the local priest. Many people attended because it was felt to be unlucky not to do so. Indeed Nicholas Ferrar was probably far from unusual when he justified being confirmed for the second time by saying that 'it was a good thing to have the bishop's prayers and blessing twice'.[42] Contemporary clergy were certainly scathing about the ordinary parishioner's ability to understand the true significance of the rite. The Bishop of Salisbury lamented in 1692 that 'of those multitudes that crowd to it, the far greater part come merely as if they were to receive the bishop's blessing, without any sense of the vow made by them, and of their renewing their baptismal engagements in it'. Nine years later Samuel Saywell commented that

Tis certain many people have very false and odd notions of confirmation and esteem it not at all, others look on it as but a Man's blessing at most, and therefore great numbers never seek it, either for themselves or for their children.[43]

Even if prompted by genuine religious sentiment the mass confirmation ceremonies were hardly edifying spiritual occasions. Criticisms about the accompanying disorder abound. Gibson noted that

a great number of parishes were obliged to attend at each place appointed for it, the noise, the tumult and the indecency with which young people crowded to the chancel, looked more like the diversions of a bear garden than the solemn performance of an apostolic office.[44]

Even more interesting is Richard Baxter's account. Apparently he and his friends ran out to see the bishop 'not knowing anything of the meaning of the business'.

The Bishop examined us not at all in one article of faith; but in a churchyard, in haste we were set in a rank, and he passed hastily over us, laying his hands on our head, and saying a few words, which neither I nor any that I spoke with, understood, so hastily were they uttered, and a very short prayer recited, and there was an end.[45]

Another question about which all too little is known is whether confirmation and the first communion were viewed as high points in the life-cycle, to be celebrated, like other rites of passage, with commensality and festivity. For the ordinary parishioner the noise and bustle may actually have been one of the attractions of the confirmation service. Indeed, from references to 'fair like confluences' and 'the country folk who pressed in to see the ceremony', I suspect that the day was treated as a holiday by the candidates themselves and by the community in general.[46] Here was an opportunity to dress up and visit the local market town, perhaps to meet friends and kinsmen and no doubt to eat and drink. By contrast, the first communion may have been a rather low key affair, of significance perhaps only to the very devout. If children had been accustomed to attending with their parents they would not have found the occasion unusual. On the other hand it may have provided some opportunity for meeting people, for commensality and for binding the community together, for we know that the annual Easter communions could attract large crowds and that before the Reformation at least the distribution of bread among householders added a social dimension to the rite.[47]

While much remains to be discovered about contemporary attitudes to confirmation, evidence concerning the point in the life-cycle when people became full church members, a question of interest to demographers, is easier to find. Sixteen is generally adopted as a cut off point when using communicant lists as a demographic source. From 1604 onwards people of 16 and over were certainly liable to be presented in court for not attending communion.[48] However, this was not the only age mentioned in official sources. Moreover, the age of confirmation did not necessarily have any bearing on the age of first communion.

In the primitive Church confirmation and first communion followed close on the heels of baptism. But there was an increasing delay between the three sacraments during the Middle Ages and by the time that the Bishop's Book was written in 1537 it is clear that few accepted the need for infant confirmation. As it said in the latter, provided that the child was 'baptized and died innocent' it would be assured of salvation. Yet it was still considered 'well done that men do present their children unto the bishop . . . when they be of so tender age as commonly they be wont to do', and literary and iconographic evidence suggests that until the Reformation children could be confirmed at any point between 5 and 10.[49] From then on, however, the emphasis gradually shifted from childhood to adolescence, a dangerous age as many contemporary works point out.[50] According to the 1549 Prayer Book confirmation was 'most meet to be ministered when children come to that age, that partly by the frailty of their own flesh, partly by the assaults of the world and the devil, they begin to be in danger to fall into sin'.[51] The young needed disciplining. They also needed the spiritual prop of communion to shield them from temptation. Yet the Church was increasingly hesitant about administering the sacrament prematurely for it was felt that young children did not have the discretion to examine their consciences or to receive the body of Christ with due solemnity. Nor did they have the ability to give an account of their faith. As pointed out earlier, it was not enough to acquire the bishop's blessing. Young people had to be taught how to lead a 'godly life' and they had to prove that they had received a basic religious training before they were 'houseled'. As far as contemporaries were concerned then what was important was the 'capacity' rather than the age, of the potential communicant; that he or she had reached 'the years of discretion'.

Given this new emphasis on training the question we need to resolve is not, in fact, whether there was an exact point in the life-cycle when the individual assumed the responsibilities of church-manship, but whether there was an accepted minimum and maximum age for confirmation and taking first communion. Children under 10 were certainly confirmed until well after the Reformation, although they were no longer encouraged to commune. In 1640 Cosin noted that 'many can say their Catechism and are confirmed at seven years old', and one of the objections voiced at the Savoy Conference in 1661 was that as soon as children could recite the articles of faith, which the Puritans alleged could be as early as 4 or 5, they could be brought before the bishop.[52] By the eighteenth century it seems unlikely that the age range was quite as wide.[53] Yet evidence from the diocese of Worcester, where a series of confirmation lists have survived, makes it clear that the clergy were happy to present children in their early teens. Some rectors specified that they were submitting those of 'ten and upwards that had learnt their catechism'.[54] A few actually noted the age of each confirmand. In Alcester, for example, three 9-year-olds and nine 10-year-olds were confirmed in 1701, roughly half the people submitted that year being under 13. This applied to a quarter of the candidates in 1703, while at the next visitation the vicar noted the 11 and 12-year-olds, those 'qualified if their age will permit', separately and added that there were several others under 10 who had been catechized and 'are desirous of his Lordship's blessing'. In the diocese of St Asaph a series of local returns dating from the 1680s also illustrates that many were confirmed before 16, the age when communion became mandatory.[55]

On the whole the authorities were content to let the local clergy decide on the suitability of each candidate during the seventeenth century. From 1700 onwards, however, efforts were made to exclude the very young, the Bishop of Chester being the first of a number of prelates who decreed that they would not confirm anyone under 14.[56] This was linked with the attack on the organization of confirmation ceremonies. But it also marked an appreciation of the problems which arose if there was a delay between confirmation and first communion. As Gibson complained, one reason why such numbers of those confirmed, did afterwards utterly disregard the Lord's Table was that they were confirmed so long before they were really fit to come to it, and either did not know, or had forgoten that one end of the confirmation was to prepare them for it.[57]

But until the latter was more regularly administered it was believed that the problem would remain unresolved. This was certainly why James Tinker of Droitwich submitted children of 8 or 9. As he pointed out, 'because opportunities in this kind haue been rare amongst us theyr parents and sureties humbly begg his lordships feavour of admittance yt they may partake of the Benefit of his prayers and blessings in this holy action'.[58] It was also one of Gibson's reasons for holding extra confirmation circuits it being 'for fear of losing the happy opportunity of being confirmed' which encouraged parents to offer their children prematurely.[59]

Not only were young children confirmed but the Worcester lists also illustrate that the confirmation of men and women of 'riper years' was far from unusual. The rector of Abbots Morton presented a list of 'all ye mature persons and children' that 'desire to receive communion' and his colleague at North Littleton distinguished between 'children desiring to be confirmed this day'; 'adult persons confirmed yesterday' and those of 'riper years'. When ages are noted it can be seen that, although most catechumens were under 20 there were always a few older people who took the opportunity to obtain the bishop's blessing. In 1701 the seven candidates from Bickhamford ranged from 19 to 33 and those from Alcester included Mary Morgan and John Abel aged 60 and 56 respectively. Was it superstition which encouraged such people to attend . . . a fear, perhaps of imminent death? Was it because of pressure from a particularly diligent priest? Or does the fact that the lists include several groups of people who may have been related suggest that some of the older candidates were inspired by the example of a younger member of the family?[60]

Although we can only speculate about individual motives, it is possible to suggest a variety of reasons why such people escaped as adolescents. Sometimes the responsibility lay with the bishop, and many went for years without holding a visitation, albeit because of ill-health, absence on parliamentary duty, or simple apathy.[61] The local clergy were also criticized for failing to present suitable candidates. But the most diligent incumbent could not cope with public indifference or with the intriguing, practical excuses which were forwarded for neglecting confirmation. Sometimes it was the inability of the young people themselves, sometimes parental opposition.[62] Lack of time and the weather also played a part, a fact that White Kennet took into account when choosing Sundays for his confirmation tours 'because the good folks have then their best cloaths, and horses to spare, otherwise we should have very few folks upon these dripping daies while they wait upon hay and corn'.[63]

Whatever the excuse, by the late seventeenth century many people evidently did escape confirmation, although Baxter's comment that 'there is not one of an hundred confirmed at all' may be unduly pessimistic.[64] But does this imply a corresponding neglect of communion or can we assume that, as Baxter went on to say, people who were never 'bishopped' were able to 'live in the parishes as reputed Christians and may come to the sacrament when they will'?[65] One objection to episcopal confirmation, as Robert Cawdry observed in 1587, was that in neglecting their duty bishops forced the clergy to disobey the Prayer Book and to admit people without being confirmed.[66] During the century after the Reformation attempts were made to maintain the correct procedure. Yet the authorities were not insensible to the problems hindering confirmation and they agreed to revise the Prayer Book ruling in 1662 so that those 'ready and desirous to be confirmed' could partake of the sacrament provided that they showed evidence of having been catechized.

This regularized a situation which, as evidence from individual parishes makes clear, was often the norm. Indeed, as early as 1577 the Bishop of Durham made a significant distinction between people under 30, who he believed should not communicate unless they had been confirmed, and those over 30 who had only to demonstrate their knowledge of the catechism.[67] At this stage, however, most bishops were less prepared to compromise and would have gone along with Hall's suggestion that the ignorance of the communicants in his diocese would be remedied if 'the precedent and godly order of our church were duly observed that none should be admitted to the communion but those that have been confirmed'.[68] It would, of course, be interesting to establish whether changing attitudes to confirmation had any effect on the average age of first communion. Unfortunately, concrete evidence is hard to find. Few vicars were as diligent as the incumbent of Ludlow who listed the new communicants in his parish between

1717 and 1732, and references to communion in diaries and spiritual autobiographies are few and far between.[69] Oliver Heywood, one of the few to mention the subject, said that he first received the Lord's Supper at the age of 14, although he added that 'I confess I was not prepared according to that exactnes required in worthy communicants and have cause to be humbled'.[70] But was he typical? Certainly by the eighteenth century, once people were allowed to dispense with the need to be confirmed first, it seems reasonable to take 16 as a mean.[71] But whether there was a wider range when Heywood was a young boy and whether local practice varied remains to be established.

It is important to stress that, whether he took first communion in his early teens or in his twenties, the young person was not immediately integrated into the parish community. The assumption of parochial responsibilities was a gradual process and one which cannot be divorced from the context of the household. The responsibilities in question can be considered under three heads: spiritual, financial and administrative. Of these the last, which included the obligation to assist in running parish affairs and, on a more intangible level, to report the social and religious misdemeanours of fellow parishioners, need not concern us here, for it was restricted to the male householder and within that sector to a fairly narrow social group.[72] But in order to put our discussion of the role of the young into a wider context it is important consider the two other attributes of 'churchmanship'.

Let us look first at the spiritual requirements. From Elizabeth's reign onwards people over 14 were expected to attend morning and evening prayer on Sundays and holy days and those of 16 and over could be presented if they failed to communicate at least once a year. The enforcement of these rulings was haphazard at best.[73] It was hard enough to persuade older people to go to church, let alone the newly confirmed, and the rector of Finmere was certainly not the only incumbent to single out servants as a problem. Unfortunately, the people who are mentioned in court records represent no more than the tip of the iceberg and they were far more likely to be householders than young, single people. In St Martin's, Salisbury, for instance, the vast majority of offenders who were presented for failing to communicate in the 1630s were married men or their wives.[74]

What is perhaps not stressed enough is that it was the responsibility of the head of the household to ensure that the various members of the family did fulfil their spiritual obligations and he was liable to be fined if they failed to do so.[75] When adolescents were presented in court, and this was far more likely to be in a parish with a particularly diligent priest or a puritan biased vestry, their father or master was often named as well. William Hutchens of Salisbury, who was presented in 1639 for allowing his servant Joane Spratt 'to rub out her book upon the Sabbath day' and his fellow parishioner George Tennum who was fined 'for suffering his wife to soe upon the Sabbath day and suffering his daughter to knit then', were certainly not unusual.[76]

It is within the context of the household too that one must consider the financial obligations of churchmanship. The upkeep of the church was the responsibility of the local congregation. Parishioners, as Burgess points out, were supposed to contribute towards items such as books, candles and the communion bread and wine. From the mid sixteenth century onwards, they were rated at intervals for repairs to the fabric. The wages of the parish clerk, the sexton and sometimes the priest, were also met by local rates and the latter was entitled to a small offering, usually of 2d. or 4d. per communicant, every Easter and to a variety of additional tithes. Being governed by local custom rather than by statute, the methods for assessing and collecting these levies varied from place to place. Nevertheless certain common features emerge when one examines local ordinances and the records which were used to facilitate their collection.

Although participation in the communion brought with it the obligation to contribute to parochial assessments, in practice individual payments were often met by the master of the household. In Pittington, Durham, it was ordered that 'every communicant shall pay 1d to the churchwardens and that every maister of the family shall pay for himself, wife and children and servants'. In Southwark the householder bought tokens for each member of his family who intended to take communion. In St Michael's, Chester the clerk's quarterly wages were met by the householding population.[77] As he grew older and rose in status, however, the individual began to assume responsibility for his own financial obligations. The point can be illustrated if we concentrate on the offerings which were paid to the clergy every Easter. In Coventry an act dating from 1558 ordered that the householder should pay 2d. for 'his wife, children, servants or others of their family, takeing their rites of the church at Easter' and in St John's

Chester householders paid a similar offering for servants, but 'notheinge for childr and prentizes'.[78] Apart from the last clause, there was nothing unusual in these arrangements. But I have singled out these two communities because evidence survives to show that the rate collectors distinguished between covenanted servants and apprentices. If individuals received an independent wage, rather than simply being allocated bed and board, they were expected to pay for themselves; if not their fathers or masters were responsible. The determining factor was not so much the stage individuals had reached in their spiritual careers, but their financial capability.

Having started to pay their own way the parishioners gradually took on more and more financial burdens. One of these was the personal tithe, a rate on the profits of trade and wages. By the late sixteenth century servants were no longer expected to give a tenth of their earnings to the church as they had in the past. But an extra element for wages was sometimes added to the Easter offering. A particularly detailed description of the way in which this system operated survives in an eighteenth-century terrier from St Margaret's, Leicester. It stipulated that at Easter 'every man servant pays 12d., every maid servant 6d. and every apprentice 2d., paid by the master or mistress; all other servants receiving wages pay for themselves'. It was also noted that sons and daughters between 16 and 21 were rated at 2d. a head but that 'after one and twenty years every son pays 12d. and every daughter 6d., all inmates ye same', by which stage it was obviously assumed that the young person would be in receipt of wages.[79]

Exactly how local officials established the age or ability of each member of the congregation remains a mystery. But a study of their notebooks and papers makes it clear that they did their best to ensure that everyone was rated correctly. The vicar of Ludlow who compiled special lists of newcomers to the sacrament has already been mentioned. In sixteenth-century Ledbury, too, the collector of the Easter tithes itemized those who 'do take wages', those who 'doe not take any wage at all' and recent confirmands under separate heads, the latter paying only half the normal offering, the waged servants an incremental rate.[80] In other parishes marginal notes besides the lists of individual contributors sometimes reveal that a young person had been rated erroneously. In St Margaret's, Leicester, we learn of people who were 'but 12' or '14 by Eastr' or, in the case of some of the sons and daughters, 'but 19 and 20'. Elsewhere amendments were made if the individual was 'unwaged' or 'had not yet received'. There was no standard procedure for collecting and enforcing parish rates, albeit the occasional assessment for repairs or an annual collection for the curate's wages. Yet the same basic principles apply whether one is talking about the sixteenth century or the eighteenth, the rural or the urban parish. A single male parishioner, for instance, may have had relatively few burdens. But once he set up his own household he needed to dip into his pocket on a number of occasions each year and was expected to pay higher rates as he rose in seniority and wealth.

Much more could be said about the laity and their financial contributions to the church. There were, for instance, many other aspects of 'giving' which can be viewed within the context of the life-cycle.[81] But having brought the individual from the stage when he began to learn something about his faith to the point when he asumed some responsibility for the beliefs and actions of others, it is a convenient point to stop and draw some conclusions. Although the surviving evidence raises many questions, it is clear that the Church authorities were far from insensible to the importance of the young. It was important for the local clergy to know how many people lived in the parish, how old they were and whether they had passed the various stages on the road to 'spiritual adulthood'. At a practical level alone this enabled them to check that everyone who was liable to contribute towards the church complied. In order to ensure the conformity of future generations it was also vital to train the individual from an early age.[82] There were periods when children appear to have been neglected . . . that much is clear. But when the church was under attack the need to ensure that the individual was adequately prepared for his or her future role in the religious community assumed far greater prominence.[83]

In some senses, the stages in the spiritual life-cycle which have been discussed were no more than symbolic. Perhaps this helps explain why the attitudes of laymen and clergy alike were ambivalent and why, however hard the authorities tried, the enforcement of the legislation on catechism, confirmation and communion varied considerably from place to place. But even if mere symbols these stages did impart a sense of formality to the proceedings. To belong to a religious community – and this was as true of a medieval guild or a dissenting sect where membership was voluntary, as it was of the parish, which theoretically embraced the entire community – implied a commitment of faith, of time, sometimes of money. It also implied some form of initiation, albeit by paying an entrance fine, demonstrating a knowledge of one's faith or participating in a ceremonial rite of passage.[84]

Acknowledgements

I should like to acknowledge the support of the Research Board at Leicester University whilst working on this paper and the help and encouragement of my fellow contributors.

Notes and references

1 T. Heywood (ed.), *The Diary of Henry Newcome* (Chetham Society, vol. 18, 1889), p.v.

2 J. Horsfall Turner (ed.), *The Reverend Oliver Heywood, His autobiography, diaries, anecdotes and event books* (1882), vol. 1, pp. 156–7.

3 Richard Baxter, *Reliquiae Baxteriae* (1696), pp. 1–2; M. R. Watts, *The Dissenters from the Reformation to the French Revolution* (1978), pp. 422–3.

4 P. Collinson, *The Religion of Protestants* (1982), p. 232.

5 Phillipa Tudor, 'Religious instruction for children and adolescents in the early English Reformation', *Journal of Ecclesiastical History*, **35,** (1985), pp. 391–2. In the Middle Ages parish guilds often assumed an educational role. Rosser, above p. 43. The growing emphasis on training in the sixteenth century is illustrated in the amendment to the Prayer Book rubric in 1552 so that communion should not be administered until the individual could 'say *the catechism and* be confirmed'. J. D. C. Fisher, *Christian Intiation, The Reformation Period* (1970), pp. 243, 251. Catholic reformers also believed that religious education was one way of strengthening their church and systematic teaching was carried out in recusant households. M. Rowland, 'Recusant Women 1560–1640', in Mary Prior (ed.), *Women in English Society 1500–1800* (1985) p. 165.

6 S. R. Smith, 'Religion and the conception of youth in seventeenth century England', *History of Childhood Quarterly*, (1974–5), p. 496.

7 E. Cardwell, *Synodalia* (1842), vol. ii, p. 510.

8 See for example the injunctions of the Bishops of Chester, York and Lincoln in the 1570s and 1580s. W. P. M. Kennedy (ed.), *Elizabethan Episcopal Administration* (1923), vol. ii, pp. 43, 119; J. Purvis, *Tudor Parish Documents of the Diocese of York* (1948), p. 129.

9   In practice it is unlikely that the obligations to ensure that the laity had an understanding of the basic articles of faith were adequately fulfilled. It would have been impossible to examine all the candidates who attended confirmation services. Nor would the clergy have had much time to check on the ability of those who wished to receive communion, although some individuals were evidently diligent in this respect. In seventeenth-century Oxfordshire, for instance, the priest at Cropredy 'doth not every sabbath day so examyne the youths accordinge to the article, but onely at such tyme as they are to recyve the comunyon', while Robert Middleton of Newport complained that he had been refused the sacrament because he 'would not then answer a question of catechising wch the sd Mr Awsten demaunded of him'. S. A. Peyton, *The Churchwardens Presentments in the Oxfordshire Peculiars of Dorchester, Thame and Banbury*, (Oxford Record Society, 1928), vol. x, pp. 249, xxxxvii.

10 M. Bateson, *The Records of the Borough of Leicester* (1905), vol. 3, p. 452. The religious character of all forms of education during this period should also be noted, the Lord's Prayer and the catechism providing a basic text when teaching children to read.

11 F. G. Emmison, *Elizabethan Morals and the Church Courts* (1973), p. 143. Emmison noted that in Essex half the presentments for neglecting catechism involved the laity and half the local incumbent, p. 142.

12 Mary Clapinson (ed.), *Bishop Fell and Nonconformity. Visitation Documents from Oxfordshire Diocese, 1682–3*, (Oxford Record Society, 1980), vol. 52, p. xxxv.

13 H. A. Lloyd Jukes (ed.), *The Visitation of Dr Thomas Secker to Oxford in 1738*, (Oxford Record Society, 1957), p. 69.

14 Paul Seaver, *Wallington's World* (1985), p. 37.

15 E. C. R. Brinckworth, *Episcopal Visitation Book, 1662*, (Buckinghamshire Record Society, 1943), vol. 7, p. 93; D. Robertson, *Sarum Close* (1969), p. 193. The problem was certainly not new for similar complaints were aired in the early sixteenth century. See A. H. Thompson (ed.), *Lincoln Visitations, 1517–31*, (Lincoln Record Society, 1940), vol. xxxiii, pp. 23, 26, 112, 134, 5.

16 W. Longstaff (ed.), *The Acts of the High Commission Court within the Diocese of Durham* (Surtees Society, 1858), vol. 34, p. 2.

17 The case arose because the girl had been nominated to act as godparent, although godparents were theoretically to be practising communicants. W. Bruce Bannerman (ed.), *The Registers of St Pancras, Soper Lane*, (Harleian Society Publications, 1917), vol. 45, p. 145.

18 R. L. de Molen, 'Pueri Christi Imitatio: The Festival of the Boy Bishop In Tudor England', *Moreana*, **xl** (1975), pp. 17–29; in several parishes in York groups of young people maintained lights in church

before the Reformation. D. M. Palliser, 'Civic mentality and environment in Tudor York', *Northern History*, **vii** (1982), pp. 104–5.

19 H. J. F. Swayne (ed.), *The Churchwardens Accounts of St. Edmund and St Thomas, Sarum 1443–1702* (1896), p. 274; WRO, SDR, Dean & Chapter Lease Book I, f. 227; Thomas North (ed.), *The Accounts of St Martins, Leicester, 1489–1844* (1844), pp. 3, 70, 190, 208.

20 Children were taken to the midsummer feast of the Salisbury Tailor's Guild. WRO, SCA, I/246/2, f. 75. They can also be found enrolling as members of parish guilds. Rosser, above p. 44.

21 Rogationtide perambulations were one of the only medieval religious processions to survive the Reformation. Donald Spaeth, *Parsons and Parishioners: Lay-Clerical Conflict and Popular Piety in Wiltshire Villages, 1660–1740*, (Unpublished Ph.D. thesis, Brown University, 1985), p. 92.

22 S. R. Smith, 'Religion and the Conception of Youth', p. 496, 7.

23 Spaeth, pp. 132–5; *Reliquiae Baxterianae*, p. 2.

24 Christopher Hill, *Society*, chapter XIII. This is still one of the best assessments of life in the Puritan household. On the establishment of pews and evidence of youths in church see R. Gough, *The History of Myddle*, (ed.) D. Hey (1981), pp. 77, 78, 117, 119.

25 The popular seventeenth-century Conduct Books were full of advice on running a 'godly household'. See, for instance: William Gouge, *Of Domestical Duties* (1622) and John Dod and Robert Cleaver *A Godly form of Household Government* (1630). John Bossy discusses catechism as a parish activity in *Christianity*, p. 117.

26 In Broad Hinton the vicar commented that 'the young people in these parts very much delight in ch[ur]ch music', Spaeth, p. 167.

27 See also Barry's comments on the schools which were promoted in early eighteenth-century Bristol. Above, pp. 169–70. By 1723, 1329 charity schools had been set up as a result of the SPCK's efforts. Watts, pp. 422–5.

28 Spaeth, p. 165.

29 Fisher, p. 237.

30 The Puritan objections were formalized in the Millenary Petition of 1604 and later at the Savoy Conference of 1661. S. L. Ollard, 'Confirmation in the Anglican Communion, 1500–1800' in *Confirmation or the Laying on of Hands* (SPCK, 1926), vol. i, pp. 109, 145.

31 Richard Baxter, despite criticizing the organization of confirmation, argued for its revival after the Civil War for he believed there was a danger of slipping into the Christian community without some formal process. Ollard, p. 137.

32 As Robert South noted when arguing for more frequent confirmation services in 1685, 'the grand rebellion of 1641, by unhinging the minds of most of the nation' is partly answerable for the neglect of parents

to see that their children are confirmed' Ollard, p. 166.

33   Ollard, p. 102.

34   W. M. Marshall, 'Episcopal activity in the Hereford and Oxford Dioceses, 1660–1760', *Midland History*, **iii** (1983), p. 115; N. Sykes, *Edmund Gibson, Bishop of London, 1669–1748* (1926), p. 219–20, G. V. Bennett, *White-Kennett, 1660–1728, Bishop of Peterborough* (1957), p. 207–26.

35   Marshall, p. 116; in the 1630s Baxter said that the minister in his village failed to send a certificate of those who had been catechized and 'we ran of our own accord to see the Bishop'. P. E. More and F. L. Cross (eds), *Anglicanism: The Thought and the Practice of the Church of England* (SPCK, 1957), p. 450.

36   Ollard, pp. 119–22. Similar crowds attended the other services Mathew held whilst Archbishop of York.

37   Ollard, p. 112.

38   Bennett, p. 227.

39   Detailed figures are given in Ollard, Appendix II and Appendix A.

40   Ollard, p. 84.

41   Sykes, *Church and State*, p. 121; Sykes, *Gibson*, p. 218.

42   Ollard, p. 188; In 1712 Wesley noted that at Epworth, Lincolnshire 'great numbers were confirmed who ought not to have been . . . and many who had been confirmed before, some of them twice and thrice over', Sykes, *Church and State*, p. 133.

43   Ollard, pp. 184, 179.

44   Sykes, *Church and State*, p. 218. At Potter's confirmation in 1732 there was 'a great noise the whole time, highly indecent', Marshall, p.115.

45   More and Cross, p. 450.

46   Ollard, p. 122, 3.

47   Bossy, pp. 64–72 on the communal aspects of the mass. Sometimes people took first communion as a family group. See, for instance, the lists of new communicants prepared by the vicar of Ludlow. Ludlow Easter Books, 1725–1734, SRO, 2881/1/78.

48   Canon 112, 1604. Cardwell, vol. i, p. 309. During the sixteenth century there was a lack of consensus about the 'ideal' age for confirmation or for first communion. In 1565 Bishop Bentham of Coventry and Lichfield asked that children over 7 should be presented for confirmation. Fourteen is mentioned in a number of other episcopal injunctions and queries, so too is 16. Ollard, p. 112; Kennedy, vol. 2, pp. cxi, 70; Cardwell, vol. ii, p. 512. A variety of ages were also mentioned in the seventeenth century although by the 1670s 16 certainly seems to have been the norm. See Anne Whiteman, *The Compton Census of 1676* (1986), pp. xxx, xxxiii.

49   H. Holloway, *The Confirmation and Communion of Infants* (1901), p. 34–7, 40–5; Fisher, p. 222. See too D. Palliser's comments on the

age of first communion in 'Some aspects of the social and economic history of York in the sixteenth century', (Unpublished D.Phil. thesis, Oxford, 1968), pp. 77–8.

50 The Statute of Artificers referred to the 'licentious liberty of youth' and said that until 24 a man was 'wild, without judgement and not of sufficient experience to govern himself'. R. H. Tawney and Eileen Power (eds), *Tudor Economic Documents* (1924), vol. i, pp. 354–8. Authors of the popular Domestic Conduct Books also stressed that children were 'for the most part . . . heady and rash for want of experience'. Gouge, p. 449.

51 Fisher, p. 239.

52 Ollard, p. 134, 145.

53 Although Denne lamented that some presented children 'almost while they had them in their arms or at least while they were of a most incompetent age', Sykes, *Gibson*, p. 222.

54 Worc. RO, BA 2504/741: 2055/741.

55 In Welshpool the youngest child to be confirmed was 10. In Llangdafan 14 was the minimum. The Notitae of the Bishop of St Asaph, 1681, 1684, National Library of Wales, SA/Misc/1466 & 1410. Copy held at the Cambridge Group for the Study of Population and Social Structure.

56 Ollard, p. 195. Wake set a minimum of 14 for boys and 12 for girls in 1724. Sykes, *Church and State*, p. 121.

57 Cosin pointed out the problem in 1640 when asked whether those confirmed at 7 should be admitted to the sacrament. Ollard, p. 134; Sykes, *Gibson*, p. 220.

58 Worc.RO, BA 2504/741, no. 101.

59 Sykes, *Gibson*, p. 220.

60 For instance, when Elizabeth Eads and Mary Green, both in their thirties, were confirmed in 1703 the vicar also submitted Mary Eads, a 14-year-old, and John Green, aged 11. The four Churchlys, who ranged from 44 to 11, and Sarah, Dorothy and John Jennings, aged 20, 18 and 15 respectively, may also be related.

61 Sometimes the sheer size of a diocese prevented the bishop from covering each deanery every three years. The confirmation tours listed in Ollard, Appendices II and A are revealing in this respect.

62 Clapinson, p. 23. Other examples of the failure to submit confirmation candidates are given in Spaeth, p. 74. For instance, the churchwardens at Codford St Mary declared that the 'infectious disease of Salisbury hindered them from bringing any children to that place'.

63 Sykes, *Church and State*, p. 119.

64 In 1685 it was reported that 'most if not all the older people' at Ibstone, a parish where all spiritual obligations seem to have been sadly neglected, were unconfirmed and the Rector of Droitwich

complained that although many of his parishioners had been catechized they would not join the other candidates in 1703. Clapinson, p. 23; Worc.RO, BA 2504/741, no. 103. The two examples are far from unique.

65   Sykes, *Church and State*, p. 132.

66   Ollard, p. 103 and for similar complaints pp. 134, 147, 185–9, 197.

67   J. Raine (ed.), *The Injunctions and Ecclesiastical Proceedings of Richard Barnes, Bishop of Durham, 1575–1587*, (Surtees Society, vol. 22, 1850), p. 14.

68   Ollard, p. 136.

69   SRO 2881/1/78, Ludlow Easter Books 1725–34. The ages of the new communicants, where they can be established, range between 14 and 22. I am grateful to members of the Ludlow Historical Research Group for help on this issue. Another revealing source is a list of 'souls quallified (as to their age) for communicating', which was compiled by the vicar of Stoke on Trent in 1701. The rector noted the inhabitants in each household with their ages and then gave the number of communicants in each unit. From the latter it is clear that he certainly believed people were qualified by the age of 16. STRO, D 1742 Bundle 55. Copy held at the Cambridge Group for the Study of Population and Social Structure.

70   J. Horsfall Turner, p. 157.

71   A brief survey of some of the official literature suggests that by the early eighteenth century there was more of a consensus on the issue than there had been during the previous 150 years.

72   In seventeenth-century Lancashire the custom of 'houserow', whereby parish office was assumed by each householder in turn, was common. In Chester too parochial responsibilities were shared by a fairly wide social group. Elsewhere parish office was confined to the local elite. A. Hodge, 'Office holding and social structure in seventeenth century Lancashire', (Unpublished paper given at the Economic History Conference, 1985), p. 3. Alldridge, above pp. 105–7.

73   See *Statutes of the Realm*, Acts of Uniformity passed in 1559 and 1593 (1 Eliz., c.2; 35 Eliz., c.1 & 2) and the Ecclesiastical Canons of 1604, No. 112. Various ages were specified in the statutes which dealt with the problem of recusancy. In 1610, for instance, an act 'to prevent the dangers that may grow from popish recusants' established a fine for people over 9 refusing to attend church and a similar ruling passed in Synod in 1640 mentioned the age of 12. Act for the Administration of the Oath of Allegiance, 7 & 8 JI c.6. Cardwell, vol. i, p. 394. On local efforts to ensure attendance see Spaeth, above pp. 127, 140–1.

74   Twenty-four couples and fourteen single men and women were reported for not receiving communion in 1636. All but one of the couples and three of the single people can be traced as householders in the parish Easter Book compiled that year. In only five of the

households in question was another member of the family included in the presentment. SDR, St Martin's churchwarden's presentments 1636; SCA, 1899, Tithe Account Book, 1634–40. Likewise, while several thousand people were presented for absence from Sunday services in Elizabethan Essex, only two cases involved children. It is possible, of course, that some of the servants whom Emmison mentions would only just have reached the age of compulsory attendance. F. Emmison, p. 89.

75 While the statutes of 1593 and 1610 imposed fines on heads of households for every member of the family not attending church, others only demanded the attendance of householders. Hill, *Society*, p. 457. The role of the householder is illustrated in a variety of church records. In the London parish of All Hallows the Great, for instance, the sidesmen were provided with 'a table of the names of the howseholders of the same parish' to help check up on absenteeism. Guildhall lib. ms 819/1 f.65. 1615.

76 WRO, SDR, St Martin's churchwarden's presentments, 1639.

77 J. Cox, *Churchwardens Accounts* (1913), p. 100, 1625. For details of this system see J. Boulton, 'The social and economic structure of early seventeenth century Southwark', (Unpublished Ph.D. thesis, Cambridge, 1983). CDRO, P65/8/1 & P63/7/1.

78 T. Sharpe, *Illustrative Papers on the History and Antiquities of the City of Coventry* (1871), pp. 6, 7. The act which regularized the system in Coventry echoed a similar ruling for London. *Statutes of the Realm*, 37 HVIII c.12. CCRO, CR Bundles 39–42. Similar procedures were adopted elsewhere. In Bristol and Salisbury, for instance, the compilers of the Easter Books provided the names of each communicant, but only gave sums by householders and older servants. S. J. Wright, 'Easter Books and parish rate books: a new source for the urban historian', *Urban History Yearbook* (1985), pp. 33, 35.

79 LRO, 18D62 13a. Incremental rates were also paid in many other urban parishes. Wright, p. 33.

80 HWRO, Ledbury Easter Books, A61.

81 In his paper above Burgess discusses gifts made at the end of the life-cycle. Surplice fees, pew rents, voluntary donations and offerings at churchings could also be considered in this context.

82 Some even hoped that the young might set their elders an example and draw them to church too. Spaeth, p. 165.

83 Indeed, interesting parallels can be drawn when one compares the legislation concerning the young with that relating to church attendance in general.

84 For a discussion of initiation in a nonconformist church see G. F. Nuttall, *Visible Saints: The Congregational Way, 1640–1660* (1957), pp. 111–13.

Bibliography

J. Barry, 'Piety and the patient: medicine and religion in eighteenth century Bristol', in R. Porter (ed.), *Patients and Practitioners* (1985)

Jeremy Boulton, 'The limits of formal religion: The administration of Holy Communion in late Elizabethan and early Stuart London', *London Journal*, **10** (Winter, 1984), pp. 135–54

C. M. Barron and C. Harper-Bill (eds), *The Church in Pre-Reformation Society* (1985)

G. V. Bennett, *The Tory Crisis in Church and State*, (1975)

M. Bowker, *The Secular Clergy in the Diocese of Lincoln 1495–1520* (1968)

John Bossy, *Christianity in the West 1400–1700* (1985)

H. M. Cautley, *Suffolk Churches and their Treasures* (5th edn, 1982)

J. C . D. Clark, *English Society 1688–1832* (1985)

Patrick Collinson, *The Religion of Protestants: The Church in English Society 1559–1625* (1982)

Mary Clapinson (ed.), *Bishop Fell and Nonconformity. Visitation Documents from Oxfordshire Diocese, 1682–3* (Oxford Record Society, vol. 52, 1980).

J. C. Cox, *Churchwardens' Accounts from the Fourteenth Century to the Close of the Seventeenth Century* (1913)

R. Currie, A. D. Gilbert and L. Horsley, *Churches and Churchgoers. Patterns of Church Growth in the British Isles since 1700* (1977)

Horton Davies, *Worship and Theology in England*, 5 vols. (Princeton, 1961–75)

Natalie Zemon Davis, 'Some tasks and themes in the study of popular religion', in Charles Trinkaus and Heiko A. Oberman (eds), *The Pursuit of Holiness in Late Medieval and Renaissance Religion* (Leiden, Brill, 1974), pp. 307–36

A. G. Dickens, *The English Reformation* (1964)

C. Drew, *Early Parochial Organisation in England. The Origins of the Office of Churchwarden* (St Anthony's Hall Publications, vii, 1954)

L. G. Duggan, 'Fear and confession on the eve of the Reformation', *Archiv für Reformationsgeschichte*, lxxv (1975)

J. D. C. Fisher, *Christian Initiation. The Reformation Period* (1970)

A. D. Gilbert, *Religion and Society in Industrial England. Church, Chapel and Social Change, 1740–1914* (1976)

K. von Greyerz, (ed.), *Religion and Society in Early Modern Europe 1500–1800* (1986)

Felicity Heal and Rosemary O'Day (eds), *Church and Society in England: Henry VIII to James I* (1977)

P. Heath, *The English Parish Clergy on the Eve of the Reformation* (1969)

P. Heath, 'Urban piety in the later middle ages: the evidence of Hull wills', in R. Dobson (ed.), *The Church, Politics and Patronage in the Fifteenth Century* (1976)

Christopher Hill, *Society and Puritanism in Pre-Revolutionary England* (1964)

J. Hurwich, ' "A Fanatick Town": The political influence of Dissenters in Coventry 1660–1720', *Midland History*, **4** (1977)

M. G. Jones, *The Charity School Movement* (1938)

J. Kermode, 'The merchants of three northern English towns', in C. H. Clough (ed.), *Profession, Vocation and Culture in Later Medieval England* (1982)

A. Kreider, *English Chantries: The Road to Dissolution* (Cambridge, Mass., 1979)

J. Le Goff, *The Birth of Purgatory* (trans. Goldhammer, 1984)

J. Wickam Legg, *English Church Life from the Restoration to the Tractarian Movement* (1914)

B. L. Manning, *The People's Faith in the Time of Wycliffe* (2nd edn., 1975)

W. M. Marshall, 'Episcopal activity in the Hereford and Oxford Dioceses, 1660–1760', *Midland History*, **iii** (1983), pp. 106–120

F. C. Mather, 'Georgian Churchmanship Reconsidered', *Journal of Ecclesiastical History*, **36** (1985)

John S. Morrill, 'The Church in England 1642–9', in John S. Morrill (ed.), *Reactions to the English Civil War* (1982), pp. 89–114

G. F. Nuttall and O. Chadwick (eds), *From Uniformity to Unity 1662–1962* (1962)

S. L. Ollard, *Confirmation or the Laying on of Hands*, **i** (SPCK, 1926)

D. M. Owen, *Church and Society in Medieval Lincolnshire*, Society for Lincolnshire History and Archaeology, History of Lincolnshire, **V** (1981)

John H. Pruett, *The Parish Clergy under the Later Stuarts: The Leicestershire Experience* (Urbana, University of Illinois Press, 1978)

Barry Reay, 'Popular religion', in Barry Reay (ed.), *Popular Culture in Seventeenth Century England* (1985), pp. 91–128

J. J. Scarisbrick, *The Reformation and the English People* (1984)

S. R. Smith, 'Religion and the conception of youth in seventeenth century England', *History of Childhood Quarterly* (1974–5), pp. 493–516

R. W. Southern, *Western Society and the Church in the Middle Ages* (1970)

R. W. Southern, 'Between Heaven and Hell', *Times Literary Supplement* (18 June 1982), pp. 651–2

Margaret Spufford, 'Can we count the "Godly" and the "Conformable" in the seventeenth-century?', *Journal of Ecclesiastical History*, **36** (1985), pp. 428–38

Margaret Spufford, *Small Books and Pleasant Histories: Popular Fiction and its Readership in Seventeenth Century England* (1981)

N. Sykes, *Church and State in England in the Eighteenth Century* (1934)

N. Sykes, *Edmund Gibson. Bishop of London, 1669–1748* (1926)

N. P. Tanner, *The Church in Late Medieval Norwich 1370–1532*, Pontifical Institute of Mediaeval Studies, Studies and Texts, **66** (Toronto, 1984)

T. N. Tentler, *Sin and Confession on the Eve of the Reformation* (Princeton, 1977)

K. Thomas, *Religion and the Decline of Magic* (1971)

A. H. Thompson, *The English Clergy and Their Organisation in the Later Middle Ages* (1947)

J. and L. Toulmin Smith, *English Gilds*, Early English Text Society, original series, **xl** (1870)

J. Walsh, 'Origins of the Evangelical Revival', in G. V. Bennet and J. Walsh (eds), *Essays in Modern Church History* (1965)

Arthur Warne, *Church and Society in Eighteenth century Devon* (1969)

M. R. Watts, *The Dissenters. Volume 1. From the Reformation to the French Revolution* (1978)

H. F. Westlake, *The Parish Gilds of Mediaeval England* (1919)

K. L. Wood-Legh, *Perpetual Chantries in Britain* (1965)

Index